THE LIFE AND SECRETS OF A PROFESSIONAL PUNTER

ALEX BIRD

THE LIFE AND SECRETS OF A PROFESSIONAL PUNTER

ALEX BIRD

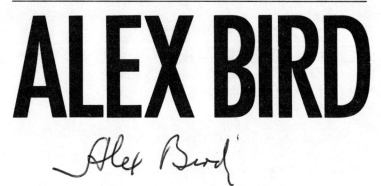

ALEX BIRD WITH
TERRY MANNERS

Queen Anne Press

A Queen Anne Press Book

© Alex Bird 1985

First published in Great Britain in 1985 by
Queen Anne Press, Macdonald & Co (Publishers) Ltd,
Maxwell House, 74 Worship Street,
London EC2A 2 EN

A BPCC plc company

British Library Cataloguing in Publication Data

Bird, Alex
  1. Bird, Alex   2. Horse race betting —
Great Britain   3. Gamblers—Great
Britain—Biography
I. Title
798.4′01′0924   SF336.B5

ISBN 0-356-10589-X

Typeset by Sunrise Setting, Torquay, Devon

Reproduced, printed and bound in Great Britain by
Hazell, Watson & Viney Limited,
Member of the BPCC Group
Aylesbury, Bucks

Having given great thought to whom I would dedicate this book, I eventually narrowed it down to three people: Peter O'Sullevan, ace commentator and journalist, who helped me with his inexhaustible knowledge; Phil Bull, whom I consider the greatest Turf authority of all time; and Johnny Foy my confidant, who invested millions of pounds for me purely on word of mouth. Johnny, a deeply religious man, died a few years ago, and I am sure that Peter and Phil will forgive me if I give his memory special preference.

FOREWORD

ON A GLORIOUS May morning, in the heart of the Cheshire countryside, I sat having coffee with Alex and talked about the forthcoming publication of his book. Fortune had already smiled sweetly on me when I was given the job of sorting out Alex's notes and tapes. But to be asked to contribute these few paragraphs is more than I would have expected.

I vividly recall taking my tape recorder and some notes with me on holiday to Arizona. I was on my own and delayed for several hours in a dreary airport lounge in New York, on a miserable Sunday afternoon. I felt very homesick for a few moments, then settled myself in a corner and turned on the tape recorder. There was Alex's familiar North Country voice recalling the drama of the Grand National and instantly I was immersed in racing again and home did not seem so far away.

I must be one of the least qualified among Alex's friends and colleagues to write a foreword to the book. He pays his own tribute to the great names of racing, including Peter O'Sullevan and Phil Bull, both of whom figure prominently in the text – and to *Daily Express* journalist Terry Manners, who has written the book with him and worked with tremendous enthusiasm and patience. I value the opportunity I have had to get to know Alex the man – not the gambler, punter, professional backer, call him what you will.

Larger than life characters always attract criticism, particularly those who smoke cigars, drink champagne and drive a Rolls-Royce. Alex has never been less than courteous and kind to me, but I should not care to be on the wrong side of him! He has pointed out that he is a mixture of cold, calculating ruthlessness and a 'softie'. It is these conflicts within a personality which make a cutting edge and expose our vulnerability. It is part of the endless fascination of human nature.

My wholehearted sympathy goes to Alex's wife Evelyn, who has suffered constant second-hand labour pains during the prolonged birth of the book, and to his family who will be extremely glad, I am sure, to see it in print.

If my small contribution has helped to bring about Alex's wish to publish this book, I am delighted, because it has been a pleasure for me.

ANNETTE MAIDEN

PREFACE

SOME PEOPLE SAY I am a legend but I do not think that is true; I only know that the opportunity to make a living backing horses as I have will not come again. Betting tax and the juggling of the odds in the bookies' favour have seen to that. Some years ago, William Hill, arguably the greatest bookmaker who ever lived, stopped me by the paddock at Goodwood. 'Good God Alex, I never thought I would see you on a racecourse again,' he said. After the introduction of betting tax, Hill had told his board that the careers of men like me were over. However, although the betting tax was restrictive and cut down my profit, I never stopped seeking new outlets for my bets or going to race meetings, because that is what I have enjoyed most in my life. From my youth I have had two rules. The first is that my word should be my bond, and the second is that I should do whatever makes me most happy. I have stuck to both. I have won fortunes at the touch of my panama hat, but no matter what I have always honoured my bets. If I had my time all over again I would choose the same path. There are those who say that a man like Alex Bird cannot be so successful without being dishonest: they do not know me. If I cannot beat the bookies honestly, I do not want to beat them at all. That is the challenge that has driven me since the days I stood watching my bookmaker father work out the winning bets in his office over the family's coal merchant's business.

When it comes to taking a final analysis of oneself, one has to be utterly truthful. I did hear the expression once that to kid other people was one thing, but one should never kid oneself.

Have I been a Jekyll and Hyde character? That is a question I keep asking myself. On one hand I have been the hardest of hard men and on the other, the biggest softie in the world. When I embarked on a racecourse career I realised I was entering a jungle and I had to be tough. There were times when I would not give an inch. Like the day I refused to lend a fiver to a skint punter who wanted the fare home from the racecourse. I took the view that if I was regarded as a soft touch, such people would never leave me alone. On the other hand I know I am very vulnerable to my innermost emotions, of which my wife Evelyn I am sure is unaware. One of her favourite sayings is: 'I have been striking flint on him for years.' However, the emotional side of my character is very evident at times. Being a royalist I can never stand at Royal Ascot and listen to racegoers singing the national anthem in full voice to the military band, without feeling the colour drain from my face. I have felt the same on Cup Final day at Wembley.

At the age of sixty eight, in the quiet of my home, I have attempted to analyse these emotions of mine. I accept I have been an introvert with a cold, clinical approach to racing, afraid to make a wrong step, virtually a coward. But often I have been a person whose outlook is carefree, possibly fatalistic, and the kind of man not afraid to take a chance. It is my carefree attitude that I find most difficult to analyse, an attitude which might baffle the most eminent psychiatrist. I have been a Lloyds underwriter for twenty two years, but I shudder to think what my income might have been had I underwritten the risks taken by people like me. To put it in racing terms, insurance companies who have covered my life have been betting 'over the odds'.

However, no matter what my qualities or flaws are I have succeeded in winning a great deal of money and keeping it, although there were times when the odds were against me. In this book is a message to anyone who has ever had a few bob on the horses. There is a way to have fun at the bookies' expense and on occasion enjoy a very big win indeed. Understand, however, that nothing comes easy. That is the moral of my story.

1

MY FATHER, JAMES Arthur Bird, was a bookmaker, the only one in Newton Heath, a sprawling semi-rural suburb north of Manchester. He ran a coal merchant's business, but his heart lay in the dusty old rooms over the coal offices, where he ran his little betting empire. It was a secretive world that intrigued me as a boy.

My sisters May and Hilda and I were brought up with the smell of coal dust and damp sacks, of horse manure and hay in the brick, wood and corrugated iron stables that housed by father's old cart horse. I was forever in awe of my father, whose life seemed to be full of colourful people and mysterious meetings at the top of the narrow staircase in the back of his coal office. One brown-panelled door divided our two worlds.

My mother, Nellie Bird, was a lonely woman, with a will of iron and a heart of gold. She ran the local grocery store, where I often helped pack the shelves with cans of mushy peas. The shop smelt of bacon, bread and coal tar soap. She never made much money on the business, because it was a time of great austerity and she could never resist a hard luck story or the hungry look of a child. I think most of her business was done on the slate, although she did not always admit it to father, for he would never have approved.

One of my biggest thrills was when mother would give me brown bread sandwiches stuffed with beef and pickle for my father. I was only allowed as far as the top of the staircase in his office. He would take the crusty lunch from me in the doorway as I peered into the room, quickly trying to take in as much as I could before the door closed on me. I was always intrigued by the strange machine in the corner, tapping out reams of paper ribbon. They were racing tapes, the lifeline of my father's business.

11

In those days a man of means could bet on credit with a bookie but the working class could not. To cater for their needs, my father employed runners, men who worked at the giant factories and cotton mills in the area. I used to watch them leave his office early in the morning, clutching small leather bags and return at night, carrying the same holdalls, jingling with coins. Years later I realised that these were betting clock bags. The runners would take them in to the factories and place workers' bets in them. Each bag would click before the time of the first race.

For the record, I was born on 26 May 1916, in an old converted inn named the Travellers' Rest, which my father rented in Briscoe Lane, Newton Heath. I am reliably informed that my father's joy turned to anger when he discovered that the registrar had written the girl's name Alexandra on my birth certificate. That was hastily sorted out I am glad to reveal. The inn was surrounded by rolling fields near the Manchester to Oldham road and All Saints Church, where I was christened.

I learnt the three Rs at All Saints Church of England School along the road from The Travellers' Rest; my playground as a boy were the roads that twisted and turned past the local gas works, the giant Avro aircraft factory, a brickmaking firm and my grandmother's farm. My mother hated me to knock about with the boys who lived in the old timber and tile cottages next to the farm. 'They're rough lads Alex, you're to have nothing to do with them', she would tell me, waving her finger in the air like a stick. The rules were laid down. I was to play only with my cousins, Harry Alcock and Ernest Brown, both my age. 'They're nice boys and never get into trouble', mother would say.

Nevertheless the activities of the rough lads were too hard for me to resist. Sometimes I would sneak out of the house and join them for a raiding party into the dump at the Avro factory. We would scale a high, wire fence and abscond with old, brightly-coloured aircraft skins, which made wonderful wig-wams in nearby fields. Our gang leader was Fred Taylor, about my height, who liked a bit of a scrap, but it was his younger brother Stan who I took a shine to. He was a quiet, shy boy. We nicknamed him Thinker, because he would make astounding long-range predictions. 'That bloody gas works will blow somebody to hell one day', he would say, pointing at the steel cones.

One a day a gasometer did explode and several people were killed. We felt the blast as we sat in the classroom. It was a tragedy that rocked the neighbourhood. After that, Stan was held in high esteem. We were all sure that he would be famous one day.

On another occasion, as we stared into the Avro factory, Stan pointed out a Japanese party who were being shown around, and said: 'Mark my words, one day those Japanese will make their own fighter planes and then there'll be trouble!' I wonder what he is doing now? Perhaps he is making a living with a crystal ball.

I first disappointed my father at an early age. A mile from our rickety old inn was an old wooden hall that served as the headquarters for the Culcheth Church Band. It was one of the leading bands in the North. The musicians wore military uniforms on most of their marches, but sometimes they regaled themselves in morning dress and black top hats, earning the nickname The Top Hat Band. My father loved the pomp and ceremony of the band almost as much as his ritual Sunday drink, a large port with a raw egg dropped in it. Every Whit Monday the musicians would march the three miles to Manchester, calling at the Travellers' Rest for refreshments. It was quite an occasion for my father. The trumpeters and drummers always seemed to step more sprightly after leaving us with a few tots of rum inside them. Father wanted me to play the clarinet and join the band, but it never appealed to me. The nearest I came to being musical was a few puffs at the mouth organ, as I sat on the water trough next to our cart horse in the yard. Something I had no say in, however, was the Whit Sunday walks when all the local churches united to march together. It was another occasion my father held in high esteem. When I was six, I fidgeted and frowned as my mother brushed me down in the kitchen for the march. She had dressed me in a pristine white outfit, a jersey, shorts, socks and shoes. I felt a cissy. As I walked with all the different congregations that day, my parents were at their usual place on the Manchester to Oldham road. I passed them, smiling as if butter would not melt in my mouth, but when the parade was out of their sight, I fell back to the end of the line. Then, as the others marched sprightly on, I cut across the fields and headed for home. The Travellers' Rest was thankfully empty but the front door was locked. I ran around the back and clambered over the fence to the stables and coal carts. As I walked across the yard I looked at my clothes. My gleaming white outfit was the colour of coal. The fence had been newly tarred and the thick, black gooey substance was all over me. I remembered that my mother used butter to get tar or grime off our hands so I ran indoors and raided the larder. Grabbing the butter I hastily rubbed it over my clothes but it made matters worse. The black marks spread. I was trying another pack when I heard the kitchen door creak open behind me. It was mother. That night, with watering eyes, I eased my black and blue bottom into my bed.

The older I got, the more the jigsaw pieces of my father's secretive world fitted together. It appeared that most men in the area knew my father and placed bets with him, and it was not long before I became one of his runners. My initiation into this life started at school. One of my teachers, Mr Cross, loved two things in life it seemed to me: beer and horses. Just before the lunch break, the short, tubby, middle-aged master would lean over me in class, thrust a piece of paper into my hand and whisper: 'Just pop that along to your father, Alex.' Before long, he did not have to whisper instructions, he just winked and passed me the name of the horse he wanted to back. I became his pet pupil and it was not my academic drive that put me in the favourite's saddle.

In 1927, my mother, who did not understand why men made such a fuss about betting, had a little flutter on King of Clubs, ridden by Pat Donaghue, son of the legendary Steve Donaghue, in the Lincoln Handicap. She asked father to put sixpence each way on the horse for her and we all laughed because it was 100–1. However, she had the last laugh when King of Clubs won, and I remember thinking then that betting could be a grand way to make a living.

When I was twelve, we moved to a house in Church Street, half a mile from the Travellers' Rest. There was nothing particularly startling about the move and I mention it only because the day we left the inn holds a sad memory for me. I kept a dozen pigeons in the loft as pets and my portly Uncle Jack, who was the new tenant, wrung the necks of every one of them, and dropped them from the loft hatch to the landing. He planned to install his fine racing pigeons and there was no room for my tatty feathered friends.

I became even more immersed in the thrills of backing horses, when, because of Uncle Jack, I realised that the game really could pay. One evening, after moving into 58 Church Street, my father said to me: 'Go and tell Uncle Jack that St. Mary's Kirk has won the Chester Cup.'

I ran all the way to the Travellers' Rest and found him tending to his prized racing pigeons in the loft. I shouted out his win to him and he popped his bald head over the hatch. 'Here lad, go and treat yourself,' he said, throwing down a shiny silver crown. As I walked back down Briscoe Lane, proudly fingering the large five shilling piece in my pocket, I felt very pleased with myself. I had been paid handsomely for just delivering a message. Uncle Jack must have won a fortune. And it was obvious there was a lot of money in the racing game.

My first experience of a racetrack came when I was thirteen and my father took me to Uttoxeter. Being at the races was a thrill but the real memory of the trip was painful. When the train pulled into Manchester station on our return, I was so excited over my day out, that without thinking I jumped off it in the opposite direction to which it was slowing to a halt, and fell flat on my face. As I lay dazed on the platform, my father pulled me to my feet and said: 'Well Alex, has this finally put you off going to the races?' I wish I could have told him then that I would one day fly to courses in my own plane.

Although I was not interested in being a great scholar, I became head boy and captain of the school soccer team, and at fourteen passed an entrance exam for high school. My parents were thrilled, but I was to disappoint them. My mind was made up. I wanted to leave. My father and I had a man to man discussion in the parlour.

'You're a fool, boy,' he said.

'Yes sir.'

'Very well then, I think I can get you a job at the Co-op. You will do well there, they have a good pension scheme.'

'No sir, I don't want to work at the Co-op.'

'What then?'

'I want to be a bookmaker like you.'

There was no arguing with me. I told him that if he would not let me work in his business, I would find another bookmaker to work with.

'Very well then, you can oversee the clock bags and cross out the losing bets, but that's all. For the time being.'

Within months I had thrown myself into my father's mysterious world, and soon he was relying on me. I learnt about the runners and got to know each man by name as I started to collect their clock bags with the jingling coins. Although this side of the business was illegal, the police turned a blind eye to it unless some local do-gooder complained. Then the police would unofficially inform my father that they would have to prosecute. He would put forward a 'dummy', a man with a pocketful of betting slips, to be apprehended on a street corner. The man would be fined ten pounds, which would be paid to him by us. He would also earn three pounds for his trouble. As the average weekly wage at that time was about two pounds, there was no shortage of volunteers. There was a sliding scale of fines: ten pounds for the first offence, twenty pounds for the second, thirty pounds for the third and so on. For this reason, a different man was put foward each time. It was all a formality to keep do-gooders quiet. I never saw my father bribe any police officers. The most he ever did was to hand out a turkey at Christmas or a bottle of Scotch worth twelve shillings and sixpence.

Soon my father, amazed at my dedication to his bookmaking business, let me work out the straight winning bets, for example, 2–1, 3–1 and 4–1. Then I progressed to 7–4 and 13–8. Slowly, I began to realise that perhaps there was real money to be made backing horses, provided a punter studied the form book. One day I spent my savings on an expensive set of hardback form guides and racing annuals. That evening, I went to my bedroom early after dinner and, armed with pencil, paper, the sporting papers and my new books I began to work. The more I studied the guides, the more I realised there was a lot to be learnt. From then on, my study of the form became a nightly ritual. If I missed an evening's work I would be eager to make up for lost time. As I worked deep into the night, I would hear my father's footsteps on the stairs. He would stop on the landing and sigh in despair.

'That damn boy is wasting a fortune in gas. Why doesn't he sleep like everyone else?' he would say to mother.

There was no reward for my endeavours in that first year but I was happy to be patient. For by this time I knew that patience and planning was as much a part of betting as form, the going, the jockey, the distance and the tactics.

One morning, however, I decided to put my theories to the test. My father's own bookmaker was big Billy Mosedale, who operated at the Ellesmere Club in Manchester. He was a typical, old-fashioned bookie who would take any amount of bets. He had an office in Didsbury, run by a nephew, and he was my first target. When the office agreed to accept my bets by telephone I knew I was at the post. I started having two pounds each way, then five pounds each way, on certain horses, but not every day. I did not bet on handicaps, concentrating mainly on races for two-year-olds. If a favourite was an odds-on chance, I would back the second favourite each way. I called these my thieving bets and I proved beyond a shadow of a doubt they were sound policy. I was winning steadily and my confidence grew. Then I hit the first hurdle. The bookie closed my account because I was too successful. However, I was not upset. I already wanted to expand my operation anyway. The question was how?

It was at this time that I met Evelyn, the girl who was to play such a vital part in my life. Slim, beautiful and dark-haired, she lived locally and worked with my sister May. She was a regular visitor to our home and even breakfasted with us. First we became friends and then in the spring of the following year we fell in love.

From the start, Evelyn seemed to understand my passion for backing horses. She never mocked me and was always there for support. When I became egotistical, she would pull me up. We were a good team. Although my father was never rude to Evelyn he would drop hints when she visited the betting office. 'Why don't you go and have a nice cup of tea at our house, love?' he would say, with the sort of look that bid her farewell.

Evelyn was never in the way when we were working but it irritated him to have a woman around. Only May was allowed in his private domain. My father never really showed his feelings and I think that is why I have always found it hard to show emotion. His only real gesture of endearment was to our brown and black striped cat Tush. He genuinely loved her and was always tickling her fur and bringing her the best meat from the butchers. At times she probably dined better than we did, but even Tush knew how to make herself scarce when father had a bad day at the office. For then he would pick her up and throw her out into the yard. 'That bloody cat is always under my feet', he would growl. Somehow it was therapeutic for him to vent his anger on her, but half an hour later he was calling her name as he searched for her with a saucer of milk.

The second phase of my betting operation began when I opened accounts with bookmakers who advertised in the press. Then I would stand in my father's office, watching the tape machine. Before me on the table would be four telegrams, each filled in with the address of the bookmaker and the stake of the bet. All I needed to add was the name of the horse. When the first betting showed, I would write in my selection, run out of the office and leap on my bicycle. Then I would pedal like mad to the post office in the Oldham Road, four minutes away, to telegraph my bet.

One day as I sped through the rain, I realised that my operation would have to be expanded yet again. The bookmakers limited the number of telegrams to four from each post office. This was to restrict the amount of money put on off course seconds before the start. If the bookmakers could prove that more than four telegrams were placed by one person at one post office, they would limit the odds to 4–1 for a win, regardless of a 10–1 starting price. Another reason was that if the telegraph operator had a backlog of bets to tap out, some would not get done until after the race. So if I wanted more than four bets on one race, I would have to go to more than one post office, but I could never cover the distance in time on my old bike. I would have to buy a car. By increasing my bets and covering two post offices, I calculated that I would soon recoup the outlay. The following weekend, I bought a second-hand fabric-body Rover for a princely fifteen pounds. Now I was the fastest backer in town.

A week later I raced down the stairs to the waiting car, clutching eight telegrams, jumped behind the wheel and sped off to the post office on the Oldham Road where I placed four bets as usual. Then onto another post office to place another four bets. I had found a winning system and it paid dividends. The only thing that ate away at my profits was the engine bearings I kept replacing.

Then the inevitable happened. The bookmakers either closed my accounts or put impossible restrictions on my betting. They did not like winners. Some wanted me to bet for a place at Tote odds, or half as much for a place as for a win. I did not blame them for taking such action. When they realised the pattern of my bets, they knew they had virtually no chance. In their circumstances I would have done the same. It was time to find another new system, using agents to place my bets perhaps. I began to think up schemes.

During this time, my father was turning his attention to other investments. 'Put your money into bricks and mortar, son, and you'll never go wrong,' he said. He started to buy houses for a few hundred pounds each and soon had a string of twenty, but each one had a sitting tenant, and he never made a fortune from them. The rents were low, the repair costs high and there was little chance of selling them later without vacant possession. They did not appreciate in value much during those times and finally became slums before being pulled down.

My father was a bookmaker pure and simple. He observed all the ethical rules of making a book. If one of his clients had a double running on and the first horse won at a big price, he would hedge the bet by placing money on the second selection to reduce his liabilities. The only misgiving he had about the bookmaking business involved betting on football because in that he had no control. Every match starts at a certain time and finishes at a certain time. If one of his clients had backed six selections and the first five were winning, he could not hedge on the sixth. My father did not want to carry on with that side of the business, but because other bookmakers were betting on football he had no option but to follow suit. He was never a big bookmaker. The most he took on a single day was £2,000 at racing, and if he lost £1,000 that was a lot to him. At football, things were different. He did not take so much money; £1,000 at the most on a Saturday. However he soon calculated that if the matches went a certain way, he could lose £8,000 or £10,000. He would have been hard put to find such a sum, but having said that, he would pay it to the full. One particular bet he hated laying was 33–1 for three draws. 'I don't care about punters backing the home side, I don't mind punters backing the away side, but I like the draw for myself,' he would say.

He was a strange man my father, superstitious, yet a contradiction in many ways. He even kept a lucky lump of coal in his office. May still has it almost fifty years on.

Father even took the same route to work. I would often stand with May at the office window, watching him cross the road from the back door of our house. 'I'll lay you £100 to a pound that he goes around the telegraph pole,' I would say. Sure enough, he would walk ten yards out of his way to go around that pole. He never changed the route.

However, he did not always follow an expected pattern. Father used to drink with the lads almost every night except Sundays, and I often felt sorry for my mother; she lived a very lonely life it seemed to me.

It was Father's habit to buy drinks for the runners who worked for him in the local pubs. One evening on his walk about a barman persuaded him to pick a dog number for the Waterloo Cup, a coursing event where the greyhounds chase a live hare. Father said he would have number fifty eight, the number of our house, and he took the same number at every pub he went to that night. Father, normally a cool man, was shocked when his number turned out to be a greyhound called Church Street. Nevertheless, the fact that it was the number of our house and the name of our street, failed to have an impact on this most superstitious of men. He checked out the dog and when he discovered it was a rank outsider, decided to have just a few bob on it, because he was a bookmaker at heart as well as by trade. Later that week, James Arthur Bird almost choked drinking his pint when a runner told him the dog had won. He had turned his nose up at a once-in-a-lifetime coincidence.

My experience with greyhounds was equally dramatic, and I particularly remember an incident in October 1935 when I was nineteen. Evelyn and I were on our way to the cinema in my 14.9 Ford, a present from Uncle Jack who by now was doing well one way or another.

'Stop the car!' Evelyn shouted. I pulled up on the road into Manchester. 'I'm not used to mixing with liars,' she said, her eyes blazing. 'My family never lie. I'm not going another yard with you!'

Suddenly it dawned on me what I had said. I had been smiling to myself as I drove along and Evelyn had asked me what was so funny.

'You would be laughing too, if you had seen the look on this young lad's face when the policeman hauled him off the wall at Belle Vue Greyhound track last night,' I said. 'The constable spotted him trying to get in free, and pulled him down by the seat of his trousers!'

I had put my foot in it. Twenty minutes earlier I had told Evelyn I had spent the previous night with friends in the local pub. It was a little white lie because I had promised never to go greyhound racing again. At the time I had hit a losing streak and she was worried that our savings were slipping away. Somehow I managed to calm her down and convince her that I was not a habitual liar.

21

My attraction to greyhounds started when I ran a book at the Belle Vue track in Manchester in the name of my father. One day however I had a disagreement over a ten pound bet with a punter. He claimed he had backed Dog A when in fact he had backed Dog B. I was certain I was right, and so was my clerk. After the night's racing we went to arbitration. The adjudicator was an official of the Bookmakers' Protection Association. My father disliked the man and was angry when he ruled against me. The next day, as I told him the story, my father said: 'How dare a man like that sit in judgement of my son! Alex you will never bet at the dogs again.'

I was nineteen when the first bookmaker ever defaulted on me. His name was Sinclair Milne from Bolton and I had been betting with him for three weeks. Each week I had shown a profit of around £300, which was not bad, considering that the limit he would lay me was ten pounds each way. In the fourth week I had eighteen bets with him, and when no statement arrived, I telephoned to ask where it was. 'What are you talking about?' he said. 'You haven't had a bet with me all week.' I may have been young but I was not green. I checked with the General Post Office in Manchester and confirmed that eighteen telephone calls had been made from my number to the bookmaker. Armed with this evidence, I set off for Knightsbridge, London, where the Tattersalls Committee adjudicated in betting disputes.

Harry Williamson, the manager of the local insurance office, had been in my father's offices when I made six of the calls and he went with me for a very good reason – as he had a small interest in my bets. I thought I had a cast iron case. I would hardly make eighteen calls to the same bookmaker to enquire after his health. The Committee, however, found in the bookmaker's favour. I was disappointed, but was determined the rebuff would not put me off, and I continued betting wherever I could get on.

Early in 1937, I approached my father in his office on an important matter.

'Father, I'm getting married on the 21st of August this year,' I said.

'Good luck to you son,' he replied, not looking up from the pile of betting slips before him.

'It's a Saturday and I'll need time off,' I continued, almost apologetically.

'You know that Saturday is our busiest day,' he said, still not looking at me.

'But getting married is more important.'

'There's nothing more important than your bread and butter, son. Get married on a week day, I can't spare you.'

'All the guests have been invited and the church and reception rooms have been booked, I can't pull out now.' He was indifferent to my plea. There was an agonising minute's silence.

'All right Alex.'

'Thank you father.'

'But be back in this office by five o'clock that afternoon!'

There was no arguing. So Evelyn and I had a white wedding. My cousin Harry Alcock was best man and the reception went without a hitch. Father did not come of course; he was too busy and was never one for weddings and ceremonies anyway.

May attended the wedding, and so did Mother who loved every minute of it. It was a well-earned break away from her weary routine. At one minute to five that day, May and I stepped back into my father's office. I was still wearing the morning suit I was married in. Three hours later I was off on honeymoon to Bournemouth.

I later celebrated getting married by backing Solitaire in the Manchester Handicap. When he won we paid off part of our mortgage on our first house in Sale, called Evander – a mixture of our names – and there was plenty left for furniture too.

The following year was perhaps a turning point for me. For in 1938 I backed a horse in the Grand National, a race that was to figure a great deal in my life. It was all in all a depressing year for the country. There was mass unemployment, widespread poverty and the threat of World War.

I was twenty two and wanted to apply for service with the R.A.F. Volunteer Reserve as a trainee pilot. With the appropriate forms already filled in and signed and lying on the dining room table, I explained to Evelyn that this was primarily for the defence of Manchester, and in the event of war, I would be based at Ringway Airport five miles from home. Evelyn protested vigorously however. 'If you think my nerves will stand my seeing planes fly overhead, wondering whether it's you about to kill yourself, you are very much mistaken!' she exclaimed. 'I can't live with you in such circumstances!' I had my wings well and truly clipped and had to stay on the ground. I went back to my form books.

I had been having some success, placing each way bets here and there, but only when I felt certain the horses were good value. Although I was showing a fair profit, I needed to test my knowledge more, and the Grand National was to offer me that opportunity.

One rainy day in March, as I sat in my father's office, meticulously reading the *Sporting Chronicle*, I came across a horse I had been aware of for some time. His name was Battleship, a miniature, eleven-year-old horse owned by American millionairess Marion du Pont, who had married handsome Hollywood film cowboy Randolph Scott. Marion had sent Battleship across the Atlantic to Reg Hobb's stable at Lambourn, to gain experience of the English fences. The following month he was to run in the National with Reg's seventeen-year-old son, Bruce, in the saddle. I knew Battleship was small but he was a reliable jumper who would stay the distance.

My finances were tight but I decided to put eleven pounds – a lot of money in those days – on Battleship, and I hoped Evelyn would understand. For she saved for us and I did not want to let her down! The next day I placed my bet, ten pounds to win at 40–1 and one pound place at 10–1 which would save my win stake.

It was a good job I had no way of knowing that the day before the race in Liverpool's prestigious Adelphi Hotel, trainer Reg Hobbs told friends: 'Battleship's owner is a lovely woman, but she must be tough to even think of running this dear little horse over those thirty gruelling, Aintree fences. He's only 15.2, too small to see over the Chair Jump, let alone Becher's.'

National day was cold and dreary. I remember standing in the little back room of my father's office smoking a Woodbine as I listened to wireless commentator Raymond Glendenning going through the race preliminaries. Minutes later the National was under way. Horses started to fall, and as the field streamed over the Canal Turn some could not make the ninety-degree bend and went into the water: but Battleship was still there. As the runners raced past the stands and out into the country for the second time, he was up with the leaders. Glendenning's voice became more excited. Battleship moved up on the rails and cleared Becher's a length from the big, strong Irish entry Royal Danieli, ridden by Dan Moore, and the improving Delachance. My horse, however, seemed to have the heart of a lion, as Bruce pushed him on. Two fences from home, my heart skipped a beat when Battleship made a mistake and lost ground.

At the last, Royal Danieli had a good lead from Workman and Battleship who was racing wide. Nevertheless Battleship lived up to his name. Bruce pushed him on and inch by inch he closed the gap with Royal Danieli on the run in.

The crowd went wild, and Glendenning was speaking so fast he was difficult to understand. The two horses were racing neck and neck and as they crossed the line the judge declared Battleship the winner by a neck. It was a decision which Dan Moore, who was to become a good friend of mine, contested for the rest of his life. Marion du Pont had been watching the race from the stands with actor Randolph Scott but she was too overcome with emotion to lead her horse in. I had won £410, a small fortune in those days, but I felt no emotion as I stood at the office window, looking at the old clay pit across the croft where I used to play as a boy. Somehow I felt my win was only a small beginning.

On 8 January, 1939 our first son Harvey was born, but that year stands out in my mind for another reason. My father grew ill, and he and mother moved in with us. Evelyn nursed him and for the first time they became close to each other. 'You've got one in a million there, son,' he would say.

By this time Evelyn had come to accept that greyhound racing was still in my blood. I always got a thrill walking away from a noisy, floodlit night at the dogs with my pocket full of white fivers and that year I bought a dog called Guiting Greenwood for twenty five pounds. She was a staying type, who produced her form at the end of the race. If a person has a weak heart he should never own a dog like this. Invariably it has a habit of finding any bad luck that is going. Although I never lost any money on her, once I realised what she was like, it took me a long time to discover she was prone to chasing other dogs but would not pass the leader.

Time and again she would streak by all the runners – except the one in front, and look big odds-on in running. Then at the last second she would hold back. It was heartbreaking. The facts speak for themselves. Guiting Greenwood had a run of nine consecutive seconds.

On New Year's Day 1940 my father died, leaving the betting business to me. Later that month however I decided to volunteer for the Navy, leaving May to run the office. The move was largely due to the man who lived in the next house to us, who had served at sea during the First World War. 'The Navy's the thing for you my boy, you get in there,' he advised. Little did I know that I would be cursing his very soul a few months later as I tossed my guts out on a destroyer in the North Atlantic.

Five days before I had to report for National Service I was disgusted to open the *Manchester Evening News* at home and find that Guiting Greenwood had been lifted two grades in class for her race the following day. I immediately rolled the paper up, marched out of the house and drove to the track. The racing manager looked startled when I burst into his office.

'I know why you are here, Mr Bird,' he said apologetically, putting up an appeasing hand. 'All I can say is that I am terribly sorry.'

'My dog has no chance in that class,' I exclaimed.

'I agree, but I was short of a runner and because of the forecast betting I put her in. Please don't worry. I will lower her three grades and promise she will win on her next appearance.'

I was still not happy, but I let the matter drop. If he did lower her three grades later, she might be able to do something after all, although I was still doubtful. Later I went for a pint at the Wilton Club in Manchester, a favourite haunt of the greyhound fraternity. A serious card game was in progress in the far corner of the room and each player was a bookmaker. I strolled across to the table where the poker-faced men sat playing the card game Koon Kan. Each of them had a pile of pound notes. One of the players was Ina Blomley, a bespectacled greyhound bookmaker, with a computerised brain, and ruddy complexion.

As the cards were being shuffled, I told them about Guiting Greenwood and my hasty visit to the track. I was still so angry that I said I would be prepared to lay my dog at 33–1, so sure was I that she could not win. Ina picked up his cards and looked at me. 'Alex, you never know, anything can happen in dog racing,' he said. He studied his cards for a moment then put them down on the table. Looking over his glasses he picked a pound note up from his kitty and thrust it in my hand. 'I am not going to let that go without this little investment,' he added.

I laid him the bet. The following day I went to Manchester races. The fact that I had to report for National Service four days later was very much on my mind and I forgot Guiting Greenwood was running. Later than evening I returned to the Wilton Club and as I walked through the doors, a great cry went up from the members.

'What's that about?' I asked the barman, ordering a pint.

'Why, your dog has won at the White City, didn't you know?' he said with a quizzical look. I did not believe him, feeling sure it was a leg pull.

'Oh really?' I said with a smile.

'What a price!' he went on.

'What was that?'

'100–1.'

Now I was certain it was a hoax, but I had to find out for my own peace of mind. The resident club bookmaker Joe Burke, was sitting at a table by himself. He was a serious man, not one to make light of

27

life and I knew he would give me a straight answer. He never joked about the business.

'Surely they're pulling my leg, aren't they?'

'Alex, as sure as I'm sitting here, your dog has won, and she was 100–1.'

They must have bribed him with a pint, I thought. Finally, I decided to enter into the spirit of things. I pulled a wad of notes out of my pocket and paid Ina, sitting at a nearby table, thirty four pounds. Then I leant across the chair to face him and said. 'If you are pulling my leg Ina, you will return this on Monday before I go into the Navy.' I left and bought an evening paper from the street seller. There it was in print: Guiting Greenwood had won at 100–1. I laughed aloud. 'What's the joke mister?' the newspaper seller asked. 'Guiting Greenwood won at the White City,' I said. 'I know, but mister, it must be a misprint, just look at the odds.'

The next day I discovered the reason behind my dog's phenomenal price. I had a drink with Herbert Howarth who was a bookmaker at the track. As he had been present when my bet with Ina was struck he opened his prices at 33–1, instead of the normal 8–1 perhaps drifting to 16–1.

Herbert explained: 'I shouted: "The owner doesn't fancy this 33–1 Guiting Greenwood!"' Then he increased the price to 40–1, 50–1 and 66–1. When the starter released the hare on its preliminary run around the track, Herbert called out again: 'Let's have some tea money, 100–1 Guiting Greenwood!' He laid the price to a fellow club member Fred Tattersall and shouted that the odds were still on offer. When the dogs came out of the traps, the starting price reporter had no option but to return the dog at 100–1. Herbert lost over £500 on the race, so he was not very pleased; that was a lot of money in those days. Guiting Greenwood's price is a record for a greyhound race in England. What made her finally go to the front in a better class race is a mystery to this day.

My navy days started at HMS *Raleigh*, in Torpoint, Devon, which was later to be a temporary home for hundreds of French refugees. They fled to the safety of England in the Dunkirk evacuation, bringing with them their cats, dogs and caged birds. I stood watching them trundle off the armada of small boats and the despair on their faces was something I will never forget.

Alex Bird's war was not really a spectacular affair and I shall recall just a few memories of it. My first ship was the ex-American destroyer HMS *Castleton*. I joined it a few days after being stationed in Halifax, Nova Scotia, where we lived in barracks on the racecourse, which made me feel very much at home. The *Castleton* was the first of Britain's 40 lend-lease destroyers from America. All the crew thought that as it was the No. 1 ship it would be called HMS *Churchill*, but sadly that was not to be.

At Halifax American sailors showed us the ropes, and I asked one of them if they were crossing the Atlantic with us. 'Not us boy,' he said. 'Those bastards are all right for cruising round the Panama Canal but not across the Pond!'

A few weeks later I discovered what he meant. I was on watch on the bridge as the Castleton rolled to an angle of forty eight degrees. She stayed there for seemingly an age but it was obviously only seconds before she got back on an even keel.

I was terribly seasick for the first four days and was only saved by a Scottish sailor when we docked at St. Johns, Newfoundland. 'Have a large whisky and chaser,' he advised. I had never heard of scotch washed down with beer before and I tried it. I can truthfully say that from St. Johns to the end of the war, I was never seasick again.

When I got back to England the first thing I did was ring Evelyn. The date stands out in my mind because 21 August, 1940 should have been a red letter day.

'How are you darling?' she asked.

'I'm O.K. I've just crossed the Atlantic and I am quite safe.'

'But what have you really rung for?' she asked.

'Nothing special apart from telling you I'm all right.'

Then came the disappointed cry: 'But don't you know that this is my birthday and our wedding anniversary?'

Next came Atlantic patrol, where we were prey to the elements as we escorted the convoys. We were constantly at action stations.

My job at sea was to look after a large complicated piece of machinery called the 'director'. By adjusting various controls it enabled the gunners to focus on the target. When not in use it was covered by a large tarpaulin sheet, many hundreds of pounds in weight. To facilitate its removal a pulley was fastened to the cross piece of the mast, way above the crow's nest.

One day I accidentally let the rope, which was threaded through the pulley, go loose and the tarpaulin fell in a crumpled heap. The bosun's mate, a tough Devonian, said sarcastically, 'Well Dickie, we will have to put it back won't we.' I looked up fearfully. The ship was rolling badly. One moment the mast was over to starboard, then way out to port. I have never been fond of heights and had it been possible I would have given someone a hundred pounds to do the job for me. Up I went, past the crow's nest. When I got to my precarious destination, I had to turn, and with my heels securing me on a steel ladder, the rope clenched between my teeth, I was able to edge along the cross piece and reeve the rope through the pulley. I had never been so scared in my life. The wind was howling and the bosun was screaming instructions to me. He must have seen the look on my face as I shouted back: 'Come up here you big fat bastard and do it yourself!' When I got back down he asked: 'What was that you said Bird?' 'It won't be long, I have almost finished,' was my reply.

On the few occasions I stepped ashore in England I would touch the ground for luck. Then I would sleep my way home, on a series of trains, trams and buses, asking drivers, conductors and passengers to wake me up at each destination. I would finally arrive at my house, greet my son and wife and fall into a deep, trance-like sleep in a room that seemed to dip and sway under me as if I was in an imaginary sea. Often I would wake up with just a few hours left to my return, not long enough for my family or my form books. The routine was home for a day, at sea for fourteen. It was hardly worth packing my kit bag.

For a while I was based at the Kyle of Lochalsh in Scotland, where the *Castleton* escorted fast mine layers north of Scapa Flow.

As this looked to be as semi-permanent a base as anything could be in the Navy, I moved Evelyn and Harvey into digs in a crofter's cottage on the beautiful Isle of Skye, where I could visit them on leave. When they arrived the ship had embarked on duties. I was fully prepared for them to have gone back home, as Miss Matheson, the owner of the cottage seemed most terse and forbidding. That was not, however, the case. Evelyn told me that it took three days to break the ice and after that, Miss Matheson and her elderly mother made her as welcome as the flowers in May. She told me that she attended all the dances at the local hall and learnt the Highland reels.

Next came the uninviting Gladstone Dock at Liverpool, and more convoy patrols. Early one morning the Admiral was piped aboard the *Castleton* for a shipboard conference before the fleet sailed for the Atlantic. As the party strolled along the deck, the Admiral leant over the rails and looked down at two cars parked on the dockside. Turning to the bosun, he pointed to the shiny new SS Jaguar, standing gloriously alongside the crates of supplies that were being loaded aboard.

'That's a fine motor the captain has got there,' he said.

'Oh no sir, that's not the captain's car,' the bosun replied. 'The other one belongs to the captain.' The bosun pointed out the old, battered American Ford standing in the shadow of the Jaguar.

'Then who does that fantastic thing belong to?' said the Admiral.

'Why, it's Able Seaman Bird's sir!'

The Admiral went off muttering, wondering perhaps what a rating was doing with such a prize. It was a lovely prize too, a measure of my success backing horses. My captain would, of course, have preferred the Jaguar to his own car. However, it was his old Ford that I drove him about in, even taking him to Manchester races. My navy life was so unusual that my friends sent letters addressed: Extraordinary Seaman Bird.

My biggest shock of the war came when I joined the aircraft carrier *Victorious*. By then I had devised a way of keeping myself afloat in cash. Crewmates would give me their addresses in Britain and when we docked in Sydney, Australia, I wrote to my sister May telling her to send varying amounts of money to their relatives. When the ratings got word that their wives, parents or girlfriends had got the cash, they reimbursed me in crisp pound notes. One morning as I sat at a table in the ship's dining room, eating a porridge breakfast, I was approached by some Scottish lads, who could not contain their excitement. They were a good-hearted bunch, all racing enthusiasts. They had been given a tip for a horse running at Randwick that day, and were eager to back him. They knew that I placed bets at a local bar when I drove the ship's jeep on errands and they had pooled their money for the bet. They asked me to put the cash on for them and I agreed. At first I tried to explain their fancied runner was racing against an Australian champion that was the 8–1 on favourite. However, they could not be dissuaded. 'The tip comes from a man who knows the brother of the trainer,' said one rating, confidently.

I drove the jeep into Sydney to fetch the ship's mail. It was a beautiful, hot day and there was plenty of time to spare after picking up the letters. So I stopped for a quiet lunch on Bondi Beach. Then I took my uniform off, slipped into a pair of trunks, and threw myself into the surf. Driving back into the city, cool and refreshed, I remembered the race and looked at my watch. I had missed it. At first I panicked, then I realised that the lads would be pleased to get their money back because their horse had obviously lost. I stopped at the bar where I normally placed my bets. The radio was on and a couple of drinkers had heard the commentator talking about the race. The colour drained from my face when they revealed that apparently the odds on favourite had been beaten, in a finish that shocked the track. A rank outsider had won. They could not remember the horse's name, but they thought the price was 33–1. I ordered a schooner of beer and downed it in one. I had not got enough money to cover the winnings and it would take too long to telegraph May back home for it. I felt sure the lads would keel haul me. Finally, one of the men discovered the name of the winning horse. It was not the runner the lads wanted to back. I sighed with relief. From that day on, I swore never to place money for others unless I could cover the win. It was a lesson I nearly learnt the hard way. There were smiles all round the mess deck when the lads got their stake back, but I could not help wondering how many would have forgiven me if the horse had won.

There was one occasion during the war years when I was very pleased with myself. In Algiers a wellwisher gave me a case of Benedictine liqueurs and because I knew that each bottle cost over fifteen pounds on the black market I guarded the case with my life. I kept it hidden and smuggled it through the docks in England, finally storing it in a cupboard under the stairs at home.

Within a few days I was back at sea again and Evelyn's Uncle Jacob, a kindly old man, volunteered to do our garden while I was away. It was thirsty work and Evelyn offered him a drink – my liqueur. He drank it from a pint mug. 'He liked it so much, I kept topping up the mug every time he came to do the weeding,' said Evelyn innocently, as I stared in despair at the empty case on my return home three months later.

'Mind you, he did seem to stagger around the rosebed a lot after drinking that stuff Alex. Was that foreign drink strong?'

There was just one consolation; Evelyn handed me some cheques that bookmakers had sent me as winnings. One of them puzzled me however. It was for twenty five pounds and came from Littlewoods. I checked the records of my bets and realised that I could not have won the money. At the time the bet was supposed to have been struck I was on convoy duty in mid-Atlantic. I returned the cheque to the firm with an explanatory letter. From that time on Littlewoods became the only company never to close or restrict my betting. I believe the reason was that I returned their money. It was just a small example of honesty being the best policy.

On 3 August, 1943 my second son Laurence was born, and I felt the tide was turning in our favour in the war. Then two years later when the atom bomb was dropped on Japan, I was on the *Victorious*, serving with the American Sixth Fleet in the Pacific. A few days before Hiroshima I saw many of our pilots die as their planes disappeared into the sea on take-off in turbulent conditions.

I remember wondering what the liaison was like between the high commands. It seemed to me that these forays by the pilots on the aircraft carriers were a needless waste of young lives when the end of the war was so near.

A few months later I was demobbed.

Back on land things had changed. I tried to make a go of the bookmaking business, but my heart was not in it.

My mother had died and I had got a taste for the outdoor life in the navy. Now I had a yearning to try the other side of the betting fence.

Finally, after a long discussion with Evelyn I sold the business to May for a token sum of £500 and went out to do the thing I loved most: go racing.

2

IN JUNE 1944 the Jockey Club set up a committee to probe the uses of photography to judge races. Its members were so impressed with the great advances in aerial photography during the war that they called in Group Captain F.C.V. Laws, Director of Photography at the Air Ministry. Two years later the Laws Organisation was set up with the aid of a grant from the Jockey Club to design a prototype camera to be tested on a racetrack at the finishing line. Tests at Newmarket and Birmingham were so successful that The Race Finish Recording Company was formed on 1 November, 1946 in anticipation of a nationwide operation. Then on 22 April, 1947, at Epsom, a judge officially called on a photo for the first time. The race was the Great Metropolitan Handicap. The picture showed Parhelion beating Salubrious by a head. The photo finish had finally arrived to a rousing welcome from punters, bookmakers and Alex Bird, for it was to open up a whole new betting world for me.

Within months the camera was in operation at Newmarket, Epsom, Goodwood, Birmingham and Doncaster. Sixty days racing was covered at a cost of eighty pounds a day. Soon more courses were to follow.

In 1948, two years after my third son Jack was born I stumbled on the secret that was to bring me big rewards at the bookies' expense.

On a blustery day at Newmarket I was so engrossed in a conversation at the paddock, that I was late getting to my usual spot by the rails bookmakers in the Members Enclosure, where I could bet in running.

That day, however, I stood down near the rails opposite the winning post. As the horses approached it was a desperate finish and a photo was called for. In those days it took a full five minutes to develop the film. As the result was awaited the bookmakers created a separate market. Like most punters, I thought that the horse racing on the far side was the winner and he was soon a big odds on chance. Five minutes later I was amazed when it was announced that the horse on the near side had got the race. I looked back across the track, picturing the scene at the post in my mind's eye. Still I could not understand the incredible result. Perhaps I had been standing in the wrong position? I went to a raised dais about 30 yards from the rails, directly opposite the post, walked up about six steps and created an imaginary line across the track. Then I decided to test the theory that was growing in my mind. My eyes would be a camera lens and I would keep my head still, seeing the horses for the first time as they crossed the line.

The next two races went by without the necessity of the camera. I stood on the dais fixedly staring over people's heads and wondered if there would be another photo finish that afternoon. Then in the fifth race my patience was rewarded. I stood rigid, not blinking as the two front runners crossed the line. I was sure that the horse nearest to me had won, but again a flood of money was going on the horse racing on the far side. For me, the race was just a test. I was not confident of my judgement so I did not bet. I stood waiting anxiously for the result to see if I was right. I was. My horse won by a head. Later that afternoon I drove back to the University Arms Hotel at Cambridge, where I was staying with Evelyn who had been shopping during the day. Over dinner I explained the phenomenon I had witnessed and could talk about nothing else.

'I don't know why, but I have a feeling about this,' I said. 'I'm sure I'm on to something. It could be that horses passing the post at speed create an optical illusion and the natural reaction of most people is to favour the horse farther away.'

Evelyn eyed me warily. She never doubted my racecourse logic, but this time she was not convinced.

'It may have just been a fluke, and there's no optical illusion at all,' she said.

'You could be right but I will stay on the line the next three days and sort it out. This is like tennis, people are turning their heads left and right, but even in tennis, a touch line judge has to keep his head still. I think that's the secret of it.'

However, I realised the danger involved in my system if I was proved right. If I was not watching the horses over the final few furlongs, as I stood rigid, creating a line across the track, I would be ignorant about what was going on in the race. If there were any incidents which merited an objection I could lose my money in the stewards' room, for although I was right in my judgement of the photo, bets were settled on the stake. Still, that was a risk I would have to take and I did have the consolation of knowing that one of my tic tac agents would mark my card if he saw anything untoward happening.

The first photo finish the following day was an obvious win for the horse on the far side, an apparent half a length and no betting on the result. Yet the verdict was only a neck. I waited impatiently to prove my theory. My chance came in the third race. It was a desperate finish. As the horses came to the line I stood as still as a board, creating an imaginary tape across the track. I could have kicked myself when, in the crucial last split second, as the runners passed the post for a photo, I turned my head just a little. That was a habit I would have to conquer. However I was sure the horse on the near side had won by a head.

The finish was identical to the race the previous day, when I thought the horse nearest to me had won. I decided to have a bet, even though I was still not fully confident. Both horses were 6–4 on and I laid £600 to win £400. The horse racing on the far side was the one punters wanted to be on and he finished up favourite. Had I waited I could have had odds against my horse. The result was announced. My selection had won by a neck! I was on to something after all.

I practised my method for the rest of the day, trying different positions and stances. Finally, I got it right, with an extra ingredient. I kept my left eye closed, and that was to be my stance on courses throughout Britain, wherever the photo finish was operated, for twenty years.

My winnings were to bring me a mansion home, Daimlers, my own plane, a string of racehorses, a private dining room at Aintree and a box at Manchester United's Old Trafford ground. I was to be a lucky man indeed. It was all courtesy of the bookmakers, my friends off the track and my enemies on it. Thanks to them and the photo finish I was to enjoy a successful career with a betting turnover of £2,000,000 a year.

During the year that my photo finish betting system was born I bought my first race horse, Quags. Little did I know what heartaches I was letting myself in for as an owner.

The three-year-old was bred by Lord Rosebery, and was out of the mare Hors d'oeuvre. He named the horse after Quaglinos, his favourite restaurant, which, he claimed, did the best Hors d'oeuvres in London.

I paid 1,100 guineas for Quags after he won the Barnham Selling Plate over a mile, at Newmarket on 29 April. He was a very genuine horse, but there was nothing special about him. I bought him purely for the pleasure of owning a horse. Trainer Jack Pearce was at the meeting and as he had been travelling head man to that great trainer Sam Armstrong, I believed he would be the ideal person for me. We came to an arrangement and he packed Quags off to the small stables he rented in Lincolnshire. I already knew Jack, having been introduced by a friend, farmer John Harrop, who lived in the same county. Jack was a meticulous man, with a sergeant major attitude that no doubt greatly assisted him in his job. However I was later to learn that being travelling head man was not necessarily the best preparation for becoming a trainer, as he spent very little time in the stables. Quag's first outing for me was a moderate race at Worcester, where he finished second. A couple of weeks later I ran him in a better class race at Doncaster and he ran terribly. As I left the stands I thought: 'There's one born every minute and you are it, Alex Bird!'

Quags had been ridden by Jimmy Foy, brother of my commissioner and great friend Johnny Foy. My confidence in the horse faded but because I wanted a runner at a local meeting, I entered Quags for The Willows Plate, over a mile, at Haydock.

The other runners were in a much higher class. I did not put a penny on him and he was returned at 20–1. Lord Derby's horse, Tolbooth, was hot favourite. There was no doubt that Tolbooth, who had been engaged in the classics, was a good thing. The only apparent danger was Valray, owned by Willie Satinoff, a slim and impeccably dressed millionaire with a zest for fitness who was later to involve me in one of the most incredible betting coups in the history of English racing.

Willie was sure Tolbooth would win, and asked me to put £1,000 on for him. I placed an extra £1,000 on for myself. I watched the race from the top of the stands with Willie and could hardly believe my eyes. Quags, again ridden by Jimmy Foy, was going very well and it was a battle royal over the last furlong between him and Tolbooth. Quags won by a neck.

It should have been apparent to the stewards, one of whom was Lord Derby, that this was one of those shock results which occur from time to time. The winner was a complete outsider and no mysterious coup had been organized. However, minutes after the race they called my trainer in. Lord Derby did not adjudicate as his horse had been involved. Jack made his excuses and finally they were accepted. The penny should have dropped then that I was a marked man, but I went blissfully on, unaware that something of a vendetta was building up against me. Time and again I was to be summoned before the stewards, when normally only the jockey and trainer are called in. Although I did not back Quags in the race, someone did have enough confidence to put money on him. I later found out that Jimmy had fifty pounds on his ride, so he must have been better informed than I was.

A few months later I was at Epsom for the Oaks. That day Hollywood legend Rita Hayworth and the Aly Khan, cut their usual glamorous figures as they took their seats in the Aly's box, high in the grandstand. The crowd was spellbound by them but my only interest was the two-horse Ebbisham Stakes taking place on the track, because this was business.

The Oaks had been won by the 6–1 shot Musidora, ridden by

that quiet Australian jockey Edgar Britt. It was a thrilling finish, but even then Romeo and his Juliet in the grandstand stole the show and when the tapes went up in the next race – the Ebbisham – most eyes were still on the balcony scene, including those of the bookmakers, who should have known better. For my own Romeo, a horse named Jet Plane, ridden by Gordon Richards, streaked up to challenge the hot favourite Solar Myth on the post. It was a desperate finish and a photo was called for. I of course had been standing on the line. Most people thought that Solar Myth, ridden by Tommy Gosling and racing on the far side, had held on but I knew different. As the two horses raced across the line, I turned and raised my topper as a signal to my tic-tac agents to place my bets. The two men, who had been waiting for the sign, were among the best tic-tac operators in the business.

They were Teddie Hayes and Frankie Powell. Teddie was a big impeccably dressed ex-Liverpudlian who lived in the Midlands. He never drank at the races and was a partner in the firm with Frankie, a small, fun-loving man who loved a tipple. Sadly that weakness was later to lead to his death. Within seconds Teddie and Frankie had put £2,000 on Jet Plane and I was amazed at the odds they had managed to get. After going in at 2–1 they continued to bet at 7–4, 6–4 and 5–4.

It was unbecoming to be seen to rush at Epsom and so I made my way casually across the lawn to see if betting on the result was still in progress. One of the bookmakers operating on the result of the photo was Percy Thompson. As I walked towards him, a well-known backer appeared at my side. The man, who I shall call X, was friendly with many bookies including Percy, and had a reputation of having big connections with some of London's leading gangsters, including Jack Spot. 'What has won?' he asked. 'I'll tell you when I have had my bet,' I replied. Then I waved him away. When it came to my investments I was the iron man of the course. Mr X went away with a scowl on his face and the extent of his bitterness I was to find out later. Percy was still taking bets on the rails.

'I'll take 5–4,' he shouted, meaning his favourite was 5–4 on.

'What is your favourite?' I asked.

'Solar Myth.'

'What price is Jet Plane?'

'Even money.'

'Even how much?'

'What do you want?'

'Even £2,000.'

'You've got it.'

I could hardly believe my ears.

I was even more amazed when I discovered some time later that if I had asked for an even £10,000 I could have had it. Percy said once: 'If the judge does not know which horse has won, how the hell does Alex Bird?' The result was announced. Jet Plane won by a head. I had relieved the bookies of another £5,000.

I never felt guilty of taking the bookies' money this way. People were beginning to say that my eyesight was exceptional but of course it was no better than the next man. And now that I had discovered that horses passing the post at speed created an optical illusion I realised something else: the wider apart the horses, the bigger the margin of error.

As I made my way across the Members Enclosure, master butcher Joss Travis, from Oldham, who loved horses and often accompanied me to the races, appeared alongside me and said: 'Be careful tonight Alex. I've been told that X is out to get you, and you know who his contacts are.'

I would not be intimidated. I knew that if it happened once, it would happen time and again because there were villains on every track.

'Tell X from me, that I will be back at the Mayfair Hotel at 6 pm. I will leave there at 10.30 pm for a meal at the Bagatell Restaurant nearby. After that, I will look in on my friend Edmundo Ros at the Coconut Grove, in Regent Street. Oh, and by the way I will be back at the Mayfair a couple of hours later.'

'Why give him a timetable of your movements?' asked Joss.

'For one simple reason. Tell him that I am leaving a sealed envelope with the hotel manager, outlining my itinerary for the evening and explaining the threat that has been made. If anything happens to me, it will be delivered to the Home Secretary!'

That is just what I did that night and nothing happened. For twenty five years I never spoke to X again, even though I saw him almost every day at race meetings.

I was always searching relentlessly for new ways of beating the bookies, but a lot of my bets were handled by tic-tac agents Teddy Hayes and Frankie Powell, transacting millions of pounds for me with hand signals on the course. They also accepted messages via the blower system, placing large sums of money for betting shops and bookmakers off-course, which was a good thing for me. If an off-course bookmaker would pay out £5,000 on odds of 5–1 to the punter, he would collect £5,000 from odds of 10–1 through the blower. If the horse lost of course, the bookie would have made half the original stake, £500. Either way the bookmaker could not lose, and that is true today. When I used Teddie and Frankie therefore, the rails bookmakers would have little idea of the origin of the bet. They could never be sure it was my money that was going on. It could be from other sources via the blower. People who are not involved in racing have no idea of the honesty and integrity of men like my two tic-tac agents. When I was betting on photo finishes, millions of pounds were invested, and I had no way of confirming with them the total number of bets. They merely showed me their cards and afterwards I made a deduction for wages. Teddy and Frankie were to do business for me for over twenty years, and I never had a single argument with them. In the south they operated with tic-tac agents working for the firm Hokey and could place money in all the betting rings. Often though, I would put money on through owners, or friends who had accounts with bookmakers. The fact that most of them lost money on their own bets was in my favour, for the bookmakers were always willing to accommodate them. Johnny Foy placed most of my off-course commissions. He had contacts with bookmakers in every town and city. I likened those contacts to the tentacles of an octopus. Each one would have another twenty contacts and in this way he covered the whole of

Britain. In later years I would stand by the telephone at home, watching a race on TV. As the horses were being loaded into the starting stalls, I would ring Johnny at his office. 'Now!' I would say. He already knew which horse I wanted to back and he would signal to five helpers sitting by telephones. They would place the money simultaneously with five different bookmakers seconds before the off. I cannot really blame bookmakers for not wanting to lay me large bets, but if a bookmaker calls out a price, and literally puts his goods in his shop window, then he should lay a decent bet. It is galling to have a bookmaker reduce my bet to perhaps a tenth of what I want and in the next breath, lay a fantastic bet with someone he considers a mug punter. Once, at Cheltenham, I had trouble getting my money on a horse with the rails bookmakers. Finally I succeeded but I had to spread my bets with ten bookies. So I was annoyed when told that a wealthy builder had backed the horse I wanted, to win £100,000 with a top bookmaking firm. Their man took the bet without turning a hair, for the company chairman of the building firm was known to be a 'Top of the Book' client. Such punters are not reckoned in the profit and loss columns. Their bets are ignored for the very good reason that their chances of success in the long run are minimal.

The more my confidence grew on the photo finish, the bigger my bets became. Although I was always confident of my photo prediction, I still lived with the nagging fear that the bookies had seen something in running that I had not. The 1949 Derby was an example that this fear could become reality itself. I was on the line for a photo between Nimbus, Armour Drake and Swallow Tail. I backed Nimbus, ridden by Charlie Elliott, to win £2,000 with Percy Thompson. He laid me the bet at what I considered very generous odds, as it was obvious to everyone that Nimbus had won from Armour Drake with Swallow Tail beaten into third place by a head. Later, however, after taking Percy's money yet again, I discovered that my bet was by no means safe. While I had been standing with one eye closed creating my imaginary line across the track, a battle royal was taking place over the last two furlongs. Nimbus was not keeping a straight course and Armour Drake, ridden by Rae Johnson, switched position. Swallow Tail swerved to the right, trying to come through, and there was a great deal of bumping. Percy had obviously seen the trouble in running, and thought that Nimbus might be disqualified. Had Swallow Tail been second, there would have been an objection to the winner. The bookies are very good at reading a race and I quickly learnt never to underestimate them.

The photo finish was a magnet to me and I felt drawn to courses where it operated. Once, on holiday at the Royal Norfolk Hotel in Bognor Regis, I could not relax and I told Evelyn over dinner, 'I shall have to go to Birmingham races tomorrow dear, just for the day.' I intended to charter a businessman's plane at a nearby airstrip and fly to Castle Bromwich airfield, which was just across the road from the Birmingham race track.

'But Alex, why?'

'Because they have the photo finish there.'

'Surely you can relax for a change, you're on holiday, and anyway, you don't need the money.'

I knew Evelyn was right. I was always dashing around the country, and a few days by the sea would do me good. It would not hurt me to forget about racing for a while, but I could not.

'I'm sorry dear. I just know that photo finish betting won't last forever. I must make hay while the sun shines.' The next day I was off.

Newmarket always had a special place in my heart, perhaps because it was where I gave birth to my photo finish system. One day at the July meeting I was late again, lingering too long with friends in the paddock. The race had ended in a close finish and there was a photo; I wasn't in time to get to the line. The Duke of Roxburgh had been in the Stewards Box, overlooking the post and I asked him who he thought had won. He immediately informed me, with some authority, that the horse on the far side was the winner. I smiled and thanked him for his advice. The result of the photo was announced and he was wrong, the horse on the near side had got up to win by a neck. 'My Lord, I don't think I will appoint you as my deputy,' I said. The serious-looking aristocrat, who knew of my reputation, chuckled. We were getting to know each other fairly well despite a bad start to our relationship. One day in the Redcar paddock I had been apprehended by an officious-seeming gentleman who demanded to know what I was doing there. I dismissed him with a wave. How dare a racecourse employee talk to me that way, I thought. 'I'm representing Mr Ollernshaw the owner of Claverhouse,' I said disdainfully. As he walked away a jockey whispered in my ear: 'Didn't you know that was the Duke of Roxburgh?'

On 27 August, 1949 I flew to Hamilton Park with Joss Travis in my charter plane. My horse Quags, ridden by Ginger Dyson, was running in the Quarry Selling Handicap. As I never believed in telling anyone of my betting intentions, I merely said to Joss: 'I will back him only if all the omens are right.'

'If you do, please put twenty five pounds each way for me,' he said.

As I had arranged to see the horse saddled, we agreed to meet outside the bar, just before the race, when I would let him know if he was on or not. I put the money on for Joss and backed Quags to win £6,000 for myself, but when I came out of the paddock, there was no sign of my friend. It was a good race, and Quags won by a head from Invoice, ridden by Jimmy Thompson. My trainer Jack Pearce and I went to buy Quags in, if the price was not too high. At the unsaddling enclosure, I met Lord Rosebery, a senior steward at the meeting. He did not congratulate me on my horse's win. In all the years I was to own horses I was never congratulated by a steward, but we did discuss Quags as he had bred him. While we talked, I was aware of frantic gesticulations from Joss in the distance. For a few minutes I ignored his wild arm-waving. Then, finally, I broke off my conversation for a moment, to nod in his direction as a signal that I had backed Quags for him.

The horse was entered for sale at one hundred guineas. At first the auctioneer looked in vain for a bid, for Quags was getting old and did not have the best of legs. His hammer was going down for the third and last time and the *Sporting Chronicle* reporter standing next to me, wrote down on his card: NO BID. Suddenly a bid came from outside for one hundred, so Jack followed with £110. The bidding went on to £800. 'Forget it,' I told Jack. He looked crestfallen, because Quags was the first horse he had trained for me. 'Never mind, I'll buy a few yearlings at Doncaster in a fortnight's time,' I said. Quags was knocked down to the person outside. But as we walked away, the auctioneer shouted 'BOUGHT IN'. I looked at Jack in amazement. 'The last bid wasn't ours, was it?' I asked. Then along came Joss, looking very pleased with himself. 'I wasn't sure if you wanted to go to £850 guineas,' he said.

The penny dropped. His frantic signal across the paddock had meant: 'Shall I buy your horse in, while you are talking?' Not: 'Have you put my bet on?' To make matters worse, as he had made the first bid, I had to pay an extra shilling on every pound for the horse, making a total of 700 guineas. The first one hundred pounds was not affected. The race was only worth £292 in prize money. Joss should have known that even if he were buying the horse in, he should never have made the first bid. Years later, I told Lord Rosebery that my conversation with him had proved costly. He smiled sardonically and said: 'Yes, I heard about that.'

It makes me laugh to think of the story now, but at the time I could have throttled Joss. The story does not even really end there. That day at Hamilton Park, I could not bring myself to speak to Joss on the flight home and I thought the penny would have dropped about his bloomer. Some time later, however, when Quags won at Haydock Park, he came to me and said: 'Well Alex, that was a marvellous performance, I was right to buy the horse in for you wasn't I?'

Not long after that I bought four yearlings, and as Jack only had a small place I purchased a training stables on the Scarborough Road at Malton, Yorkshire for him. He paid me a peppercorn rent and became established but not as my private trainer because he took on other owners.

The following year I arrived at Aintree for the Grand National in my shiny black American Buick, with Evelyn and Nancy

Thornton. Her husband Bill was too busy running his bookmaking business to join us. There was great excitement on the course, for the Royals had just arrived, King George VI, Queen Elizabeth, Princess Elizabeth, Princess Margaret and the Duke and Duchess of Kent. The Queen and Princess Elizabeth jointly owned Monaveen in the big race, but my money was on the brave and sturdy jumper Freebooter, trained by clergyman's son Bobby Renton.

When I told people that the Grand National was one of my favourite races for investments, they invariably expressed surprise. 'But that's surely a gambling race because it's the most hazardous in the world,' they said. The fences dressed in spruce, were upright and daunting. Many had (and still have) drops on the landing side, which caught out the unsuspecting horse. Aintree was no place for a chancy jumper accustomed to brushing through the top of park course fences. So my thorough homework on the form book usually revealed a horse which could be relied upon to really jump those mighty fences. Such a horse was Freebooter. A month before the National I had won £6,000 on him at Cheltenham and I was sure he had everything it took to win at Aintree.

Evelyn and Nancy found a picnic spot on the crowded course but it was not exactly in a marvellous position. It was just thirty yards from the ladies' loo and as we sat, tucking into our beef and ham sandwiches, a long queue of frustrated women filed into the little brick-built convenience, gazing hungrily at our spread.

'You'll never guess who we met Alex,' said Evelyn.

'King George?' I mused.

'For heaven's sake I'm serious.'

'All right then, who?'

'Fred Truelove,' said Nancy excitedly.

'What's so special about him?' I asked.

Fred was a bookie from Yorkshire, who placed hundreds of thousands of pounds in bets for me. He was a man with a shrewd brain, and he, along with Johnny Foy, had placed my commission on Freebooter.

'He insisted that Nancy and I had one hundred pounds to nothing with him on the horse.'

'In that case I wish you both luck,' I said, wondering why they seemed more excited about the possibility of winning one hundred pounds, than the small fortune I stood to gain. Nancy, Evelyn and I went to the top of the stands to watch the race. There were forty nine runners. Monaveen was easy to spot, with a star on his forehead. From the off Freebooter, ridden by Jimmy Power, was nicely placed. I felt confident of success until disaster almost struck at the Chair Fence. As the horses streamed over it, Freebooter took off too soon and crashed down on the landing side, throwing Jimmy up from his saddle. My heart almost stopped. In a split second, Jimmy managed to throw his arms around his horse's neck, and hang on for dear life. Somehow, Freebooter managed to stumble on, but he lost ground. I considered burning my bundle of betting vouchers. I glanced at Evelyn and Nancy and noticed the disappointment on their faces.

When I continued to watch the race, I was heartened because amazingly Freebooter was going strong again. He jumped Becher's superbly second time round, and came away from the fence lying second to Mr J.V. Rank's Shagreen, with Cloncarrig, ridden by Bob Turnell third. The Queen's blinkered Monaveen was going for a gap in the fence, behind a riderless horse. Then Shagreen fell, and two from home the race lay between Cloncarrig and Freebooter, both finishing strongly. 'Come on Jimmy,' I said quietly to myself. The two horses jumped the next fence together, Freebooter literally floated over and Cloncarrig fell. I put my binoculars down, as Freebooter cleared the last on his own, and galloped home to win convincingly. Wot No Sun, ridden by Arthur Thompson, followed him in, with Action Major third and Rowland Roy fourth. I smiled as I watched the frantic actions of the bookies in the ring, for I had just taken them for £70,000.

I celebrated my good fortune in the Aintree bar with Nancy and Evelyn, who was a little concerned about my generosity. Almost anybody who was anybody seemed to join the party. That night we went to Manchester's Midland Hotel. Nancy's husband joined us there and the party went on until the early hours. Then I suddenly announced that we should visit an old friend, Billy Booth, who ran the Grapes Hotel in Oldham. I drove Evelyn, Nancy and Bill there, a little the worse for wear.

When we arrived, I thumped on the door of the hotel and Billy threw it open. 'Alex I've been saving a little something for such a special occasion.' He produced the biggest and oldest bottle of scotch I had ever seen. I never drank whisky but how could I refuse his generosity? I toasted my success again, with a tumbler full to the brim. Then we laughed as I related the story of how the year before Evelyn and I had walked the two-and-a-half mile Aintree circuit, with friends. Among them was businessman Frank Swift, who had brought his new bride, a beautiful Swiss air hostess named Doris, to Aintree for the first time. We were walking past a high wall, with jagged glass on top to prevent people sneaking into the course from the road, when Doris suddenly stopped. 'Oh no, those poor horses, it's too cruel!' she announced. 'They must cut themselves to ribbons when they jump that!'

How I drove us all home from the Grapes I will never know, but I do not think I went faster than fifteen miles an hour. I still felt much the worse for wear at Leicester races two days later. Nevertheless I soon perked up when I heard that I was rumoured to have cleaned up a cool £250,000 on the National.

3

IT WAS ONE o'clock on a sunny Sunday afternoon in July 1950. I did not know it but this was to be the day when a brief telephone call would make me the centrepiece of one of the biggest attempted betting coups ever. My wife Evelyn and I were sitting at the bar in our new home, Franklyn, with Bill and Nancy Thornton. I still miss the rambling grey-stone house, nestling in a Cheshire village, for some years later I was to sell it to Manchester United Chairman Louis Edwards. The robust boss of a northern meat wholesalers died there, in the study where I burned the midnight oil studying the form books.

I had been playing tennis with Bill on my court near the end of the drive, that led to the Macclesfield Road. Both of us were tired but I was more exhausted than he was. Playing against Bill, a former Lincolnshire hay and corn merchant turned bookmaker, always left me feeling more dead than alive. As I sat in my tennis whites, my thoughts wandered. Evelyn was talking to me and I was responding automatically to her for my mind was on Newmarket later in the week. I have always had a great ability to continue a conversation when my thoughts were on something else. I stared out of the window at the lawns and thought of the girocopter I planned to buy. I had already built a landing pad on my vegetable garden. The 'copter was made by an American firm with a reassuring sales patter. It guaranteed that if the engine cut out, the blades would automatically whirl in reverse, so that you floated down to safety like a petal. That sounded good to me and the fact that I could stroll out of my house, step into the machine and fly to the races direct instead of driving down to my plane at Ringway airport. My eldest son Harvey was training for his pilot's licence and I had visions of him ferrying me around. (Unfortunately, as I was about to proceed with the venture some time later, the company was to go bust and come down to Earth like a lead balloon and not a petal.) My floating thoughts were interrupted by a phone call from Willie Satinoff.

'Alex, can you spare two seats on your plane to Newmarket on Thursday, one for me, the other for Johnny Hughes?'

'Just for you I'll make room Willie, even if I have to leave the pilot behind.'

Willie laughed, then his voice became serious: 'I need to sit next to you Alex, it's important. We must have a chat, but I can't tell you anything now.'

I was intrigued by Willie's secrecy. Little did I know that dapper owner of the Manchester-based company Alligator Rainwear, was hatching a daring plot. If it came off the bookies would be caught at the post – but the odds against success were long. There were too many unknown factors. The scheme would have graced the pages of a Dick Francis novel, had he been writing then instead of risking his neck riding in steeplechases.

Willie went to keep-fit classes at the Manchester YMCA every day. He hated ostentation and steered clear of lavish parties. In his mid-forties, this perfect gentleman hardly drank and was in bed by ten o'clock every night. Whenever I saw the name Satinoff I thought of some snobbish women who were discussing the card at York races. 'Satinoff,' one of them said: 'A fine old English name', I resisted the impulse to intervene and say: 'A more wonderful Englishman you could not wish to meet.'

He had one weakness, however. He was an easy touch – an astute business man unable to resist a hard-luck story. Willie, who owned a string of race horses trained by Harold Wallington at Epsom, had one burning passion, Manchester United. They were his pets. He travelled abroad with them and was friends with every member of the club, including manager Matt Busby, secretary Walter Crickmer and legendary players Tommy Taylor, Alan Chilton, Roger Byrne and the greatest of them all, Duncan Edwards. Sadly it was his burning obsession with the Busby Babes that was to lead to his death some years later.

Willie always worried about other people's money. He hated to see them waste it. On Grand National Day in 1949, his guests in his private box at Aintree were his great friend Tommy Appleby, manager of the Manchester Opera House, Hollywood star Stewart Grainger and actress Jean Simmons. Grainger was caught up in the excitement over the big race. He had no idea what to back and kept going through the card with his pencil, pausing at each horse.

'It's got to be Cromwell,' he announced with some confidence. 'What do you think Willie, shall I have one hundred pounds each way?'

Willie hated being put on the spot. 'Nothing is certain in the Grand National I'm afraid Stewart,' he said rather apologetically. 'Please don't waste your money, just put a tenner on it and leave it at that.'

Grainger's confidence in Cromwell waned. He thumbed through the card again, anxious to place a bet as time was running out. Willie stepped in to calm the star's nerves.

'Look Stewart, you're appearing at Tommy's theatre with Jean in *The Power of Darkness* by Tolstoy. That's Russian, so why not have a bit of fun on Russian Hero?'

Grainger was delighted. Surely this was an omen. It all fitted, he had to back it.

'One hundred pounds each way, Willie?'

'For heaven's sake no. It's a rank outsider at 100–1. Just have a quid each way and enjoy the race,' Willie replied.

So the famous film star put two quid on his fancy. However, from the off you would have thought he had backed it to win thousands. As the horses thundered round the gruelling course, he was leaping about in his seat. On the final turn this outsider, which had fallen in the betting to 66–1, was going strong and Grainger was uncontrollable. Throwing his fists in the air and screaming support for his horse he was attracting almost as much attention as the race. Then the incredible happened. Russian Hero raced across the line to win with Grainger hoarse from shouting. For days after, the Press were chasing the story. They really thought the Hollywood legend had backed the outsider to win a fortune. They just would not believe the exhausted actor had returned to his hotel with only £133 profit.

On Thursday 13 July, following Willie's secretive telephone call, I was up early to discuss the day's racing over the phone with my manager Stanley Platt. This studious, tidily-dressed, slightly corpulent man in his mid-40's, would spend six or seven hours a day pouring over the form books, working out handicaps. It had become his passion. He was a quiet, unassuming person, well suited for his former job as an undertaker. Whenever I passed his bungalow in my car at night I used to lay odds with myself that he would be in the front bedroom with the light on, studying the form books.

As race course timing was so important in my assessment of horses, especially two-year-olds, it was inevitable that I should work with such a professional. There were times when I would meet half a dozen 'clockers' at a vantage point on top of the stands, always opposite the finishing line. It was interesting to note their comparisons. That was how I sorted out the most reliable and consistent men, and it was how I met Stanley. He asked me if he could co-operate in my rating system and timing, and I agreed to give it a trial. From that day, until he died many years later, we had a very successful association. He came to my house every Sunday and we compared our notes and ratings for the previous week. As the years passed he moulded himself into my system and methods, and later it was most unusual if we varied by more than 1 lb in weights in our estimates.

As I had about ten horses in training Stanley was able to assess the best handicaps for me, leaving me free to concentrate on my bets. When the Racing Calendar came out each Friday with the published weights Stanley spent sixteen hours between then and Sunday assessing the best handicap. In those days there was no computerisation of handicaps. Each handicapper had his own personal opinion and I have known times when two handicappers varied by as much as 30 lbs. Apart from saving me so much time, it was most important that my trainers should know the best handicap.

On that morning of the 13th we went carefully through each race on the Newmarket card. In the third, the Reach Selling Plate, Willie had a horse running named Royal Alligator, trained by Harold Wallington and ridden by a virtually unknown jockey, Fred Hunter.

The favourite was Mavourneen Rhu, also trained by Wallington, with Kenny Gethin the stable jockey on top. Royal Alligator had not run since April when, very backward, he finished in the middle of the field in a better class race. Stanley and I put a question mark against the horse and left it at that. Little was known about his ability or that of the jockey. We had no idea Royal Alligator was the key to Willie's precarious scheme.

Later that day I drove to Ringway airport where I was greeted by pilot Dave Lancaster. The small good-humoured and good-looking man in his early thirties ferried me to courses throughout England and Scotland for many years in my Rapide bi-plane. It cost me £3,000 to buy but word soon spread about my new acquisition and before long people were opting for a free ride to the races. Finally I created a private company called Ringway Aircharter Services Ltd. I charged about six pounds a seat on the plane. From then on it was always a strictly business arrangement for everyone and as I always carried about seven passengers, the trips began to pay for themselves.

Waiting for me in the sunshine at Ringway was Herbert Howarth, a big backer in his own right. As we stood talking by the hanger, Willie arrived with his racing manager Johnny Hughes. Willie, in a dapper grey suit, looked serious. I could tell he had a lot on his mind. Johnny however was as jovial as ever. There was always great competitiveness between us. I once gave Johnny a lift in a chartered plane to Edinburgh to see my horse Slipshod run. This was one of my best named horses. It was by a sire called Slipper out of a mare Careless . . .

The flight took so long that I realised we would miss the race and I told him that I had backed my horse heavily.

'Right I'll have a tenner each way with you Alex,' said Johnny.

'This horse will win so you ought to have a pony (twenty five pounds) on,' I told him. He did. When we walked through the gates of the course, the doorman told us my horse had won at 5 to 1.

Johnny laughed and said to him: 'That bloody Alex Bird. Never before has he told me to back a horse before a race, but this time he told me because he knew there was no chance of me spoiling his market miles above the Irish sea. Blimey, he's even frightened to tell his bookmaker what he wants to back!'

Then Johnny made the classic remark that was to be repeated on courses throughout the country for years: 'They say that Alex Bird won't even go to bed with his wife the night before he has a fancied runner, in case he talks in his sleep.'

Johnny was well-known for his witty remarks. Once at the Haydock water jump in front of the stands a horse called Bollinger splashed his back legs. 'Bollinger's in the water,' someone shouted. 'Better than water being in the bleeding Bollinger,' Johnny replied.

However, back to the day and as I settled down beside Willie on the plane I could tell he had something on his mind. We were not in the air for long before he unfolded his scheme.

'Alex, Royal Alligator has the beating of Mavourneen Rhu by ten to fifteen lengths,' he whispered, looking over his shoulder making sure no one else was listening.

Even though Royal Alligator, named after Willie's rainwear company, had not run for three months, he had improved tremendously and shortly after his initial race won a trial very easily. News of this gallop spread like wildfire, Willie explained, and the lads working for Harold Wallington could hardly wait for the horse's next race. He was the talk of the stables. Unless the memory of that gallop was erased from their minds, there was no chance of Willie getting a decent price. For the intelligence network of bookmakers is amazing. If they had run MI5 during the war it could well have been shortened. I have been racing all my life on both sides of the fence, but I have yet to discover their true source of information. They have access to stable talk and performances on the gallops. They sift through thousands of whispered reports and often know things long before the owners.

Bookmaker Fred Truelove once told me that he always knew of

the capabilities of the horses in a leading northern stable. 'Mrs X,' he said, 'has had fifty bob each way and that makes the horse a certainty!' She was the trainer's mother-in-law.

The bookies are always ahead of the game. Take an average race for two-year-olds. The horses have never been out in public, yet somehow the bookies formulate a market. An owner could sometimes expect to be able to have a bet at reasonable odds, but there is no chance if the horse has shown even a squeak of ability at home. By the time the owner walks into the ring, his two-year-old that has never run in public could well be favourite or second favourite.

Willie was faced with this problem. There had to be a cover-up, but it was not possible to stop Royal Alligator from doing his best in gallops without running the risk of teaching him bad habits and having the horse think that was what he had to do on the racetrack.

'From the day we realised his ability, nobody was allowed to ride the horse in his work, except Kenny Gethin,' Willie went on. 'And Gethin never rode without carrying at least two stones of lead concealed in the lining of his waistcoat.' Only three people knew of this, Gethin, Harold Wallington and Willie. Even the stable lad who looked after the horse was not told. So each time Gethin took Alligator out, he did not have to restrain him as he could not reproduce the ability he had shown in the initial trial.

The lads went cold on the horse and decided not to risk their money. Royal Alligator was moderate after all and that is what the whispers said. The message went out on the bookmakers' incredible network. Gethin had done his job properly, but even then Willie had to take further precautions. The next part of his plan was to be absent from the course along with his trainer Wallington. This would be taken by the bookmakers to denote a lack of confidence in the horse.

'When we touch down on the heath I'll leave in disguise,' Willie announced. He opened his bag revealing a large, light brown raincoat, dark glasses and a hat. It was like something out of a gangster movie. 'Harold is picking me up in a car, he'll be in disguise too,' said Willie, who was revelling in his master plan. He explained that the key to the plot had been to put unknown jockey, Fred Hunter, on Royal Alligator. Stable jockey Gethin was on the favourite Mavourneen Rhu and all the signs were that Rhu was the horse the stable fancied. 'Hunter is a good work rider, he can handle it,' Willie whispered.

The veil of secrecy was so tight that even Hunter believed Rhu was the better horse. He had no idea Royal Alligator was a potential winner. Jockeys are not allowed to bet but some do. Usually they do not know their mount is fancied until they receive their trainer's instructions. Then those who risk a bet secretly signal to someone to back a horse for them. They might touch their caps, scratch their ears or carry their whips in a certain way. No one was suggesting that Hunter would do that, but nothing was being left to chance.

'When Hunter gets up he will be told that Royal Alligator's form has deteriorated so much he hasn't got a chance,' said Willie. 'He will go down to the start unaware of the horse's ability.' Willie explained how Gethin would tell him when he got to the starting gate, and added with a smile: 'I hope Hunter doesn't fall off in surprise.'

He went on: 'I want you to put a monkey (five hundred pounds) on Mavourneen Rhu for me in the early stages of the betting and that will further convince the bookies that Royal Alligator is not fancied. When his price drifts I want you to step in and put £8,000 on my horse.'

I knew this would be a daunting task as the market on the July course was notoriously weak. I would need help. My mind started working overtime. I wanted £4,000 on for myself, making £12,000 in all. The plane landed on the Newmarket heath and Willie slipped into his raincoat, put the collar up over his ears, stuck on his dark glasses and pulled down the brim of his hat. I smiled as I watched him dash from the plane looking like some Chicago gangster, to a waiting black limousine with the shadowy figure of Wallington ducking down in the back seat. Who would have thought that this fleeting figure was a modest millionaire, friend of the stars, and the toast of one of the greatest soccer clubs in the history of the game? The car sped off to Willie's hideaway, a nearby hotel. The rest of us

got a taxi to the course three miles away. As we drove there I began
to revel in Willie's brilliant plot to foil the bookies. There was
nothing dishonest about it. It was just a clever piece of strategy, that
might or might not come off.

I did not dislike bookies, indeed I had many friends among
them. When it came to business however I was their target and they
were mine. All's fair in love and war. Nevertheless there was
mutual respect between us, and I have seen that to be the case with
many professional backers and bookies throughout my career.

The course was not crowded that afternoon, and the betting
market was not particularly strong. I stood in the sunshine,
enlisting the help of the five people who were the final key to the
attempted coup. I did not reveal the name of the horse I wanted
them to back. I said that ten minutes before the race I would be
standing by the rails bookmakers and would signal the horse to
them. Then, when I raised my Panama, they were to go into
different parts of the ring at the same time. My betting platoon
listened intently. There was Herbert Howarth, Frank Stringer, a
quiet, sometimes intense man, who had a hotel in the Midlands and
was chairman of Coventry City Football Club; Billy Carter, my
great friend and a professional backer; Teddy Hayes and Joe Israel,
who traded under the name of Hokey, the southern tic-tac firm. My
helpers dispersed, synchronising their watches. As I strolled to the
paddock bar there were some nagging doubts in my mind. I knew
that the bookmaker's spies must have already reported the absence
of Willie and Wallington from the course, but things could still go
terribly wrong. If the undercover millionaire and his trainer were
spotted deliberately keeping a low profile in the nearby hotel, the
game would be up.

Meanwhile my team of backers had to be synchronised and
strike before the bookies realised what was happening. The five-
furlong Reach Selling Plate started at three o'clock. When the
betting opened I invested £500 at 4 to 1 on Mavourneen Rhu and
the horse became 3 to 1 favourite. That resolved the doubts with the
bookmakers that Mavourneen Rhu was the stable's favourite.
Meanwhile the price of Royal Alligator drifted to 7 to 1. The race

drew nearer but I waited. Mavourneen Rhu was still favourite. I leant against the rails. There were ten minutes left before the off, nine, eight, I waited, then signalled the horse. The bookies did not know what was hitting them. There was confusion everywhere and they were demoralised. The horses were at the starting gate when Herbert Howarth parked himself alongside burly, seventeen-stone William Hill, one of the most courageous bookmakers I have ever known. The bespectacled, trilby-hatted, six-footer was betting for the firm. The first price he offered on Royal Alligator was 7 to 1 and Herbert asked him for £1,000 to 140. Hill then went 6 to 1, 5 to 1, 4 to 1, 3 to 1, 2 to 1 and each time he offered the horse, Herbert stepped in and backed it to win £1,000. My other backers were spread throughout the ring. Over at the starting gate, while my helpers were taking on the bookies, Hunter was easing Royal Alligator into position when Gethin on Mavourneen Rhu passed alongside. 'Go for your life – you're certain to win and take home a fabulous present,' Gethin told him and within seconds they were off.

I could hear people shouting but there was no time to watch the race. One by one my helpers reported back from the action and handed me their race cards with their bets marked on. None of them had been able to get the full amount that I had requested on the horse. I was still trying to do my sums, when Willie appeared out of the blue like a ghost. He had not even gone to the paddock to watch his horse being saddled from a discreet distance. I was glad however to see he had dropped his gangster disguise, and was again dapper in his sober grey suit.

'How much did you get on, Alex?' he asked.

I could hear the horses getting nearer.

'I honestly don't know, Willie. I'm still trying to work it out, look, take the racecards yourself.'

'No I trust you, Alex. Just hazard a guess.'

'About £5,000 and you have probably backed Royal Alligator to win £15,000. His last price was 13 to 8,' I said hurriedly still studying the racecards. 'Marvellous, Alex. Tell me for certain after the race.'

Willie then dashed off to tell Wallington who had miraculously appeared about twenty yards away. For the first time I looked up at the race. Royal Alligator was so far in front he won in a canter pulling up. I stood smiling in the sunshine on that wonderful day, when the only people on the course to be taken for a ride were the bookies! In the comparative calm I totalled up the bets and went to find Willie at the unsaddling enclosure to tell him the good news. Hunter was taking off the saddle and Willie was watching as I parked myself alongside him.

'Willie, I've backed Alligator to win just under £23,000 and your investment was £7,300.'

The pleasure on his face was a joy to behold. I told Willie that none of the men who carried out the operation so well, had managed to get a bet on for themselves. He immediately told me to deduct £3,000 from the winnings and distribute it as I saw fit. After deductions his net profit was £19,585. I left Willie with his trainer for as it was a selling race he had to buy his horse in. As I walked away he shouted: 'Alex, order the champagne, I'll settle the bill later!'

'Nothing would give me greater pleasure,' I replied with a smile. We would toast the men who had made the day such a joy, the bookmakers.

Many people have since told me that I was entitled to one third of the winnings because I had wanted £4,000 on Royal Alligator myself. However, I was asked to invest money by a friend and until I had done so, I was not entitled to have a bet.

On the flight home I wrote Willie a cheque for £19,585. He waved it away saying the money was not due until the following week. 'Take it now Willie, while my current account can stand it,' I joked.

Willie made a photostat copy of my cheque as a memento of his great coup. In February 1958 the millionaire went abroad with his favourite football team, and was killed. He died in the tragic Munich air disaster along with so many of the Busby Babes he loved so dearly. When his body was recovered from the wreckage of the aircraft on that cold, snowswept runway, the copy of that cheque was found in his wallet. I heard later that had he not been killed, he would probably have been the next chairman of that fabulous club. God bless you Willie.

The 1950 flat season was quite a year for me. During that time, my mind had been on my horse Newton Heath. I had bought him as a two-year-old at the Doncaster Yearling Sales for 1500 guineas in 1949, and named him after my birthplace. He won two races for me at my local tracks Haydock and Manchester. The latter gave me particular pleasure because it was the Sale Plate and I was still living in Sale at the time.

However, during the week of the Royal Alligator coup I intended to have a very good bet on the horse. I entered him for the Trial Selling Plate over a mile at Newmarket.

He had been unplaced in his previous race the Carlisle Bell, a much better class event. I knew Newton Heath was much better than a selling plater, so I had decided to go for it in a big way. I flew down to the course with Herbert Howarth, one of the people I had enlisted to back the horse for me.

He approached prominent Tattersalls bookmaker, Lou French, who was listing his opening prices. 'What's this? A horse from the North, trained by Pearce, never heard of him. He wouldn't know where the bloody weighing-in room was!' said Lou. My team backed Newton Heath down from 10–1 to $5\frac{1}{2}$–1. It was easy for Newton Heath. Ridden by Doug Smith, he won by three lengths from Bill Rickeby on Parfigures. I picked up £10,000 from the bookies and Herbert had also had a big bet, but his greatest pleasure came as he drew his ready money from Lou and told him: 'Now those mugs from up North have collected!' It cost me 1,500 guineas to buy back Newton Heath after the seller, but who was counting?

By the end of the season, it was obvious that Newton Heath needed soft ground to be at his best. 'If the horse shows any ability over hurdles, I want him to have a race or two to keep him cherry ripe and then we will have a crack at the Lincoln Handicap,' I told my trainer Jack Pearce. I knew that the Lincoln was invariably run on heavy ground. In his first few races over the jumps, Newton Heath did well. In December 1950, he finished second in the East Lancashire Hurdle at Haydock Park, over one and a half miles. Ridden by Vic Speck, he started as an outsider and I had a little each way on him, just to cover expenses. Then he finished third at Wetherby on 20 January, 1951, in the Rudgate Novices Hurdle over two miles. Ridden by Percy Wigham, he was 5–2 favourite, and I backed him to win £2,000. At Manchester, two weeks later, he came second over two miles, with Martin Moloney riding, and then on 8 February, at Haydock, Arthur Thompson rode Newton Heath to victory in the Ashton Novices Hurdle. After the race I booked Arthur to ride the horse in the Slaphouse Novices Hurdle at Ayr on 16 March. Arthur won again, cleverly beating Woodland Tale, ridden by R. Cross, by three quarters of a length. Later that afternoon, Arthur took a spare ride on Dreamy Legend in the Blair Quhan Handicap Steeplechase over three miles. Dreamy Legend fell at the eight fence and was destroyed. He had broken his neck. Arthur was lucky he escaped with a broken collar bone, but broken bones could not hold back the plucky jump jockey. With his arm strapped high, looking like a policeman on point duty, he travelled back to Ringway with me in my plane. He planned to go to London by train the following morning to see a top bone specialist, and I had invited him to stay at my house overnight.

'I'm sorry that we can't keep you company this evening,' I explained, 'but Evelyn and I have arranged to go to a local tennis club dance with Bill and Nancy Thornton.' What jump jockeys are made of I do not know, but they are a tough breed. Arthur insisted on coming to the shindig with us. He was a joy to watch as he danced the night away with his arm in a frame, high above his partner's head.

The highlight of the evening was when he took his chances in a novelty dance with a heftily-built girl. When the music stopped, each man had to pick up his partner, and race to the far end of the room. Arthur was beaten by a short head in a photo finish, an honourable defeat indeed. That evening was a great success, but afterwards I could not help but think that had we not gone to the dance and sat at home talking by the fire instead, Arthur would have told me what happened when he rode Newton Heath that day. He told my trainer, but not me, and it was something that would happen again with a devastating result.

Two weeks later Herbert Jones, a young apprentice who claimed a 3 lb allowance rode Newton Heath in the Lincoln. He had sweated off 4 lb in a Turkish bath to do the weight, but even so, he had to have a tiny saddle and still put 2 lb over weight. The horse, specially trained for the event, looked a picture. He had done a particularly good gallop on Filey Sands, with my horse Signification. I had backed Newton Heath to win £40,000 ante-post, but on the morning of the race I was far from confident. The going on the preceding day was good, and naturally I wanted it very heavy. Lincoln City were playing Oldham Athletic at home, and kick-off was at 11 am. My friend Frank Swift, who ran a group of cotton mills and was a director of Oldham, asked me to accompany him to the match, and I readily agreed.

We sat down in the Director's Box. The majority of the crowd were standing in the open air, and when Oldham kicked off, heavy rain started to fall. Within minutes, the pitch was a quagmire. The unfortunate spectators had no protection at all against the deluge. To this day I cannot remember who won the match. I only remember grinning like a Cheshire cat, as I looked at the sea of newspapers over the heads of the crowd. My mind was not on the football. Every drop of rain that fell was in my horse's favour, he would revel in the wet. My only worry was that if the rain did not stop, the race might never take place. At the course, that afternoon I pressed my bets and backed Newton Heath to win a further £20,000.

Before the race, Jack was nervous. Newton Heath was not the easiest horse to saddle, because he blew out a lot. As the trainer struggled with the girth, the belt broke. Jack had no option but to run to the weighing room to get a new one. He was not a young man, and it was a considerable distance. He arrived back exhausted to find the paddock deserted, except for Newton Heath. The other horses were well on their way to the start. Jack hurriedly re-saddled the horse and told Herbert to get the starter's assistant to check the girths, before the off. When Herbert arrived at the post however, the starter was understandably tetchy, having kept everyone waiting in the rain and raw March wind. Ignoring Herbert's plea, he ordered him into line and despatched the thirty five runners within seconds. The huge field fanned out across the course and it was impossible to see which horse was making the early running, but Herbert had Newton Heath lying handy behind the leaders. Newton Heath was running a cracking race and at the distance took the lead. Herbert thought he had it in the bag when he got a shock. His reins seemed longer. The saddle was slipping back. Instinctively, he twisted his fingers in the horse's mane and held on for dear life, unable to help Newton Heath at the finish. In the last few strides, Joe Sime, riding Barnes Park, got up to beat Newton Heath by half a length. These things happen in racing. I lit a cigar and strolled to the unsaddling enclosure, to congratulate my great friend Harry Lane, who owned Barnes Park. I bought the Pathe Gazette newsreel of the race, and whenever I wanted to torture myself, I played it over and over again. I did not see Arthur Thompson until June, when I went to Newcastle races for the Pitman's Derby.

I met him by the paddock.

'I don't know why Jack did not run the horse with a breast girth,' he said.

'Why?' I asked.

'Well, when I won on Newton Heath, at Ayr, I told Jack never to run him without one, because I could feel the saddle slipping, a furlong out.'

Jack had never told me about the problem.

After the traumatic Lincoln, I only had one other gamble on the horse. It was at Hurst Park, a now defunct course, in the shadow of Hampton Court. The betting was very weak and I placed the whole of my commission away from the track. The race was the Walton Handicap Hurdle over two miles, a few days before Christmas. I asked Arthur, who was in his native Ireland, to ride for me, and he kindly postponed his festive celebrations to fly over from Dublin.

It was not the best of days. The weather was misty, it had been raining all morning and the going was getting softer by the hour. The race drew near but there was no sign of Arthur. Finally, the jockeys had to be declared. I had no option but to find another rider so I engaged Vic Speck, who had ridden Newton Heath on his first outing over the jumps in December 1950. When the horses were in the first furlong, Arthur appeared. His plane had circled London Airport for over an hour because of the bad weather, but he still had time to get to Hurst Park, so he leapt in a taxi and told the driver to step on it. The cabbie assured him he knew the way. An hour before the race he delivered Arthur to Sandown Park. So the jockey had no chance of getting to Hurst Park in time for his ride. There was a rousing finish to the race and Newton Heath was just beaten. I knew that had Arthur been on board he would have won.

In the hectic and carefree days of the 1950s the rules and regulations for small planes were nothing like as strict as they are today. A pilot virtually had a licence to land and take off anywhere. They were crazy young men in their flying machines, as I was to discover to my cost.

There were times before I bought the Rapide when my heart was in my mouth on bi-plane charter flights. I and other passengers skimmed hedges, once landed in a ploughed field and at times used our binoculars to focus on the name of a railway station below, as the pilot circled lower and lower having lost his bearings. On one occasion as our plane came in to land we were picked up by a strong wind and deposited 300 yards from the runway in a meadow. The narrow escape was Bird luck playing its part again. Once I went from Ringway to Newmarket in a twin-seater plane. The visibility was bad and the pilot was a relatively inexperienced youngster. We soared over Buxton, the highest point in the Peak District, without being sure where we were. Using my binoculars I managed to identify the pub below, but the young Biggles could not hear me over the din of the engine and I had to go into an elaborate demonstration of the name. I played a make-believe violin, flapped my ears and licked my paws. Finally, just as I was exhausted with the game, my pilot realised it was the 'Cat and Fiddle' and almost fell out of the cockpit with laughter. Using more sign language we agreed the visibility was too bad and we returned to Ringway, laughing all the way.

The next day that plucky young pilot took the same plane out again. He died an hour later in a horrific crash.

One August morning in 1951, I chartered a plane to go to Sandown Park. My passengers were Frank Swift, Laurie Brown, a business man in textile machinery and Joe Allmark, a slim, well-dressed professional backer who loved a joke. We all arrived on time at Ringway and were surprised to find our pilot intently studying some maps in the dining hall, when he should have been sitting in the plane. Niggling worries set in, but we put the incident behind us and trooped across the tarmac to the plane. We had not long settled down in our seats when the plane started to rumble over uneven ground. As I was sitting in the front, I opened the door to the cockpit.

'Where are we going?' I shouted over the din of the engines.

'I'm looking for the perimeter track,' our confused-looking pilot replied.

I closed the door and tried to settle back wondering why a trained pilot had lost his way before take-off. Meanwhile we rumbled on over the bumps. A stiff drink would soon be the order of the day to steady our nerves.

Then our pilot really shook us. He pointed the plane towards a nearby road, while revving the engines full pitch. If the brakes had failed, we would have whizzed into any oncoming traffic. Anxiety swept over me. I looked at Frank and Laurie and saw the fear in their faces, but by now, joker Joe was in his stride.

'Didn't you see him down those four large whiskies at the bar as he was reading the maps?' he quipped, roaring with laughter as the rest of us forced a nervous smile. I could not stop myself – once again I opened the cockpit door and peered in. The pilot appeared to be inspecting the water in the batteries.

Frank and Laurie decided to bail out. They got up from their seats and were walking to the exit door, when the plane suddenly took off and gained height at an abnormally rapid rate. We were now over Congleton, about fifteen miles from Ringway when we started descending at speed. Once more I opened the cockpit door and stuck my head in. There was our pilot peering at his maps, unfolded over the joy stick and controls. I patted him on the shoulder not wishing to make him jump, in case we lurched into yet another strange manoeuvre. My touch shook him into reality and he pulled back the joy stick. Up we soared again with Frank and Laurie, faces white, compressed into the backs of their seats for the roller-coaster ride. Nothing could have been further from their minds than the Sandown meeting. Joe however was still in great form.

'I'm not worried – I've nothing to lose – but you lads better start worrying you've got money,' he shouted, laughing.

'You're so bloody right, I've got £15,000 my wife doesn't know about hidden under the floorboards,' shouted Frank, with a look of anguish.

His fear and the twinkle in Joe's eyes were more than I could stand. I shook uncontrollably with laughter, tears streaming down my face. I reached for my handkerchief but realised I had left it at home. There was nothing for it, I pulled out my shirt and wiped my eyes on the lap. Laurie was angry at Joe's wisecracks in a time of great danger and vowed he would never speak to him again – if there was an again. Happily things settled down and we all relaxed, feeling quietly confident that the pilot had finally got over his teething problems, although we all had a nagging doubt about landing. After some time smoking, talking about the meeting and studying form, it suddenly occurred to me that we had been travelling for about two hours. Once again I felt anxious and stared out of the window. Another forty five minutes went by and I could not restrain myself.

'We've been travelling for about two hours forty-five minutes,' I announced.

'So what?' asked Frank.

'Well, the plane has only enough fuel for three hours!'

'Did you tell him we were going to Sandown, Isle of Wight or something?' asked Laurie, with a look of fear on his face again. 'Christ we must be well over the English Channel by now.'

I nervously pressed my nose against the window and nearly fell out of my seat. About half a mile away was a whopping great airliner coming our way. I rushed into the cockpit and my heart stopped when I saw the state our pilot was in. He was sweating buckets, with his head pushed forward as he stared intently out of the cockpit window, clutching the joy stick in sheer panic. I touched his shoulder and he violently shook my hand away. I felt sure this was it. The end. I went back to my seat, too full of gloom to say anything that would put Laurie and Frank's mind at rest. I waited for the inevitable and reflected that I would never again enjoy a summer race meeting or see my wife. This was my last furlong. I wondered if they had Havanas in heaven. Suddenly the note of the plane's engine changed and we were descending through the clouds. I saw a runway under us.

'He hasn't put the flaps down,' I shouted.

'Bloody tell him,' shouted panic-stricken Joe.

Frank and Laurie were compressed into their seats their lips too frozen to speak.

'Not likely – hold tight!'

There was a terrific bump and we landed, skidding to a halt at the far side of the airport with ambulances and crash tenders racing towards us. When we shakily got out of the plane, we realised we were at Croydon. One of the rescuers raced up to me and shouted: 'Where the hell have you been? You've had the whole of London in a panic.'

Our pilot had the last word. He stepped calmly from the plane, which could only have had a teaspoon of fuel left and asked politely: 'What time do you want to return?'

There were only two words I could say . . . and they are unprintable.

The charter company sent another plane to take us home. His journey took three and a half hours and his claim for seven hours flying was rejected out of hand!

4

ON THE MORNING of 21 September, 1951, at the height of my photo finish bets, I received a letter that shook me. It was from the Inland Revenue and read:

'I would be pleased if you could send me a copy of your accounts for the first year in business as a professional backer.'

A month later I sat before a young Irish tax inspector, in his pre-fabricated office in Didsbury, Manchester. He was anxious to know the reason for my phenomenal success and I surprised him when I opened my case and produced bookmakers' statements of every bet I had made since I was a teenager. For ten minutes I sat quietly as he went through the pages; it must have become clear to him that I had made money on an each way system of backing in non-handicaps. Then he came to the statements which revealed consistent winnings of £500.

'Ah, what have we here?' he asked, clearly hinting that there could be more in the figures than met the eye. The bets mostly related to horses ridden by Irish jockey Martin Moloney, brother of champion jockey, Tim Moloney. I had first seen Martin ride at Leicester and was convinced he had great ability. From then on I backed him in every race he rode in England. I developed a staking method on his mounts. I backed his first horse to win £500. If that horse lost, I backed him to win £500 next time, plus what I had lost on his previous ride. I continued backing this way until he rode a winner, then I reverted to my original stake. It was, of course, necessary to guard against a losing run and a limit had to be fixed. So I set myself a ceiling of £4,000. Once I reached that, I would write off the loss and start again. 'In all, I won about £60,000 on your very fine countryman,' I told the inspector.

'Ah yes, Martin is a great, great jockey,' he mused, hiding any disappointment he may have felt on discovering that everything was in order. He made some enquiries about my photo finish bets, then we drifted back to the subject of Irish jockeys and finally parted amicably.

Winning money by betting on objections was another nice sideline for me in my career at this time, until the day something happened at one course that stopped me in my tracks.

In the preliminary betting before a race, I had £2,000 to £1,000 on the favourite with one layer. That was a very big bet for any bookmaker to lay on a small track. I fully expected the odds to shorten to 6–4 or less, but the horse held its price until shortly before the off. In fact I was most dismayed to hear the bookmaker call 9 to 4, followed by 5 to 2. Then a friend of mine approached me in the stands. 'You have done your money, Alex,' he said. 'I know for certain that the horse is not trying and so does the bookmaker.' I paid particular attention to the race and could almost see the jockey blink through my binoculars. It was a steeplechase event, and half the field had fallen by the time the horses got into the straight. Then the leader fell at the second last and I could see the favourite I had backed, going very well, just behind the new front runner. I remember thinking to myself: 'Now, if you are not trying what are you going to do my lad?' The horses popped over the last fence and the favourite's jockey sat with a double handful. He then did what I had never seen before or since. He took a pull on the rein and the horse veered to the right, almost colliding with the other runner. The jockey on the favourite then made a theatrical gesture and almost stood up in the saddle. After that he apparently rode for his life in the last furlong but was beaten by a narrow margin. As I wondered for how long the jockey would be laid off, even warned off, an announcement was made. The second objected to the winner. I could hardly believe my ears. Then the penny dropped, he was trying to justify his action by blaming the other jockey: a crafty move. He would get off with a twenty five pound fine, and of course the stewards would overrule the objection. I proceeded to put £3,500 on the first past the post. Minutes later, to my amazement, the objection was sustained. Johnny Hughes, a great judge of horses in running, was standing with me. He had also backed the first past the post.

'You never stop learning at this game, Alex,' he said, and revealed that he had been told at an early stage in his career never to bet on objections in the last race of the day. The reason he said was that the stewards were reaching for their coats or had downed one port too many. I did not back on objections for many years after that. When I decided to again, it was only if something was very obvious and could be checked by patrol camera.

Early the following year I went into the Park Ward car show-rooms, just off London's Edgware Road, knowing exactly what I wanted – a special-body Rolls Bentley. I explained my unusual colour scheme to a dapper salesman who had an Eton accent.

'I want a new Rolls Bentley painted in crimson and gold, my racing colours!'

The salesman did not bat an eyelid.

'Certainly sir, may I suggest crimson bodywork, with perhaps gold wheel arches?'

The order was duly placed, but when I returned home full of excitement over my new purchase, Evelyn was none too pleased.

'You'll make a spectacle of yourself in a car like that, and I certainly won't ride in it! You'll just be showing off!' she said.

She was right of course. God knows where my ego would have taken me if it were not for that wonderful woman. I picked up the phone and re-ordered the car, in black.

Mrs Brotherton, owner of my National winner Freebooter, had a similar Bentley, painted in her racing colours, blue and grey. That was what had given me the idea, but it was certainly a more sober colour scheme than I intended.

That year I backed Freebooter in the National again, but there was another good jumper on the scene called Teal, who impressed me tremendously. He was trained by Neville Crump, at Middleham and owned by Harry Lane, who had told me the horse was a potential National winner in the spring of 1951. Harry was a

Stockton-on-Tees engineering contractor and director of Sedgefield Race Course. Weighing about twenty stone, white haired, hatless Harry was so large that when he visited his trainer's home Neville's wife Brownie kept her fingers crossed that he would not break the chair he always chose to sit on. The seat sagged so much, his bottom almost touched the floor.

A few months earlier I had travelled to Hamilton Park races with him and five other men, all squashed in a chauffeur-driven Daimler. The weight was obviously too much for the car, as big as it was, and we got a puncture. For half an hour, as we stood around in the road sipping champagne and eyeing our watches, the chauffeur struggled with the jack, trying to get the wheel off. The more he struggled, the more impatient Harry became, until eventually he could stand it no more. 'For Christ's sake!' he shouted, marching over to the boot of the car. He put his back against the body and gripped the bumper with his hands. Then, in one effortless movement, lifted the Daimler off the road. 'Now get that bloody wheel off, I want to go to the races!' he said.

From what Harry had told me I felt Teal might have the beating of Freebooter.

In fact, Harry was so confident that he was taking his 600 employees to Aintree to see his horse win. On the same day, my own horse Signification was in the fifth race. This would be quite a meeting. Signification was very backward as a two-year-old. As he was by a great staying sire, Precipitation, he wanted a distance of ground. The last race I had run him in as a two-year-old was at Newmarket. He lost at least six lengths at the start but at the finish he was running on very strongly and was only beaten by about five lengths by the winner. The well-respected publication *Race Form* must have had one of its off days, because Signification was not noted in the summary of the running. There was no indication that he was travelling very fast at the finish and came home sixth. Had the handicapper had this information he would have given the horse much more weight than he allocated him. I could not believe my eyes when I saw the handicap which was published three weeks before the Liverpool meeting. Signification had only got seven

ALEX BIRD

stone three pounds. I had told my trainer Jack Pearce in the previous autumn that I wanted the horse for an early race and he had subsequently kept him well on the move. I stressed that I did not want the horse tried in any way, and only one jockey was to ride him in his work, Johnny Greenaway.

Johnny later told me: 'You've got a horse and a half there, Mr Bird.' His words were enough for me. I did not need Signification to have a trial. If I had arranged one the world would have known that I intended to have a big gamble on the horse.

I intended to back Signification to win £50,000 and I was arranging the most unorthodox preparation for him.

Meanwhile, I steadily increased my bets on Teal for the National to win an equal amount. He was being ridden by Arthur Thompson, who chased home Freebooter on Wot No Sun in 1950.

On the big day at Aintree I had invited several guests to dine with me in the room that I had started to hire each year. One of them was my racing helper Norman Baxter who walked with the aid of a stick, because he had a caliper. He had been a friend and confidant and we had travelled many thousands of miles together to various race meetings. He was a great judge of the form book and having been weaned on greyhound racing, timing was an important factor for him. Times are the be all and end all of greyhound racing, and although people do not attach the same importance to timing for horse racing, I have never agreed with this.

In my private room, my waiter, Beard, who worked for the Royal Family, was immaculately turned out in a waistcoat and bow tie. He was waiting for me with a drink. This marvellous, thin and dapper man was to become a great friend of the family.

Although I had backed Freebooter and Teal I had not yet placed a bet on Signification. That would have to wait until I knew the result of the National, and even then I could not be seen by the bookies or their spies to put a bet on myself or the odds would fall immediately.

Unknown to me at the time someone else on the course that day had everything at stake on the big race. The investor was a man named Les Armstrong, from Timperley. Les was the husband of

73

Nancy Thornton's home help, Jenny Armstrong. He loved a flutter on National day and had saved a fiver for the outing, enough to pay for the petrol for his motorbike, get into the course and have his bet. He arrived, on his Norton, with hope in his heart and his racing equipment strapped to his back – a kitchen stool on which he planned to stand during the racing. Nancy had told Jenny that I had backed Teal and she had passed the message on to Les who backed the horse for the first leg of the Tote double.

And so the jockeys came out for the big event.

So confident was Arthur Thompson when he went to saddle up on Teal, that he turned to the other jockeys and said, 'I shouldn't bother to come out if I were you!' Neville and Brownie Crump laughed at the remark, as they wished him luck along with Harry Lane.

Evelyn and I watched the race from our usual place at the top of the stands. From the off the forty seven runners surged forward in a wide, jagged, multicoloured wave to break and reform over the first fence, where Russian Hero was the first faller. Teal, in a good position, was followed by Freebooter, ridden by Bryan Marshall, and Brown Jack II. At Becher's the second time around Teal, who was leading, made a mistake and Freebooter went ahead with Legal Joy third, Wot No Sun fourth followed by Derrinstown. I was not worried because I could see that Arthur was riding the race of his life. He pushed Teal on and was soon leading Freebooter by a length as the field headed for the Canal Turn. Freebooter took the fence too soon and fell, taking half my bet with him. The race was now between Legal Joy, Teal and the improving Royal Tan who was about six lengths behind. Then Royal Tan made a blunder and threw his jockey at the next fence. Finally I put my binoculars down as Teal wore down Legal Joy on the run in, to win by fifteen lengths. I had won £50,000. As I reflected on my good fortune, I remembered how Teal had been offered for sale by his Irish breeder, Mr G. Carroll of Clonmell for just £2.10s.0d. – with no takers. He was later sold with another horse for a bargain thirty five pounds the pair.

There was a great celebration as Teal came into the winning

enclosure. The crowd swelled around him and Neville and Brownie were caught up in the throng. As I watched the celebrations my thoughts were on Signification.

Meanwhile punter Les Armstrong was wondering what horse to back. Time was running out. Then he saw that my horse was running. It was an omen and he named it for the last leg of the Tote double. I had enlisted six agents to place my bets on Signification. Each one had been allocated four bookmakers. They were to go into the ring simultaneously when they saw the first jockey head down for the starting post. One of my helpers was Charles Turiff, chairman of the giant public company Turiff Construction. He had been with us at a party in Manchester's Midland Hotel the night before, and had already laid his plans. 'Just leave it to me Alex,' he said. 'I know exactly what to do.' When the first horse headed down to the start, Evelyn and I again took our places in the stands as my helpers went into action. Betting at Aintree that day were the fearless bookies William Hill, Max Parker, Willie Preston, Jack Burns and Laurie Wallis. Charles, walking with a slight sway and deliberately slurring his words as if he had had a bit too much to drink, approached Laurie on the rails and said that he wanted to bet on Signification.

When Laurie first came out racing in 1934, he had such an innocent manner that the regulars gave him six months, but by 1952, he was one of the biggest rails operators. Laurie, thinking Charles was easy pickings, offered 100–6, so the businessman put £600 on to win £10,000. My agents continued to hit the bookmakers in the final minutes and it was the first time I ever saw a horse backed off the boards. As the horses were off, I glanced down at the bookmakers' boards at Tattersalls and could not see one with a price against Signification. The starting price was 7–2. How the starting price reporters from the *Sporting Life* and the *Sporting Chronicle* obtained their odds, I will never know. They must have checked the very last prices which were laid and returned them.

Meanwhile Les Armstrong had pushed his way as near to the rails as he could get, then he stood on his stool squeezing himself up through the throng. Signification was going like a rocket and as the horses hit the last two furlongs, the plucky punter was so overcome with excitement he lost his balance and fell into the crowd.·

Landing on his bottom, his legs and arms were entangled in people's feet. By the time he had fought his way back on the stool, the race was over. For about thirty seconds, as the crowd dispersed, he did not know the result. Then he saw Signification's number go up in the frame. I had scooped another £50,000 and Les had won the biggest bet of his life. As he raced off to the Tote payout, he realised he had forgotten his stool in his excitement and he had to rush back to pick it up. Then puffing and blowing, he sped across the grass with it like a wild man. He reckoned up what his probable winnings would be. Basing his calculations on the starting prices of 100–8 and 7–2 he thought it would be about thirty pounds, more money than he had ever had in his life. However, the best news was to come. As he stood in the queue at the payout, the Tote announced that the ten bob double was worth £389: an absolute fortune. Of the twelve people who had won on the Tote double, I had given the tip to six. When Les got to the counter the girl cashier said: 'I'm sorry sir, you'll have to take it in small change I'm afraid, all one pound notes!' Les replied: 'Lass, you can give it to me in bloody halfpennies for all I care!'

As he stood on the course, clutching his wad of notes, Les suddenly realised he might get robbed and panic swept over him. He hurried to the corner near the gentleman's loo and unfolded his copy of the *Empire News*. Looking to see if anyone was watching, he carefully wrapped the newspaper around the notes, and thrust the package inside his jacket. With one hand gripping the precious bulge in his coat, and the other holding the stool, he made his escape. This was indeed Les's lucky day because he spotted forty constables marching out of the gate in two parallel lines and rushed in amongst them. It was an escort fit for royalty. Jumping on his Norton minutes later, he raced home at breakneck speed, but when he got in, his wife Jenny was not there. He hurriedly unwrapped his precious package and spread the one pound notes over the kitchen table. Then he went and quietly sat in the lounge. Later that evening Jenny returned. 'Oh Les, what on earth have you done luv?' she shouted from the kitchen. She really believed he had robbed a bank. The couple lay awake all night with the money stuffed under their mattress. The next day they put a deposit on a house of their own.

Racecourse bookies generally take their losses very well and in the early days of my career I often looked along the rails expecting to see glum faces when a hot favourite won. I never did. The bookmakers chatted away just the same without a trace of sorrow, but after Signification won I looked quickly along the line before I went to see him unsaddled and the bookies were pole-axed. I began to wonder what else I could have done to win more money. I checked myself. It was a greedy outlook. I was being what I nicknamed an 'after-the-race-merchant', someone who goes on about the past and what might have been.

Signification's price on the Tote was 34–1, for he was not tipped by a single correspondent; as he was not talked about, had never been in the first three and had not had a trial at Malton, there was no way anyone could have known about his form. As I was placing my money I could perhaps have got £1,000 on at Tote price with bookmakers and won another £34,000 – and to think I never gave it a second thought! I was, however, well satisfied with my £100,000 winnings that National day and so was Charles. I sent Neville Crump £500 to be divided among the stable lads. Sadly Teal, who ran so courageously, died a few months later of a twisted gut.

As for Neville, I will never forget the story of one of his Grand National winners a few years before. It still makes me chuckle today.

Neville loved the smell of Grand National day. The former cavalry captain, born to be a horseman, had his first National winner with Sheila's Cottage in 1948. When his daughter Sarah married a market gardener, they went off to live in a house in Worcestershire named after the horse. Sheila's Cottage was owned by John Proctor, a Lincolnshire farmer and hotelier, who started working life as an errand boy. However in later years he grew to love drinks more than horses. Neville once told me: 'I was watching the National and it looked as though Sheila's Cottage had a chance of winning. I turned to look for the owner and saw him sitting down, swigging a bottle of brandy. "Look here, we could win this," I said. He replied sternly: "You do your job and I'll do mine, you look after the racing and I'll take care of the brandy." He did not see his horse jump one fence, but when he got to the unsaddling enclosure, I'm sure he saw three Sheila's Cottages.'

One bookmaker I thought highly of at this time was Percy Thompson, a man with a penchant for doing things in style. Whenever he went to racetracks in the North, he would hire a complete floor at Manchester's prestigious Midland Hotel, and arrive with his entourage in a fleet of six Daimlers. Percy was probably the greatest board bookmaker of all time. He had friends on every course in the country and I never heard a bad word said about him. He had a string of thirty horses in training, and nearly brought off some tremendous coups, with Coubrador in the Cesarewitch and Philadephe II and Querneuville in Lincolnshire Handicaps. Starting price reporter Geoff Hamlyn said that Percy was a godsend. He would tap his board at Royal Ascot and say quietly: 'Any horse to win £5,000.' Geoff added: 'As soon as one race was over he was up with the prices for the next however many runners there were, but occasionally there was a significant omission, one of his own horses.'

Strangely, it was with Percy that I was to have a narrow escape financially.

Shortly after my Teal and Signification victories Evelyn and I were staying at our usual River Suite in the Savoy Hotel, London, when the receptionist rang.

'Excuse me Mr Bird, but a Mr Thompson would like to see you.' I was surprised, but I told her to send him up to my suite.

'He would prefer to see you in the lounge, sir.'

When I told Evelyn, she raised her eyebrows.

'Be careful Alex.'

'Why?'

'Remember when we met Percy and his wife in the Colony Restaurant last night?'

'Yes, but so what?'

'Mrs Thompson made such a fuss of me, that I think her husband has come to borrow money.'

'Don't be ridiculous darling, this man is big in the business. There is no way he would want to borrow money from me.'

Evelyn was unimpressed with my argument, and she made me promise not to lend him money. I met Percy in the lounge and we exchanged pleasantries. After a while, as we sat sipping coffee, he said. 'Oh, Alex, I wonder, would you be kind enough to let me have £20,000 just for two or three weeks?' He went on with a complicated tale about why he needed the money as I fidgeted, feeling uncomfortable. Evelyn's words kept ringing in my ears. Percy saw the doubt on my face and even offered to make out a post-dated company cheque.

I hesitated, finding it hard to refuse him bluntly. I muttered something about promising my wife I would not lend money and having three boys growing up. We were both very embarrassed and I was relieved when we shook hands and he left. Had it not been for Evelyn I would have lent him the £20,000 or even more. For me, Percy's company, Percy and Warwick and Thompson Ltd., was as solid as the Bank of England. One week later the firm went bust. The news hit the betting world like a bombshell. I felt very sad. The man was a great character. The cause of his downfall was the number of bad debts owed to the company, running into hundreds of thousands of pounds. By law betting debts are not recoverable.

I have lost count of the number of times my horses have won, unbacked by me. Backed or unbacked they always ran strictly on their merits. Nothing was ever fixed, regardless of what some of the stewards of the Jockey Club might have thought.

At Newcastle on 15 April, 1952, my horse Vatellus, ridden by Herbert Jones, was running in the five-furlong Ellswick Handicap. I had seen Vatellus at Malton the previous week and I was not happy with him. The horse had not lost his winter coat and looked like a shaggy Dartmoor pony. I felt sure that another horse Weensland, had the beating of him.

Weensland was ridden by pipe-smoker Joe Sime and trained by Sam Hall. I considered him a good bet and put £1,000 on. That day I flew to Newmarket from Ringway in my private plane. Later I was so engrossed, studying the form of a French horse as I stood by the paddock, that I forgot about the Vatellus race. Then Herbert Howarth, who I had told on the plane that Vatellus was not fancied, came up to me and said with a hint of sarcasm: 'Congratulations Alex, Vatellus has won at Newcastle. Weensland was second!'

Another unexpected win occurred at Manchester when my horse Armada News ran in a three-runner race. Paddock experts could see that this big boat of a horse was so backward he had no chance. He started as a rank outsider, but as often happens in three-horse races, the other two jockeys were content to let the outsider make all the running. The trouble was they allowed my horse to get a hurdle ahead and it was not until entering the straight, that they realised their mistake. Armada News powered on and increased his lead, winning by several lengths, but the stewards were not amused. They summoned the two losing jockeys to appear before them and fined each one fifty pounds, a fair sum in those times.

In 1952 timing by the camera became available at Ayr, Ascot, Epsom, Newmarket and Salisbury. Each week, I thought the game would be up and the bookies would rumble my photo finish system. Instead, my success went on and on and now I had won 500 consecutive photo finish bets at an average of £500 a time. My profit from those wagers was soon to soar to £$\frac{3}{4}$ million. National newspapers were to call me Eagle Eyes and the *Daily Express* ran pieces on me under the headline: 'Watch The Birdie'. Still no one knew the secret behind my bets. However, during these years I never stopped studying the form books that were my bibles, timing horses and finding new outlets for placing my bets. I had learnt that the only way to make big money backing was to have nerves of steel.

At Newmarket in July 1952, I stood in my vantage position as Flush Royal and French Design raced across the line in a close finish for the thirty six horse Cesarewitch. I was sure the 33–1 shot Flush Royal, racing on the near side and ridden by Willie Nevett, had won. Flush Royal was owned by bookmaker Jimmy McLean, whose flowing white hair and cape made him look like a Scottish laird. A well-known backer who was standing by the rails, approached me.

'I've backed Flush Royal to win £50,000 Alex, do you think he has won?'

He looked anxious.

'Yes,' I said confidently.

'Would you like to preserve the condition of my heart then, by betting me £50,000 to £1,000 that you are right?'

It was a good bet for him. He could not lose. He would either get £50,000 from me if the horse lost or £50,000 from the bookies if it won, less my £1,000.

'I'll take it,' I said.

Some people felt that it was a wild bet for me and they were worried about what would happen to *my* heart. In fact, it was a good investment. Flush Royal won by a neck from French Design, owned by Sydney Banks and trained by George Todd. The backer was delighted to pay me. Meanwhile I was pleased for Flush Royal's owner Jimmy. He was a good, honest man, who enjoyed owning horses. I always felt sorry that he never won the race dearest to his heart, the Ayr Gold Cup, which is Scotland's equivalent to the Derby. He would have given his right arm to take home that trophy. My own horses were to win it three times.

Another example of my confidence over the photo finish happened at Manchester races that same year. My great friend Melville Davies approached me asking what horse had won.

'It's the nearest I have ever seen in my life, Melville. It could be a dead heat,' I said.

Melville went to Johnny Foy and told him what I had said. He got 33–1 on my prediction and sure enough it was a dead heat.

Although 1952 was to be my most successful year as a racehorse owner, I was beginning to consider replacing Jack Pearce as my trainer.

Signification started the ball of success rolling with his win at Aintree on Grand National day. He went on to win the Ebor Handicap at York over a mile and three quarters, on 20 August, Herbert Jones rode him and he won by an easy length and a half. That day I had one hundred pounds on him at 10–1, just to cover presents as Jack had told me that the horse was a little over the top. Two weeks later came the big Ayr meeting.

It started well for me. My horse Kesrullah, trained by Alec Waugh at Newmarket, won the Arran Plate by an easy five lengths and I considered him a good thing for the Buckhound Stakes at Ascot the following month.

Then came the Ayr Gold Cup in which I had entered my horse Vatellus, ridden by Herbert Jones.

On the Wednesday before Friday's big race, I watched Edgar Britt on Landing Craft in the Craigengillan Nursery Handicap over five furlongs. All the runners were racing on the far side where the going was supposedly better. Then, Landing Craft started to veer to the stands side, and from then on, raced alone. This was a most unusual manoeuvre and everyone, thinking the horse was out of control, watched the runners on the far side racing to the line. I was on the line, waiting hopefully for a photo finish. As the horses drew nearer, I stood rigid and closed one eye in my well-practised stance.

I saw Landing Craft on the stands side flash past and to me was a half a length winner, but the judge was unaware of the horse and concentrated his gaze on the far side, giving Sky Girl as the winner by a length and a half. Later that evening at the Turnberry Hotel, I discussed the race with Edgar and asked him if he thought that he had won.

'Honestly Mr Bird, I had my head down all the way so I just don't know.'

'Well, in my opinion Edgar, you won by at least half a length.'

From then on my mind was set on tactics for the Gold Cup. On the big day I told Herbert Jones in the paddock: 'I want you to come down the stands side.' He was surprised. 'But Mr Bird, why?' I explained what had happened with Landing Craft and in the end he had to agree that the tactic was worth a try. There were no starting stalls in those days. Vatellus was drawn number eight of thirteen runners. Geoff Littlewood on Royal Hamlet was drawn ten, Blackpool Tower, ridden by Ginger Dyson was drawn thirteen and G. Colven was drawn twelve on Byland.

When Herbert started to edge to the right on Vatellus at the start, Geoff and Ginger asked him what he was playing at. Herbert told them: 'Mr Bird has instructed me to run down the stands rails!' With that, Geoff and Ginger, riding outsiders, agreed to run with him, and Colven, an apprentice, had no option but to go with them.

Vatellus was possibly the fastest horse in training and led by several lengths for four furlongs. He was dying at the finish but just lasted home, holding on for a head victory. The other three runners who accompanied him, finished second, third and fourth. The other jockeys were taken completely by surprise. For years after that day, the stands side was considered to be advantageous and nicknamed Mr Bird's Side in the jockeys' room. *

After that race Evelyn, my three sons and I returned to the Turnberry Hotel. The manager greeted us, dressed in full regalia like a Lord Mayor. 'Mr Bird, you have brought great honour to my hotel,' he announced. 'You are the first owner of a Gold Cup winner to stay here since Mr Jimmy Rank before the war, and I congratulate you.' He asked if he could show the cup to his staff and it was ceremoniously paraded around every room and hallway. Later, the under-manager asked if he could show it to the cooks and down it went to the kitchen. Afternoon tea was brought up to my suite, where my boys were joined by some of their friends, and what a tea it was. All the sweets were in my racing colours, crimson and gold.

That evening when we entered the dining hall with our guests,

---

* There was confusion at Ayr on Friday, 21 September 1984, after the judge Bob Speer announced the wrong winner of the Ladbroke Ayr Gold Cup. Able Albert was racing alone tight up against the stands rails and Alakh headed the main bunch on the far side. The judge announced that Alakh had won and called for a photo for second place. But after checking the negative he realised his mistake and quickly corrected the result, making Able Albert the half-length winner.

the band struck up: 'See the conquering hero comes', and all the other diners applauded. We sat down to eat at a long table placed in the centre of the room decorated with autumn flowers, in crimson and gold. The colours were repeated wherever possible, in the food, starting with melons and ending with trifles. It had been quite a day, and it was quite a night too. That great character, trainer Sam Hall, organised the dancing and I cannot remember what time we went to bed.

My concern about Jack Pearce was by now increasing. Signification, again ridden by Herbert, ran in the Royal Caledonian Hunt Cup at Hamilton Park on 29 September, over a mile and a half. He had beaten White Ensign, owned by the Duke of Roxburgh, easily in the Ebor, and met him on only 6 lb worse terms. As a three-year-old, I was entitled to expect Signification to make the greater progress, but that day he was beaten seven lengths, finishing fourth out of five runners. White Ensign won easily. Watching from the stands I noticed my horse hanging to the left, but did not think too much about it until a few weeks later.

Meanwhile my mind was on Kesrullah again, who I had entered for the Buckhound Stakes at Ascot on 11 October.

It was the last race of the day and although I put £7,000 on the horse, his price did not shorten significantly. That puzzled me, but I did not see any sinister reason behind it.

However, Kesrullah ran a terrible race. I put my binoculars down in amazement as he tailed off.

'What the hell happened?' I asked trainer Alec Waugh.

The normally unflappable man who had worked in Germany for nearly thirty years, was bewildered and upset.

'I can't understand it, Mr Bird.'

In my mind I knew the dopers had been at work.

Mr Waugh, perplexed and still distressed, went off to find the racecourse vet, even though a positive test result would have been embarrassing for him. As it was the last race of the day, the vet had disappeared from the course.

The trainer tried again to get a dope test done when the horse arrived home from Ascot. It was Saturday night and he had to wait until the next morning. Finally, I was not surprised when the test proved negative. The delay in analysing the horse's blood was too long. However, I was surprised when I received a phone call from Mr Waugh a couple of days later.

'Just to let you know that Kesrullah is well. He moved nicely in a gallop this morning, and I would like to run him at Newmarket tomorrow.' I was silent for a moment. In view of Kesrullah's dismal performance at Ascot, there was no way I could back him for another race so soon. The event Mr Waugh had in mind was the Scarborough Stakes over a mile and a half, the same distance as the Ascot race. The going was similar and Kesrullah would again be ridden by Tommy.

'Now listen Mr Waugh, if the horse succeeds, the stewards will have to make an inquiry because of the difference in running. That's the last thing I want at the moment. I would prefer not to run the horse. It's too early.'

'We have nothing to be afraid of Mr Bird. Please trust me.'

Eventually he convinced me that all would be well and we decided to run the horse. That day I did not back Kesrullah and after watching him win by an easy length and a half, I did not wait for an announcement over the loud speakers, summoning Mr Waugh, Tommy and I to the stewards room.

I was in camp on the dot.

Normally at an inquiry, the trainer and jockey invent an excuse for the performance of their horse, if they have not got one that is credible. Very often they will blame the pace or the going for the performance. That day, I was determined I would stick to the truth, no matter what. I went in and faced the stewards who sat stony faced as I told them that I had £7,000 on Kesrullah at Ascot and produced the bookmakers' statements, laying them on the table before me. 'However, gentlemen, I did not have a bet today. Not even to cover presents for the jockey and the stable lads.' The stewards seemed amazed. I don't think they had ever been confronted with no excuses. They accepted that there was nothing criminal about Kesrullah's turn round in form. My trainer was right. There had been nothing to fear.

By now I had realised that my activities were bound to arouse the interest of the Jockey Club. When people do not understand something, or are uneasy or apprehensive, they often over-react.

I was a professional backer. Most people had no idea how much research and appraisal went into the mini computer inside my head before I backed a horse. That is why I never called myself a gambler. I was an investor. The world of gambling was populated by shady characters who would use intimidation, deceit and deception for financial gain. That was not for me. I was determined to stand or fall with my honesty and integrity intact.

A few days after the Newmarket race I went to the meat factory opposite my stables in Malton. I loved the firm's sausages and bacon, and as food was still in short supply they would be a welcome addition to my table. The manager was in very high spirits. 'We have all won a lot of money on Signification this year, Mr Bird. So have the sausages on me,' he said.

'What about Hamilton?' I asked. 'Didn't you lose all your winnings on that race?'

He looked at me in surprise.

'But Mr Bird, my workers and I did not back him there because Mr Pearce told us he was having tendon trouble.'

It was the second time Jack had not told me something important. The other had been when he omitted to inform me of Arthur Thompson's advice never to run Newton Heath without a breast girth, thereby costing me £60,000 in the Lincoln Handicap. There would not be a third time. I took Signification away from him and sent the horse to trainer George Todd at Manton. I had it in my mind that Signification could win the Ascot Gold Cup, the following year, but I told George I was not sure he was sound. Some weeks later, the trainer rang to tell me that Signification had broken down. He never ran again and I sent him to stud.

Because of the virtual closed shop among breeders he could not get enough mares so I sold him. He went to stud in South Africa where he was to sire the winners of every classic race in the calendar.

Over the following few months I began to take the rest of my horses away from Jack. As Quags had broken down badly in a selling race, Jack took him back off my hands, with a promise that the horse would spend the remainder of his life, in peaceful retirement at Malton. The last time I saw him he was going grey and almost as broad as he was long. Alec Waugh had a couple of my horses at Newmarket. The rest went to a man I had heard a lot about, Towser Gosden. His stables were at Lewes and he trained horses for Tommy Degg, a big backer who had a haulage business in Stoke on Trent. Billy Carter was Degg's manager, and chief adviser, and organised many a betting coup for him. Towser was tall, smart and very much a gentleman. My association with him was to be long and happy.

5

In 1953 STANLEY Matthews was the King of Soccer, National Service was the blight of the rock 'n' roll generation and the young Queen Elizabeth was crowned in a glittering ceremony that took the nation's mind off meat rationing and austerity. The Coronation National was won by Early Mist, trained by Vincent O'Brien and owned by Joe Griffin, nicknamed Mincemeat Joe because he owned a sweet and fruit preserving firm in Ireland.

The first time I visited Towser's house his wife Peggy and their two children, Sally and John, were waiting to greet me in the lounge. I had flown from Manchester to London and taken a taxi to Lewes. Sally and John looked puzzled and I laughed as they lifted my riding mac and inspected my back. Towser had been pulling their legs, telling them that Alex Bird flew to racecourses every day of his life under his own steam. They were even more confused by a cartoon in the *News of the World* a year earlier, depicting me as a bird with wings. It showed me perched on a tree, wearing a bowler hat, with a pair of wings sprouting from my shoulders. The caption was simply: 'Signification'. The horse was the paper's tip for the Ebor Handicap at York. Sally put my mac down. 'Mr Bird, where are your wings?' she asked. Now she is married and living in South Africa, and John is a successful trainer in California, with Robert Sangster among his patrons.

When I joined the stables there was some dismay in the camp. Tommy Degg knew I was a big backer and naturally thought I would spoil his market. So the first thing I did was to assure Billy Carter and Tommy that I was not interested in backing any of their horses. From the time I joined the stables, until I left, I kept to that promise. There was always to be a friendly liaison between us and we usually managed not to run our horses in the same race. Tommy was a great one for entertaining, especially at his local meeting in Chester. I was always invited to his table and he was a generous host.

By now luck was playing its part in my photo finish bets. At Goodwood in 1953, I was on the line for a close finish in the four-horse Bentinck Stakes, over a mile and six furlongs. This time I was not sure that the horse racing on the near side, High Stakes, ridden by Gordon Richards, had won. However I was so surprised when the bookies offered him at 6–1, that I just had to have one of my fun bets – the odds were such good value. So sure were the bookmakers and punters that Hornet III, ridden by Australian Rae Johnstone, had won on the far side that he was 20–1 on. Evelyn was with me and I left her guarding my position on the steps, in front of the royal box, while I went to the rails and placed £300 on at 5–1. Minutes later the winning number went up in the frame and even I was surprised that High Stakes was the victor.

Later that afternoon there was an announcement. A mistake had been made and High Stakes had not won after all. The picture was superimposed on another negative, and the winner was Hornet III. Fortunately for me there was nothing that could be done as the bets were settled when the blue 'all right' flag was hoisted. I jokingly said that I was considering refunding my winnings to the bookies. Then a friend told me what they were saying about me, after hearing that once again I had won on the photo – only this time it was a false result. 'They are saying you bribed the judge, Alex,' said my friend. The bookies were joking of course, but the remark convinced some people that there must be something in it. I thought I would add fuel to the flames and said casually, 'That is not true, I have only given him a few petrol coupons!' Incredibly some of them swallowed that one.

The Bentinck Stakes made history. Nothing could be done about the mistake over the winner because at that time the rules did not allow the judge to alter his decision once the 'weighed-in' signal was given. As a direct consequence of that terrible blunder, the rules were altered to permit him to vary his decision subject to confirmation by the stewards. To help the exposed judges, The Race Finish Recording Company started to install mirrors on the far side of the courses to give them the benefit of a reflected view from the other side.

The photo finish was often at the centre of controversy, like the day in July 1953 when Tote forecasts were paid out on wrong placings at Newmarket. The result involved my own horse, Ayr Gold Cup winner Vatellus. The judge announced that Devon Vintage was the winner of the Coronation July Cup but called on the evidence of the camera to determine the minor places. To the majority of onlookers there was little doubt that Vatellus had finished second ahead of favourite Set Fair. My jockey Manny Mercer confidently rode Vatellus into the place reserved for the second horse and Eph Smith steered Set Fair into the third stall. However those punters who had forecast Devon Vintage to win the five-horse race from Set Fair, heard with delight that they had won. The official verdict was first No. 5 (Devon Vintage), second No. 1 (Set Fair) and third No. 2 (Vatellus). The totalisator forecast dividend for Nos. 5 and 1 was declared and successful backers received 15s 2d for a 2 shilling stake. Minutes later the official photo of the finish was displayed in the appropriate frame and there was anger on the course. Set Fair was marked third on the picture, which showed unmistakably that Vatellus was second. The punters who forecast 5 and 2 would ordinarily have received a handsome dividend. Unhappily nothing could be done. The blue flag signifying the weigh-in had been raised and the totalisator had paid out. Rule thirty nine of the Rules of Racing states: 'The judge must announce his decision immediately, or after consulting the photograph and such a decision shall be final. This rule shall not prevent a judge from correcting any mistake. Such correction being subject to confirmation by the stewards.' So instead of receiving the eighty pound prize money as owner of the third horse, I received £160 as owner of the second. However, there were a lot of unhappy punters holding winning tickets which were never paid.

Another method I found of beating the bookie was a direct result of owning horses. In 1953, using Johnny Foy, I planned a coup with my horse Companion Way, a five-year-old, one of the few horses still being trained for me by Jack Pearce. Companion Way was a decent flat horse who won the Carlisle Silver Bell for me in 1951. Jack told me that he had popped the horse over a few hurdles and he had shown great aptitude for the game, but did not like heavy going, so we decided to strike while the ground was firm, and run him early in the season. We chose the West Country for his inaugural race. It was on August Bank Holiday Monday at Devon and Exeter. The problem was how to get £3,000 on the horse. There were half a dozen flat meetings, as well as jump meetings going on, and the bookmakers did not want to know about betting on the smaller courses. At that time an owner was not obliged to declare a runner, so it was possible to make multiple entries for a horse, and decide where it was to run on the day of the race. The Press Association liked to be informed of the stables' intentions, so they could put out a separate list of probable starters and jockeys for the morning papers. Jack rang the agency's sports desk, telling them that Companion Way would probably run at Catterick in a handicap. There was no need to mention Devon and Exeter because the Press did not formulate probable starters and jockeys for the small meetings.

On the day of the race, Johnny placed my bet, not mentioning what meeting Companion Way was running at. Just the name of the horse was all that was required. The bookmakers assumed that Companion Way would run at Catterick and my bets were eagerly accepted. It looked an open race, and they must have been licking their lips in anticipation of blowing my money back to the course to reduce the price. They were probably surprised when the Catterick runners came through on their tape machine to see that Companion Way was a non-runner. It was not until they opened the sports pages of the newspapers next morning that they discovered my horse had won at Devon and Exeter and they owed Alex Bird several thousand pounds.

Nowadays, such a coup is impossible. Horses have to be declared and if one does not run, questions are asked by the stewards of the Jockey Club.

I still have a replica of the Carlisle Silver Bell won by Companion Way. The inscription says: 'The swiftest horse this bell to take, for my Lady Daker's sake.' Perhaps it should read: 'The swiftest horse a coup to make for the bookies' cash to take.'

On Sir Winston Churchill's eightieth birthday that year, when presents were sent to him from all over the world, I wanted to give him my horse V-Sign. (Vatellor-Significant.) To have seen the former Prime Minister give his famous victory sign when the three-year-old horse won a race, would have been a joy to behold, but Evelyn pulled me up by the reins for being too ostentatious, and on reflection she was probably right.

It was around this time that I got the same feeling about a National horse that I had for Freebooter and Teal. It happened at Manchester races when I was with trainer Bobby Renton. We were both thankful that a shower had passed and as he brushed the rain off his bowler hat, I pulled out two Havanas and passed one to him, but when I offered him my silver cigar cutter he pushed it away.

'No Alex. That's not the way to do it.' He tore the end of the cigar off with his teeth and spat it out on the soft grass. 'That's the real way,' he said. I never used a cutter again. Bobby lit his cigar.

I was celebrating victory with the cool, tough trainer of champion chasers, who had stables near Ripon, Yorkshire. We had just watched his hurdler Tudor Line win a race easily. It was owned by diminutive Yorkshire lass, Mrs Edna Truelove, wife of bookmaker Fred who had since died.

'I tell you now Alex, that horse is going to win next year's National!' I looked across at the small, unthreatening fences on the Manchester course and in my mind's eye put them in the shadow of those daunting Aintree fences. I smiled at Bobby's confidence. 'Aren't you a little optimistic Bobby?'

'Just remember this one Alex,' said the man who was to train horses until he was eighty three. Then he turned and walked off to the unsaddling enclosure, at his usual sprightly pace. I watched him disappear into the crowd on that cold day, wondering if he'd lost his senses. The National was a gruelling race for hardened jumpers. What chance did a novice hurdler have?

Even so, I remembered how I had stood alongside Harry Lane at Birmingham races in 1951 watching his horse Teal win a race and Harry had said the same as Bobby: 'That's next year's National winner Alex!' As I strolled to my car my heart began to rule my head. Tudor Line would be my biggest National bet ever. I would put enough on him to make me a millionaire in a day.

A few weeks later I took my family on holiday to Kitzbuhel, Austria, where I was to encounter fruit machines for the first time. There were half a dozen in an après-ski restaurant and my sons, Harvey, Laurence and Jack, were itching to spend their pocket money on them, mesmerised by the apples and pears that spun at the pull of a handle. I told them to button up their pockets. 'If I had two of those machines, I could have a yacht in the Mediterranean and would never have to work again,' I said. Being an investor and not a gambler I never had any wish to risk my money that way. Neither did I want to go to casinos. What the losing percentage was for the punters there I could not work out, but it must have been fantastic.

I would never bet an even money chance on the spin of a coin. However, if someone laid me 21–20 against, I would have spun a coin all day.

Pools betting also amazed me. Punters lost an average seventy percent of their stake, and the chances of winning that dream fortune were infinitesimal – and still are.

The world of betting at this time was different however and I cannot imagine any bookmaker now, being party to the kind of things that went on.

Late one afternoon bookmaker Laurie Wallis called in to see me at Franklyn, on his way home from Haydock Park. It had been a fair day for him. He had won about £1,500. But there was a look of apprehension on his face as he told me about his client F.W. Dennis, a wealthy landowner from Lincolnshire. 'I don't think I will keep that profit for long,' he said, accepting a glass of champagne. Laurie sat in the chair by the fire and made himself comfortable before going on. 'Mr Dennis had a winner today at 100–8 and I know he will be having at least £200 on the horse later.'

I was amazed. Laurie told me how he allowed Mr Dennis to bet when racing was over. At 5.30pm every day, when the meetings were finished, Laurie would ring Mr Dennis and give him the starting prices. Then his client would bet on practically every race.

There was enormous trust between the two men. Perhaps it was because Laurie came from Lincolnshire too. For the bookmaker firmly believed that his client would never cheat. Mr Dennis always backed his own horses and later that day Laurie rang him from the Midland Hotel.

As he started to reel out the starting prices, on the race that Mr Dennis's horse had won, his client roared down the phone: 'Don't tell me the betting on this race. I already know the result. My trainer has sent me a telegram telling me my horse won at 100–8. Now I can't have a bet!'

Mr Dennis had several trainers and he always instructed each one not to send a telegram with the result. The winners were not broadcast until late in the evening so he could bet in blissful ignorance, but this was a new trainer and he had not been given the instructions. Although Mr Dennis showed a loss on his bets, he liked to back outsiders with Laurie at Tote odds, and one day he caught the bookie by surprise. When a horse called Winsome Princess won at Yarmouth, at 33–1, Mr Dennis invested ten pounds each way at Tote odds – and netted nearly £5,000.

During the 1950s when the TV show What's My Line, starring Gilbert Harding, Lady Isobel Barnett and Barbara Kelly, first appeared, bookmaker Sydney Berman was betting on the rails under the name of Briggs Berman. The popular Sunday night programme, where the celebrities had to guess the occupations of guests, was introduced to England by famous bandleader Maurice Winnick.

Maurice enjoyed backing horses and one day at York, approached Sydney, asking for £1,000 to £400 on a runner. 'You can have one hundred pounds to forty,' the bookmaker replied.

Maurice was surprised. Normally at York a bookmaker on the rails would lay a horse to lose £1,000, but at that time Sydney was still making his way.

'Do you know who I am?' asked Maurice.

'Oh yes, you are Mr Winnick.'

'Do you know that I have a programme on television called "What's My Line?"'

'Oh yes, I watch it Mr Winnick. It's very good.'

'Would you like to appear on my programme?'

The bookmaker nodded excitedly.

'You'll do well,' said Maurice. 'Nobody will ever guess you are a bloody bookmaker.' Then he turned and walked away.

In 1954 I began to lay my plans for the Grand National and Tudor Line. Bobby Renton had purchased the horse from Dan Moore's yard in County Meath. One cold winter's day he had stood gazing into a horse box at the stable. He shook his head. 'No, he's too small,' he said, looking at the four-year-old horse inside. Dan showed him to the next box. Bobby went in and carefully studied the horse. 'Maybe,' he said. Dan led him to the third box. Again Bobby studied the horse inside. This time he climbed on him and sat bareback for ten minutes not moving a muscle and then dismounted. The expression on his face showed it was a hard choice. Finally, he bought the horse in the second box. His name was Freebooter, who was to have phenomenal success in the Grand National, but Bobby never forgot the horse in the third box – Tudor Line – and the following year returned for him.

The small four-year-old that Bobby discarded was Hattons Grace. Vincent O'Brien later trained him to win the Champion Hurdle at Cheltenham for three consecutive years.

To find a National winner, and to back him at the right odds requires patience and dedication. On 4 January I backed Tudor Line to win £1,000 in the Evertime Chase at Ayr. His starting price was 3–1 and he won by four lengths. Within days I managed to put the winnings on him at 50–1 for the National.

On 16 January I went to Sandown to see Tudor Line in the

Londsborough Chase. I backed him to win £6,000. His starting price was 9–4, and he won. Minutes after the race I started to place part of the winnings on him for Aintree, but I had trouble backing the horse and had to spread my bets here and there, averaging about 33–1. Slowly, however, my investment began to build up, and the more I saw of Tudor Line the more confident I became. On 3 March he ran in the Mildmay of Flete Challenge Cup at Cheltenham. I backed him to win £15,000 and his starting price was 11–4. For the first time in my life I decided to put all my winnings on for Aintree and go for the grand slam. Over the following few weeks, I schemed to increase my stake on Bobby's chaser. By the time I had finished, I stood to win nearly £500,000 on the Grand National, and word was spreading about the investment.

The phone just would not stop ringing at my home as the racing journalists pressed for more information about my bets on Tudor Line. 'I'll be glad when it's all over – I go to bed with the sound of a telephone ringing in my ears,' Evelyn said.

'Then they'll be ringing to find out how much I've won,' I teased.

'I'll move out to the garage then!'

'Oh, I forgot to tell you darling, I'm having a telephone extension put out there.'

I was not joking. I had converted the loft over the rambling garage block at Franklyn into a billiard room, and because it was a couple of minutes' from the house, I needed a telephone there too.

'In that case, I'll have the bedroom soundproofed,' Evelyn said adamantly. I laughed, but somehow I had a niggling feeling she meant it.

On the first day of the Liverpool meeting there was already a feeling of excitement building up for the big race two days away. The favourite for the National was Irish Lizard, ridden by Michael Scudamore, the father of Peter Scudamore, who was to become champion jockey. But many Turf experts tipped Churchtown and Royal Tan, the new Griffin challenge, again trained by Vincent O'Brien and ridden by Bryan Marshall.

I found Bobby Renton standing by the entrance to the

weighing-in room, as jockeys gathered around the scales, and I interrupted his thoughts. 'How's Tudor Line?' I asked, feeling a little embarrassed because I asked him the same question every time I saw him.

'Alex, he's wonderful.'

'How does he compare with the immortal Freebooter?'

'He's a better horse than Freebooter ever knew how to be!'

That was exactly what I wanted to hear. Bobby went on to tell me about Tudor Line's well being. He had complete faith in the horse. Thanking him I turned and started to head for the stands. 'In fact, I'm so confident, I'm leaving the pricker off for the race,' Bobby called after me. I stopped in my tracks. That small brush was always fitted to Tudor Line's bit to stop him jumping to the right, which he had a habit of doing. The National was run on a left-handed track, so a tendency to jump to the right could be a serious fault, especially when the horses had to negotiate the Canal Turn. Bobby soothed my worries.

'Have a cigar Alex,' he said, offering me one.

I lit up as he explained his reasoning.

'I've had Tudor Line with the pricker off and he's so easily handled, you would think he was a dressage horse.'

'Bobby, it's a left-handed track, and if you're wrong . . .'

'Alex, the pricker isn't necessary any more!'

Bobby was adamant. He was a shrewd trainer, and when it came to National horses, he was one of the best in the country, along with Vincent O'Brien and Fred Rimell. I accepted his judgement, but as I walked away, doubts still lurked in my mind.

'I hope you're right Bobby: there's half a million riding on him,' I shouted back and the trainer laughed.

'It's as good as in the bank,' he called after me.

Tudor Line had a good jockey in George Slack. The hard-working horseman started riding in 1937 but did not have a winner until 1947. Never in those ten tough years did he stop trying. Slack was no Bryan Marshall, but he was honest and courageous and that was a vital ingredient to Aintree success.

On National eve I walked into my lounge where my black

labrador Sammy was pretending to be asleep on the rug in front of the fire. He knew what I wanted all right. 'Sammy, my cigars.' He still kept his eyes shut. 'Sammy, cigars . . . I'm counting to ten Sammy.' His eyes remained closed but he could hear me. 'One, two . . .' One eye opened. 'Three, four . . .' The other eye opened. 'Five, six.' He raised himself up, then slowly padded his way to the bar. He returned with a king size jar of Upman cigars between his teeth, looking as if I should have known he was dreaming about the bitch across the fields. Once he would have fetched the cigars as I entered the room and clicked my fingers, but as he grew older, I had to count. At first he responded to two, then four and that night six. Finally, he was only to get the cigars at nine. Sadly that was to be his age when he died.

We arrived at the Midland Hotel for the Grand National Eve celebration party. The great musician Joe Orlando saluted me from the bandstand as I took a seat at the end of my table, which was decked in serviettes and flowers in my racing colours, crimson and gold. I remember thinking how lucky I was to be able to live that way.

We had a wonderful evening. Matt Busby and his wife Jean were there, along with Charles Turriff, Tommy Appleby and his wife Margaret and a dozen other guests. When the vintage port and cigars arrived, Charles, a great joker, moved up the table to sit next to me. He knew that I had backed Tudor Line to win a fortune, but he did not know for exactly how much.

'Come on Alex, how much money have you really backed the horse to win?' he asked.

I rose to the bait, my confidence in Tudor Line, bolstered, I'm afraid, by the champagne and port, I leaned back in my chair, looked him in the eye and said:

'Charles, my old friend, this is the greatest certainty I have ever seen in a Grand National, and as you know I have had one or two successes in the race before.'

He laughed as I recalled the victories of Freebooter and Teal. I was loving every minute of it.

'I have backed Tudor Line to win so much money that I have a pile of vouchers this high . . .' I stood up and stretched my hand in the air to signal the enormity of the bet.

'Never mind the amateur theatricals Alex, how much in hard cash? After all, I am a businessman.'

'Honestly Charles, I do not know exactly how much money I have backed the horse to win. It's absolutely crazy, in all my life I have never backed a horse to win more than £70,000, now I think it's around half a million.'

Charles's mouth dropped open and he stared at me with disbelief. Now I was on the run in and heading for the line. 'I am very lucky to have been born in the same era as a horse like Tudor Line,' I said loudly, wondering if I really ought to have another glass of port. 'I'm also lucky to have been born in the same era as a man like Bobby Renton.'

'But Alex . . .' I would not let Charles go on. I put my hand up stopping him in mid-stream. My ego seemed to have captured the attention of the entire table.

'You, Charles, are lucky to have been born in the same era as a man like Alex Bird!' Evelyn gave me a frosty look and I knew I had overstepped the mark again, but I could not stop myself, and anyway I was only joking.

'In fact Charles, I'm so confident of Tudor Line's chances that I wonder if you would do me a favour?'

'Anything Alex, but don't tell me that you've put so much on Tudor Line that you want to borrow a fiver for another cigar until you collect your winnings.'

We laughed in those, early, tired hours of the morning. Charles poured himself some more port and listened intently.

'I want you to back Tudor Line to win another £10,000 for me.'

'Are you sure?'

'My dear friend, absolutely, but there's no way I can put the bet on myself, it would be refused.'

With the port finally gone, we sleepily rose from our table and made our way home. Charles came back to stay at Franklyn with us. As I lay awake in bed that night, I could have kicked myself for letting my ego rule at dinner.

Charles was a happy-go-lucky businessman who had made me double up with laughter at a party in my home a few months earlier. We had dined at the Bridge Hotel in Prestbury, Evelyn and I, Matt and Jean Busby, Bill and Nancy Thornton, and several others, but as usual the party had to go on.

I invited the orchestra and guests back to Franklyn. The champagne flowed and the musicians played. Matt Busby sang 'I Belong to Glasgow' and we all danced. Suddenly Nancy burst out laughing as Bill produced an old fiddle he had bought in a second-hand shop for a few bob. Standing in front of the fireplace, he started playing it. The noise was awful, for he could not play a note. We all laughed our hearts out as the orchestra joined in the mêlée. Then Charles marched up to the fireplace, but his hand up the chimney and smothered Bill's face with soot.

'Ladies and gentlemen, I present the Black and White Minstrel Show,' he announced. He brought the house down. Charles was always the last to leave our parties.

'Alex, life is short, you've got to enjoy yourself,' he would say in fatherly fashion, but at 4.00am when all the guests had gone, I always ended up saying: 'Charles – you've got to go, I'm turning the lights off.' In the end that is what I did. Then he would slip away to meet the dawn.

It was a beautiful, clear day at Aintree. The horses wheeled and cantered to the start as I took my place at the top of the stands with Evelyn, Tudor Line's owner Edna Truelove and my great friend, textile businessman Bob Salm, who I met on a skiing holiday in Arosa some years before. He had a palatial house in Surrey, and the garden was so big he needed three full-time gardeners. I watched jockey Bryan Marshall going down to the start on Royal Tan and took heart from the fact that not since 1885 had a rider won the great race two years running, and anyway Royal Tan had not won a race for over two years. However any horse from O'Brien's stables could not be dismissed lightly. The thirty eight-year-old father-of-four and trainer extraordinary was an unhurried figure, who always quietly whispered instructions to his jockeys in the parade ring. He was a small and polite man who took over his father's stables when he died. He had a reputation for being a marvellous judge of a horse. If he took a liking to one, he was never put off by an unfashionable pedigree. He had bought Royal Tan for Griffin after it finished second to Nickel Coin in the 1951 National.

I fixed my binoculars on Tudor Line, with George Slack in checked silks on top. The horse looked good as he cantered down to the start and I began to plan my celebrations for that evening. 'Can you see my horse Alex?' said Edna. She was only five feet tall and could not see over the crowd, even on tip toes. 'Yes he's looking very fit,' I said. Then I added in gentlemanly fashion: 'Don't worry if you can't see the race, I'll do a running commentary for you.' I had always imagined myself as a bit of a Raymond Glendenning, Michael O'Hehir or Peter O'Sullevan. I watched Churchtown go to the post. He was to have run in the colours of Mrs Vincent O'Brien, wife of the horse's Tipperary trainer, but the horse finally ran in the flame and green colours of Mrs Geoffrey Kohn, who was bought a share in Churchtown as a present from her stockbroker husband for her fiftieth birthday and tenth wedding anniversary.

The race started and the horses surged forward, the colourful silk of their jockeys making a wonderful spectacle. At the first, Tudor Line made a mistake which caused him to canon into the prostrate Swinton Hero. Alberoni fell, almost bringing down his stable companion Royal Tan. At the fourth, I was surprised to see master tactician Bryan Marshall on Royal Tan desert his favourite position near the rails and steer a course near the outside. To my horror Tudor Line was jumping to the right and at Becher's he blundered. I continued my eloquent commentary for the excited Edna, standing on tip toes with her fingers crossed. 'They're going to the Canal Turn . . .' I saw Slack glance back to see few horses behind him. Then the field streamed over the Canal Fence. This point is always a dramatic moment in the race. The five-foot jump is followed by a ninety degree, left-handed turn. Horses which do not jump the fence on the angle, usually lose valuable lengths. In the days before the Canal was fenced off, many riderless horses, especially tubed horses, would gallop straight on into the water. Sadly, some were drowned. I held my breath.

101

'What's happening Alex? Where's my horse?'

'Going round the Canal Turn, my dear.' I saw Tudor Line pulling to the right again, and Slack was having a tough ride. The horse went over and landed with his jockey fighting every inch of the way. How Slack managed to wrench his horse round that sharp turn I will never know. Needless to say, he lost a lot of ground.

Halfway through the race – approaching the stands – Tudor Line was so far behind that I thought he would be pulled up. Slack was almost willing his horse on. I contemplated making a bonfire of my betting vouchers and looked down at Edna. 'I'm sorry my dear, you have absolutely no chance.' At the thirteenth, Legal Joy crumpled and fell. Jockey Dave Dick threw his cap at the ground in anger, and then turned to find the horse unable to rise. He had broken his neck. The field streamed past the stands in a glorious, colourful wave, and out into the country for the second time. I could see several jockeys pulling their horses together and kicking them on, some with more ambition than ability, cheerfully setting out on a hopeless second circuit, Tudor Line with them. Others were content to let their horses hunt round, to see how many still stood after Becher's and make the best of their way home. Slack must have been desperately tired after his gruelling first circuit, but he carried on, looking for a miracle. Suddenly I could scarcely believe my eyes as Tudor Line started making his way through the field. At each fence he veered to the right but Slack pulled him over. 'That jockey must have the muscles of Tarzan,' I said, interrupting my lucid commentary. Miracles do happen at Aintree, and within a short while Tudor Line had galloped past so many horses that he was up with the leaders. 'He's in with a chance now,' I shouted to Edna, who could hardly contain her excitement. Slack looked as if he had cured the horse's involuntary habit of pulling to the right. I think he must have been so tired that he merely sat still. Then between the Anchor Bridge turn and the second last, Churchtown, one of the leaders, faltered. He was later found to have burst a blood vessel. Tudor Line bravely galloped on and at the second last was in the lead. 'I think he's got it,' I shouted, above the roar of the crowd. Then came the last fence, the crucial point of the race.

Slack, knowing how much ground Tudor Line had made up in that final circuit, felt that if he took a slight pull on the bit and gave the horse a breather, he would preserve his strength for the long exacting run in. As the horse felt this slight pressure, however, he returned to his old habit of going to the right and lost four lengths. Royal Tan then took the lead. Slack gathered his horse and he gradually made up the lost ground. He was flying to the line and inch by inch he gained on Royal Tan. Royal Tan could not shake Tudor Line off. The question was whether the winning post would come in time for Marshall. The two horses crossed the line together. It was a breathtaking finish, worthy of a Grand National. Mystified Edna looked up at me and asked: 'Well, did we do it?' The judge's official verdict was that Royal Tan won by a neck. It was the shortest neck ever seen by some racing people. As the judge was positioned in the line I knew it could just be an optical illusion, but from where I stood, I was satisfied that we had been beaten. One more stride however, and I was equally sure we would have won. The result was Royal Tan 8–1, Tudor Line 10–1, and Irish Lizard 15–2 favourite third. Churchtown was fourth. Twenty nine horses ran. Sadly four were killed: Dominick's Bar, Paris New York, Legal Joy and Coneyburrow. As Evelyn, Bob Salm and I walked down the stands, Bob turned to me and said:

'Alex, that was your finest hour.'

'Bloody 'ell, what do you mean? There I was almost a millionaire in a day and in a second it had all gone, all because the pricker had been left off.'

'I mean, what you said to Edna. With all the despair you must have felt, you still put your arm round her shoulders and said: "Never mind love, you will win it next year." I couldn't believe it.'

In the member's enclosure 5,000 champagne corks popped in celebration, and on the inside of the course the win was toasted in picnic-flask tea, cockles and jellied eels. On the way to the car I strolled through the unsaddling enclosure. As Royal Tan was led down a lane of cheering racegoers, beaming Joe Griffin danced an Irish jig and threw his hat in the air. The successful owner was joined by his thirty-year-old wife, Peggy, laden with diamonds, pearls and a mink stole. Friends crowded round, hugging and kissing them. Joe gasped: 'I'm speechless, life's wonderful, bring on the champagne.' Then he shouted to press men: 'I had a few pounds on my horse, but I'm not saying how much.' Mrs Griffin told them: 'We're a great racing family, all our five children have Shetland ponies, and I have a horse!' Then Griffin sent a dozen bottles of champagne to the jockey's room. It was a great Irish treble again. Mincemeat Joe, O'Brien and Marshall. There was no taking it away from them. This was their day not mine. That night Griffin threw a celebration party for seventy at the Adelphi Hotel. It was the talk of Merseyside. The guests included winning jockey Marshall, of course, and his wife. People could hardly be heard against the constant popping of champagne corks and music. On the menu were Dublin Bay prawns, chicken and asparagus, flown in specially from France. Griffin always did things in style. The good conduct medal that night must surely have gone to disappointed jockey George Slack. He motored back alone with his thoughts to Cumberland immediately after the race and took his wife out to dinner. Then he spent Sunday playing with his two children, aged nine weeks and eighteen months. When asked by reporters how he felt about the race, he nobly replied: 'It was a hard ride, but it is an honour even to finish second to a jockey like Bryan Marshall.'

People never understood why I did not feel any emotion about losing. But winning and losing was my business just like buying and selling. I suppose, however, that in spite of my optimism over Tudor Line I did not really think that I would win £500,000. It was like the brief optimistic moment when I was to think I might win the Derby with my horse Amourrou. That story comes later.

On the Monday following Royal Tan's victory Peter O'Sullevan wrote in the *Daily Express*: 'It was the most dramatic National for sixteen years, since Battleship beat Royal Danieli by a head.' I smiled to myself as I sat reading the paper in the living room. Battleship launched me on a fantastic run of Aintree successes, was Tudor Line to be the last? I smiled even more when I read Tattenham in the *Sunday Express* on 25 March, 1954. He said:

'Slack thought Tudor Line would have won if he had jumped straight at the last. He didn't, and one of the biggest gambles in racing history came unstuck.' I wonder who he was talking about?

When O'Brien and Griffin finally took their winning horse home to Tipperary 25,000 people packed the tiny market town of Cashel to welcome them. On a hill, high above the houses, blazed a monster bonfire, as two bands headed a parade through the streets below. Griffin and O'Brien were carried shoulder high, to a floodlit dais, as the crowd went wild. There was only one black spot on the horizon. The Irish National Hunt stewards had suspended O'Brien for three months because of the inconsistent running by four of his horses, including Royal Tan and Early Mist. That did not take away from the glory of the day however and to the cheers of the crowd, Griffin and O'Brien stood grinning on the dais as Michael Davern, a government official and local innkeeper, declared: 'The decision of the stewards to withdraw Mr O'Brien's licence is due to jealousy!'

A few months later the dopers singled out another of my runners for their target on a cold windy day at Haydock Park.

I arrived at the course, looking forward to having a bet on my horse Orthopaedic. When I saw the expression on Towser Gosden's face, I knew that something was terribly wrong. I had never seen him so distressed. Towser rarely swore, but that afternoon he could not stop himself.

'Those bastards!' he said fiercely, clenching his fist. 'They've got at Orthopaedic.'

Towser loved horses even more than racing, and what had happened had upset him deeply. His travelling head man had summoned him to Orthopaedic's box. Towser looked at his sickly horse, his head low, almost touching the ground. The trainer bent down and gently patted him. There was saliva running from his mouth. Towser raised the horse's head and saw that the bottom part of his lip was almost completely burnt away. Dopers had obviously tried to force a capsule down him, and the horse had resisted, refusing to swallow it. The capsule must have snapped in his mouth. I jointly owned the horse with Maurice Moss, who had joined us by the paddock and was listening intently to the story. Maurice grew angry and spoke loudly. 'Towser, you must go to the stewards and tell them what has happened.'

Towser, still distressed, tried to cool Maurice down. The trainer faced being warned off over the incident, but Maurice was like a dog with a bone and would not let the matter drop. His voice grew louder still, and people were beginning to listen as he remonstrated with Towser. Finally, I stepped in.

'Calm down Maurice, don't say anything. Let us go for a walk and talk.'

The strong-willed businessman was going full steam and raised his voice to me in protest.

'I want this doping matter settled now!' he repeated.

'Stop it Maurice! You're not dealing with your secretary now, you're dealing with me. Just be quiet and let us walk around the corner.'

I led him by the arm and we strolled out by the paddock where I explained what the inevitable verdict for Towser would be.

Finally, Maurice agreed to say nothing. It was the only time we were to have a difference of opinion.

I went home that night, wondering who was behind the cruel doping. I never found out.

It was in the 1950s that bookmakers offered staggering fixed odds on football, but they scrapped their generous offers just in time to save them from extinction.

In my early years, apart from my interest bet on the FA Cup or the League Championship, I was not keen on betting on football. However, around this time a change took place in the structure of fixed odds betting on the game. There had always been healthy rivalry between the William Hill organisation and Ladbrokes, but now things had developed into a price war. From an initial 33–1 for three draws, one of them extended the odds to 35–1. The other retaliated with 40–1. Then it went to 45–1 and finally 50–1. The odds for four draws meanwhile, increased proportionately. Before, they had been 100–1 for four draws; now they were in excess of 250–1. The smaller bookies were following the lead of the big two. As the odds on three draws were 50–1, I could not resist a bet. After patient perusal of the forecasts of forty football tipsters, I invested £160 to win £8,000 on three draws. But I saw a warning light. When I told Johnny Foy to execute the commission, I instructed him to spread the risk around as many bookmakers as possible. It seemed to me that a bookmaker would lose so much that he might be forced into liquidation. My three draws came up and that was the last time I got such lucrative odds. The following week the bookmakers slashed their fixed prices by half and just in time. For on that Saturday, there was an unprecedented number of draws. It was touch and go whether the big firms could pay out their full amount. Had one particular match been a draw, instead of a narrow win, they might even have been forced into liquidation, carrying with them many of the smaller firms who had been forced to increase their prices to keep in step.

Not long after, the Chancellor of the Exchequer placed a twenty five percent tax on fixed odds betting to bring it in line with Tote betting on football. That was the end of fixed-odds betting coupons. No way was a punter going to pay such an exorbitant levy and interest dwindled. No more coupons were printed. However, at the end of the day, the tax was fortuitous for bookmakers. Sooner or later the day would have come when there were so many draws, and so many winners at fixed odds, that they would have been unable to meet their liabilities. Today the government must be happy about the way the betting industry is organised. Betting shops are licensed properties and the Treasury collects eight percent of turnover.

In the days of fixed odds football there was great support for the idea of a Tote monopoly. It was mooted by owners and trainers as well as Totalisator managers. So the bookmakers had to be careful: their image had to be pure. I often wonder what I would have done had bookmakers been declared illegal from that time.

There was no way I could have bet at Tote prices. I would have had to retire gracefully to the garden.

6

THE WORST HORSE I ever owned was Teething. How I managed to show a profit on her I will never know.

One day in 1954 Towser rang me at home to say that he had seen a beautiful chestnut filly, by Luminary out of a mare called Dribbles. When he advised me to buy her I was most surprised as he did not normally train fillies and I certainly did not back them, because I found them most unreliable. However, I agreed to let him bid for her because I had a feeling that she could be exceptional. We named her Teething. Had she been a colt I could have called her Stanley Matthews, the greatest dribbler of a football I ever saw.

As a two-year-old Teething was rather backward and had only one race. I was most hopeful that, when she came to hand as a three year old, she would develop into a useful horse. However, in her first four races, she did not show us very much and did not unduly trouble the judge. Towser was disappointed, but suggested we persevere with her as she would probably be better over a longer distance, especially at the back end of the season when fillies normally make some improvement. But I was tempted to tell him:

'Yes, she certainly wants a longer distance, the further the better – South Africa or perhaps Puerto Rico!'

Nevertheless, I refrained for fear of questioning Towser's judgement, which was normally one hundred per cent.

All in all it was a successful year for me, capped by Orthopaedic winning the Ayr Gold Cup. Joint owners Maurice and his wife Rene thoroughly enjoyed a celebration evening with us at the Turnberry Hotel, but sadly it was their last visit before they were brutally murdered as they slept in their French villa home on the Cote d'Azur. To this day their killings have not been solved.

I did not think about Teething again until October, when Towser rang to say that the horse was moving well at home and was capable of winning a race, especially in heavy ground in November.

In the last week of the season she was duly entered in a selling race at Liverpool, and also in a race at Manchester for maidens. When the handicap came out for the Liverpool race we were delighted that the filly was only given 7st 2lbs. As the weights were published two weeks before, we had plenty of time to look at Manchester. Why we double entered I do not know, because it was hardly possible to get a lower weight in a selling race, but nevertheless we had made the Manchester entry and so spent some time on it. I doubt whether, in the many years that I had been studying horses, I had come across such a race. It was bereft of any form. There was just one horse which we put a question mark against. She was a filly called Gladness, trained by Vincent O'Brien in Ireland. She had had only one race as a two-year-old, finishing way down the field. The fact that she had not run as a three-year-old until the very last day of the season seemed to suggest she was pretty useless, but we thought perhaps O'Brien was trying to get a race out of her and then send her to stud. * Nevertheless we decided to go for the Manchester race, and I thought that if I backed Teething each way, I could hardly lose my money.

'If three horses beat us she goes to the Knacker's Yard,' said Towser.

The day of the race dawned and the going was heavy, which I knew would suit Teething and I had £1,000 each way on her. However rumours were flying around the course that Gladness had some ability and this was reflected in the betting as she became a short-priced favourite. When Gladness came into the paddock, all

---

* I rate Vincent O'Brien as the greatest trainer in the world. He has won three consecutive Champion Hurdles, three consecutive Grand Nationals, four Cheltenham Gold Cups and the Derby five times. Nobody could do more than that. It was ironic that Vincent should choose a race at Manchester to produce this filly who had obviously been beset by leg problems. I did ask Phil Bull, king of the ratings, how he placed Gladness and Teething in his calculations. He said he rated Gladness approximately a furlong in front of Teething.

the best judges remarked how well she looked. I was not a particularly good judge of a horse's appearance but she did seem special. Compared with her the rest of the field looked like hairy dogs. I had backed my filly at 8–1, so if she was placed I stood to win £1,000. But if Gladness did not come up to expectations, I would gain £10,000.

The race needs little description. From the distance, Gladness cruised to the front and won, pulling up by eight lengths. Teething finished second and I was satisfied with my £1,000. Little did I know at that time that my horse, possibly one of the worst in training, had been beaten by a filly that turned out to be one of the greatest of all time. The following year she was to be entered for the Irish Lincoln, and the handicapper had no alternative but to allot her top weight as she had not had more than two races. At that time it was necessary for a horse to have had three races before it could be handicapped. Obviously O'Brien had a programme mapped out for her and ran her with jump jockey Pat Taafe on board. She finished second. Naturally Gladness was not fancied, having this safe top weight, and she started at 25–1, the biggest price of any horse in the race.

In all, she was to run twelve times in four seasons and O'Brien clearly had trouble with her. However, her wins were to include the Ascot Gold Cup, the Goodwood Gold Cup and the Ebor Handicap under top weight, where she cantered in by six lengths. Her final race was as a six year old, when she was to finish second in the King George Vl and Queen Elizabeth Stakes at Ascot. There, her tendons, which had given her so much trouble during her racing life, were to give way, and that was to be the end of the road for the filly.

In 1964 the greatest mug punter who ever lived was taking on the bookies with a vengeance. His name was Joe Sunlight and every time I met him I tried to understand him, but I never could. The small, gentle Manchester architect, bet astronomical sums on horses for over forty years. He was a Russian emigré, and he designed and owned Sunlight House, an office block in

Manchester, once the tallest building in Britain. This brilliant man, who wore the same grey overcoat with a green velvet collar for over thirty years, had the gambling bug in a big way. He would often back several horses in a race and his daily turnover sometimes exceeded £10,000. However, Joe was by no stretch of the imagination a winner. He owned a Rolls-Royce car, but also caught buses and travelled second class on trains.

Joe lost about £50,000 in 1954. That was his settlement figure. In fact he lost double that, because he only paid the bookies an average ten shillings in the pound. They treated him as a top of the book punter and did not calculate his bets in making a fair book. They ignored his wagers as he only settled at the end of each year for half his liabilities. Then the slate was wiped clean and the bookies were happy. Geoffrey Hamlyn, the starting price reporter for the *Sporting Life*, once claimed that Joe paid a bookmaker just £7,000 for a £35,000 liability. Joe had no chance of making racing pay but he believed he was a close student of the book and could evaluate a horse's chances by the look of the runner in the paddock.

One day I went to the Turkish baths in the basement of Sunlight House and was surprised to find Joe, sitting on a stool taking the money and handing out the towels. After he had collected sufficient readies, he was off to the Gus Demmy betting shop on the corner of Deansgate, fifty yards away. When he lost the money he returned to collect another few pounds which he used to bet on the last couple of races.

Once I was staying at the Majestic Hotel in Cheltenham, when I received news over breakfast that the day's racing was postponed because of the snow. I decided to stay until the end of the week, hoping the meeting would still take place. As I made my way through the dining room, I saw white-haired Joe, standing at the window, staring out at the snow and looking as if he had a lot on his mind.

'How are you Joe?' I asked.

'Very well, Alex, fit and confident.'

'Confident about what?'

'That I will get a good return when I back the winner of the Champion Hurdle this week.'

'How do you know you will back the winner?'

'Because I've backed seven horses in the race!' He pulled a racing newspaper and bookmakers' vouchers from his pocket.

'But there are nine horses entered. What if one of the other two wins?'

'Oh, I'll be backing them on the course,' he replied earnestly.

Joe was such a contradiction. He was a business genius with a mathematical mind, and yet he just did not realise his method could not pay.

'I've backed them to win varying amounts at varying prices,' he added, beaming with satisfaction as if he had pulled off some great coup. The thought never occurred to him that if he backed each horse to win say one hundred units, his total investment would be 120 or more and therefore he would be showing about a seventeen to twenty per cent loss on his bets.

One Sunday morning I paid a visit to Arthur Talkington, who worked for course bookies and bred dogs in Northenden, on the outskirts of Manchester. I found Arthur, nicknamed Talkie, still smarting from an encounter with Joe the day before. Talkie had been to the races in the South where he had lost all his wages, except for a pound, just enough for the taxi home from Manchester Station. At Euston Station in London, as he walked along the platform to catch the train north, he saw Joe in his familiar grey overcoat with the distinctive green velvet collar. The millionaire and Talkie exchanged greetings and got into a second class compartment together. 'He suddenly announced that he was going to the dining room and would I like to join him for a little something?' said Talkie. 'Of course I agreed, in view of my financial situation. We had a meal and just one glass of wine. I didn't want to take advantage of Joe's generosity, if you understand what I mean. I told him it was very kind of him to invite me to dine with him and he said how much he had enjoyed our chat when we finished the meal. Then the dining car attendant came around and said: "Together sir, or separate?" Joe said: "Separate."'

Talkie was too proud to ask Joe for a loan. His bill came to fifteen shillings, leaving him with just five shillings. He passed the precious pound note over to the attendant and told him to keep the change. Poor Talkie had to walk home through the rain from Manchester Station. It took him two hours and he was drenched to the skin. When Joe died in 1979 he left over five million pounds.

There was always a healthy respect between the regular backers and the bookmakers on the track.

It was around this time that professional backer Ted Mason was pitting his wits against them.

When he was within earshot of a few bookies, he would boom: 'Bookmakers, I hate them. There's nothing I would like better than to eat a bookmaker's heart for breakfast, cut very thin, cooked with a little bacon and a couple of eggs.' Then Ted, a big man from Worcester, with a forbidding expression on his face, would smack his lips with relish. Most bookmakers would laugh his remarks off, but one, Bob Collington, always rose to the bait.

'You won't have my heart for breakfast,' he would vow. One day, Bob got his own back. Sometimes, when a horse was a certain winner, perhaps thirty yards from the post, Ted would call out: 'I'll bet one hundred pounds to a carrot!' In a more serious mood he would transform that statement into a way of making money. If a horse was approaching the last fence a distance in front, he would shout: 'I'll bet one hundred pounds to five pounds on.' A punter who had backed that horse would perhaps lay him the bet, insuring his investment whatever happened. Once at Birmingham, Coloured Schoolboy one of the quickest and best jumpers for years, ridden by that great steeplechase jockey, Fred Rimell, was about 200 yards in front coming to the last jump. Ted knew a good thing when he saw it. His face beamed as he shouted: 'I'll bet one hundred pounds to five pounds on Coloured Schoolboy.' A punter by his side said: 'You can bet me that on!' Then disaster struck. Coloured Schoolboy got too close to the last fence and down he came, costing Ted one hundred pounds. Slowly, deliberately, he began to count out the money in one pound notes for the smiling punter.

Bob Collington was standing nearby, watching and laughing. He waited until Ted was halfway through counting, then moved in. '64, 65, 66, 67, 68 . . .'

'What did you back in the race Ted?' Bob enquired, with great interest.

Ted angrily muttered 'Schoolboy!' and miscounted.

'Bloody, bloody, bloody . . .' was all he would say, as he gathered up the notes to count them again.

Seconds later, as Ted was halfway through his count again, Bob sent in a colleague to ask how he had fared in the race. Ted replied, saying how unlucky he had been, then thumped his fist down on the notes, swearing because he had miscounted once again. The punter looked worried as Ted became even more tense, and he started to count for the third time. Bob was in his element. This time he waited until Ted got into the seventies, then sent a third man to ask about the race. Ted lost his count and his cool. He swore loudly, cursing at everything and everyone. Then controlling his rage, he explained what had happened to Bob's agent, who listened intently. The agitated punter began to wonder if he would ever get his money. Bob sent in another person before Ted realised it was a set up. He took a deep breath, clinched his teeth and raised his bowler hat. He knew that Bob had eaten him for breakfast.

At this time I was having my own personal battle on the racecourse. The government had increased the duty on champagne by five shillings a bottle and the racecourse caterers had raised their prices. However, they went overboard and increased the price by ten shillings a bottle.

I always look for value for money, whether it is in betting or in life generally. So it came as no surprise to my friends when I decided to take on the percentage men who dealt in racecourse champagne.

As caviar and oysters were my favourite food, it followed that champagne was my favourite drink. Bentleys, the purveyors of fish, invariably had a fish bar at all the southern racecourses and big

Northern meetings, like York. As I needed to watch my weight, champagne and oysters were an ideal diet. On a normal day at the races, I would arrive an hour before the first event and head straight for the oyster bar. Being a regular customer, the oyster openers on most of the courses immediately prepared three dozen specials (the layer oysters). If I was on my own, I would take a bottle of champagne with them. Usually, however, four friends would join me and we would each in turn buy a bottle of champagne. This was an important and integral part of my day and I never stopped feeling that I was lucky to be able to enjoy my life this way.

Some people wondered how I carried on with such a diet. It was my belief that a high protein diet of meat and fish, with green vegetables, accompanied by champagne or wine, but never spirits, could only be good for anyone's health. While my luck was in I would continue to try and live this way. However, I did not like the percentage increase on champagne and I protested vigorously everywhere I went, arguing that such a move encouraged inflation. One catering manager finally agreed to let my friends and I have each bottle at an increase of only five shillings. Alas this continued for only a short while. Soon he felt obliged to charge me the full price again. 'From now on I will never buy champagne on a racecourse,' I told him and asked my regular drinking companions to support me, but they felt unable to do so. 'Life is too short for acrimony,' said one of them, Jack King, a West Country farmer with a taste for horses and the bubbly. My personal champagne strike was to last for twelve months. Then I decided to have my own bar at each course. I bought a deep freezer container and installed it in the back of my car. From then on my car boot became a meeting place for my friends, with chilled refreshments on tap. The practice was to last for thirty years.

On 11 May, 1955 I arrived home from Newmarket. Over dinner I told Evelyn that my horse Gloaming, a two-year-old, looked promising. That day he had run in the Spring Stakes over five furlongs and, ridden by Harry Carr, the Queen's jockey, had finished third. Before the race trainer Alec Waugh told me that he thought Gloaming would make a very nice horse. If he could finish in the middle of the field, he would eventually win races. When Evelyn and I retired to the lounge for coffee, I made an extravagant remark. 'You know, Gloaming might win next year's Derby for me!' Evelyn then came out with an equally unexpected statement, which almost made me fall off my chair. 'You can give him to me then,' she said casually. My wife had never owned a horse before. She had never shown the slightest interest in them, and that was good for me because when I got home from the races, it was refreshing to play bridge, rather than talk about horses. Even when I stayed in London for a southern meeting I preferred not to talk about racing in the evenings and I know many others in the sport felt the same way. But some people found it hard to switch off even at play. One Newmarket trainer I knew threw a party for his staff but was so dismayed when they talked shop that he brought on a naked black woman to grab their attention. All she had on was a white turban.

'Look,' said one of the lads, 'It's Lord Derby's colours – black with a white cap!' The other boys laughed and returned to their conversation about racing.

I complied with Evelyn's wishes over Gloaming and over the following few days the transfer of ownership was made.

Three weeks later on 1 June I had my own horse Orthopaedic taken from Lewes, Sussex to Catterick, a round journey of about 700 miles. He was running in the Ferngill Handicap Stakes over seven furlongs and his jockey was Jimmy Lindley. It must have been obvious that the horse was not making the trip for nothing, and after placing bets totalling £6,000 I decided to stay away from the course – not only because my presence would have alerted the bookmakers, but because it was a weak and sensitive market. I went fishing instead at Hay-on-Wye with the man who taught me everything I knew about salmon, Ray Woolliams. He was a gentleman in the Noel Murless mould. I met him through Stan Platt who was his neighbour. Ray's father and grandfather were ghillies on the Wye, but Ray's life was not entirely devoted to fish – he loved horses too. That day I persuaded Ray, who normally had five shillings on a horse, to put ten pounds on Orthopaedic. We called at the Boat Inn for breakfast as we had done in the past. The landlady, who knew me well, asked if I had anything worth backing.

'How much do you normally have on?' I asked as she poured the tea.

'Just five shillings or a pound maximum, Mr Bird,' she said.

'In that case put five pounds on Orthopaedic in the 4.15 race at Catterick,' I told her. She almost dropped the teapot.

She offered to bring afternoon tea to us when we had finished and we readily agreed. At about five o'clock she came down to the river bank with a steaming pot of tea and buttered buns.

We were still immersed in the fishing but the smell of the buns was too much to resist and thankfully we started to tuck in. As we did so the landlady stood hovering over us with a bewildered expression on her face.

'What's wrong?' I asked.

'Aren't you going to ask how your horse got on?'

'Oh, yes of course,' I said. From time to time during the afternoon I had been thinking about the race, but I finally got so engrossed in catching salmon that I completely forgot about it. After all, once I placed a bet I never worried about it, no matter what the stake.

'Orthopaedic won Mr Bird – now doesn't that make you excited?'

If I felt any emotion at all, it was that I was pleased for her. I went back to my fishing. Patience is one of my virtues. Mix it with my inherent fear of losing and you will understand why I am such a cautious backer of horses. I am inclined to withdraw when I am losing and bet bigger when I'm winning. That is a clinical approach. Few people would admit that they are chasers, but it is a natural instinct. I have known many cases where people have backed two, three or four losers during an afternoon and have increased their stakes for the last two races. Sometimes they have managed to come out even or ahead but generally they lose.

Discipline is important. If things go wrong, hold back. It is just like skiing. If you are on a slope and you are falling, the thing to do is

117

put your weight on the lower ski and lean out from the mountain, but instinctively people lean into the slope and come a cropper.

Plenty of people believed that I was heading for a fall. They whispered that I would go broke like all the other nine-day wonders. They did not realise that I was an investor not a gambler.

I never had a strict limit as such but if things went badly and I lost say £25,000 in a fortnight, then I would pull in my reins a bit. I would prune my betting and set myself a target of three months to get the money back, although it usually took less than that. If I had been a gambler, I would probably have got the money back quicker, but I would have lost it all in the end.

My family doctor at this time warned me to stop betting at once, 'The bookmakers will get you in the end,' he said. 'I have been interested in racing in a small way all my life and everyone loses eventually.'

I told him that I would stop as soon as I had a losing year. I did, one year, show a small loss after paying my considerable expenses, but as the gross profit was still handsome, he allowed me to go on. Friends used to tell me I would be skint if I continued to do such things as charter a plane for four consecutive days to go to Newmarket and not have a bet. My reply to them was:

'I will be skint if I have a bet to justify my expenses!'

An example of the patience I am prepared to devote to racing is underlined by a race at Royal Ascot, the Queen Alexandra Stakes. It is the longest in the calendar, two and three-quarter miles. After careful research, I found out that, as this distance was beyond the limitations of the ordinary horse, it was useless to consider form over a lesser distance, even two and a half miles. Armed with this knowledge, I eliminated all the horses which had not been placed or run well in the race; the following year, if nothing qualified, there was no bet. In the last thirty five years, I have had twenty five bets. Only two have lost. The Brown Jack Stakes used to be over two and three-quarter miles and I took into consideration horses that ran well in that race. Now the distance has been reduced to two miles, so it has to be disregarded.

A few days after the Orthopaedic race Evelyn's horse Gloaming ran at Manchester. Again ridden by Harry Carr he finished a disappointing fourth in the John O'Gaunt Stakes. Then we ran him at Royal Ascot on 15 July in the Chesham Stakes. Neither Mr Waugh nor I fancied the horse's chances. However, it was one of the few meetings Evelyn attended, so we were happy she had a runner there.

Gloaming, with Harry on top, was outclassed in the race, finishing fifth, but Evelyn enjoyed the day, particularly as the Aly Khan, representing his father, the Aga, smiled and nodded to her as we left the paddock.

My wife only saw Gloaming run once more. It was at Haydock Park and he finished fourth. Then she lost interest. Mr Waugh died a few months later and I transferred the horse to Towser's yard. After two more unsuccessful races, he advised me to tell Evelyn to get rid of him.

'He goes like a bomb on occasions, Alex,' he said. 'But you can't rely on him.'

I put the matter out of my mind and the months went by. Little did I know that Gloaming was to have a surprise in store for me.

Early in 1956 my mind was once again on the Grand National.

That year I backed the Queen Mother's horse Devon Loch, to win just £5,000 in the big race, far short of the staggering £500,000 for Tudor Line. Bryan Marshall should have been the jockey, but he could not ride because of an injury. So the legendary Dick Francis took his place.

Responding gallantly to Dick's prayers for a Royal victory, the horse was at least five lengths ahead by the Aintree elbow on the long run in. I saw Dick look around for non-existent danger and as he drew further and further away from E.S.B. I made an undignified sprint to the unsaddling enclosure, holding my bowler on my head against the wind, to be sure of getting the best place to welcome the Queen Mum and her winner. It was deserted when I got there, but for National Hunt steward, Sir Edward Hanmer. Huffing and puffing, I said:

'Isn't it wonderful?'

He stared at me coldly and replied:

'Yes I suppose it is.'

Soon the crowd gathered and along came the winning horse with the trainer leading him in, but it was not Devon Loch. It was E.S.B., trained by Fred Rimell, who was cheering and shouting. I thought it was nice to be second, but could not recall a runner-up being given such a welcome before. I turned to the man beside me. 'Where is the Queen Mother?' I asked. He looked at me as if I were a greenhorn. 'What do you mean mate?'

'Where is the Queen Mother and the winner Devon Loch?'

'Devon Loch fell mate, didn't you see it?'

I didn't believe him. I tried to reconstruct my thoughts. It *was* the last jump I saw Devon Loch safely over, and I saw Dick looking round. How on earth could he have fallen? It was only later that I heard of the traumatic event when Devon Loch staggered and fell only yards from the winning post. My own horse Tobasco was running in the following race, but I did not go into the paddock. I sat on a seat away from the crowd, stunned.

Devon Loch struggled to his feet after his fall and was led away sound. He seemed suddenly to take an imaginary jump, slip and pancake to the ground. To this day his fall remains one of the racing world's great mysteries.

A few months later Towser and I entered Orthopaedic for the Stewards Cup, over six furlongs, at Goodwood. As Jimmy Lindley the stable jockey could not do the weight, we had to look elsewhere, and I suggested Willie Snaith, a very good lightweight jockey. However, he already had a possible mount in Epaulette, trained by Sam Armstrong, and owned by South African millionaire Jack Gerber. 'Epaulette has no chance,' said Towser. 'I saw Willie ride him in a race at Brighton, a few weeks ago, and he finished last. And the horse was unplaced in a very moderate race at Alexandra Park, where he was an odds on chance!'

Armed with this knowledge, Towser approached Willie at the Newmarket paddock on 18 July. I still laugh today when I recall the showdown. There was Towser, over six feet tall, staring down at Willie, four feet nothing. 'I would like you to ride Orthopaedic for me in the Stewards Cup, Willie. If you can give me your assurance, I will book you for it.'

'I'm sorry sir, I'm riding Epaulette for Mr Armstrong. I am retained by him so I shall have to ride.'

'Oh no, Willie,' said Towser sternly. 'You're surely not thinking of riding him. He was tailed-off when you rode him at Brighton, and he had no form at all. Are you sure you were trying in the race?'

'Oh yes sir, I was trying. The horse has improved a lot since then, and he takes his chance at Goodwood.'

Towser stepped closer to Willie and, with a sombre expression, asked him if he knew the Lord Chief Justice Jeffries, known as the hanging judge. 'No sir, I don't.' Towser told him that when the Lord Chief Justice condemned a man to be hanged, he donned his black cap. Then the trainer removed his trilby, and bending down over Willie, with a look of compassion on his face, said in a serious tone: 'May the Lord have mercy on your soul!' Poor Willie went white.

Orthopaedic, ridden by Kenny Gethin, was not placed in the Stewards Cup on Tuesday, 31 July. Jack Gerber's horse Epaulette came second, beaten by a head by Matador, ridden by Eph Smith.

Jack Gerber later became a very special friend of mine, and when I stayed with him on holiday in South Africa, I related the story of Towser and Willie to him. Prior to arriving in the country Evelyn and I had been staying at the Reeds Hotel in Madeira. Currency restrictions were tight and we were running out of cash. We were waiting for a friend to arrive, who would lend us some money to see us through the holiday. He was a wealthy Frenchman, and I thought all would be well, for things were getting desperate. It was a question of whether Evelyn had a cup of tea or I had a glass of wine. The man never came. There was only one thing for it. The liner *Caernarvon Castle* had docked at Las Palmas, en route for South Africa. We were fortunate to be able to get a cabin and from then on we were allowed to cash cheques legally. The next morning on the high seas I sent a cable to Jack Gerber, asking him to book us into a hotel in Cape Town. His reply was brief and to the point:

121

'You are booked in at Lancelevy.' That was the name of his luxury home. Jack, who made his money in the steel business in Yorkshire, met us at the quayside in his Rolls-Royce, which he shipped over from England on every visit. He had a new Rolls Royce every year over the thirty years I was to know him and I doubt if he ever exceeded 7,000 miles in any one of them. He drove us to his fabulous mansion in St. James's Cape Province, with its beautiful gardens overlooking the Indian ocean. That evening, as we sat in his sumptuous lounge drinking port after dinner, I told him: 'It is as well you did not win the Stewards Cup with Epaulette. Your stable might have been in trouble with the stewards for such a turnaround in form.'

Jack put on his monocle looked at me and said: 'Alex, my horses are always trying!'

Towser meanwhile had a penchant for witty remarks. Once, at Hurst Park, he had a runner – Greenbatt – which he did not fancy at all. The horse was owned by Billy Carter. It was the last race, and Towser, Billy and I watched from the stands. I had not had a bet because I never backed horses other than my own in the stable, and anyway, it was common knowledge that the horse was not cherry ripe. At the distance, I could see Greenbatt, ridden by Jack Crowhurst, pulling double. Jack was not a fashionable jockey, but a very good work rider at home. Towser did not need me to tell him how well the horse was running and he said quietly: 'Come on boys, start cheering!' We responded immediately, shouting ourselves hoarse. Because Tommy Degg and I had horses with Towser, people assumed it was a gambling stables, and they could be forgiven for thinking that Towser was also a big backer. That was far from the truth. His normal bet was twenty five pounds, and very occasionally fifty. He once told me that he was considering having one hundred pounds on a horse. I did not sleep for a week wondering how much I should have on and how to find enough bookmakers to accommodate me. For if Towser was having such a big bet in his terms then the outcome of the race was a mere formality. That afternoon, however, any one would have thought

Towser had a fortune on Greenbatt. The horse won by a neck and we went off to the unsaddling enclosure. 'Well done Jack,' Towser told the jockey, and then we retired to the bar. The real reason for Towser's assumed jubilation was that if the public saw a horse win when it was not cherry ripe, they would seize on him next time out as a good thing. Over a glass of champagne, Towser said: 'That was a jolly good performance lads.'

'Yes, the horse must have been a lot more forward than you thought,' I replied.

'I don't mean the bloody horse Alex, I mean the performance of Billy, you and me. I think we all deserve an Oscar!'

On 21 July, a few days after Towser had approached Willie Snaith at Newmarket, we ran Gloaming in the Hagley Handicap over six furlongs at Worcester. Towser had tried Gloaming with blinkers and he had gone exceptionally well. So he felt Evelyn's horse could just pull it off in the little race.

Needless to say, Evelyn was not going to Worcester. She was staying at Champneys, a nature cure centre at Tring. Towser planned to watch his beloved county cricket team, Sussex, play at Brighton that day, and I was going to Ascot. That left Towser's wife Peggy as the stable's sole representative on the course. On the morning of the race I cast my eye over the fourteen runners in the *Sporting Life*. The fact that the horse was undertaking the long journey from Lewes to Worcester would influence bookmakers and backers. They would reason that he would not be making the trip for nothing. I thought a fair price for Gloaming would be 6–1, and it was then that I decided to contact a man named Idris Isac. Idris was a chemist in Stoke-on-Trent. A calculating man with a broad Welsh accent and a sharp brain, both for dispensing prescriptions and taking on the bookies. He lived two doors away from Billy Carter and I had met him a few months earlier at Haydock Park. He told me that over the years he had built up a chain of connections – people who would put money on horses for him. Each person was limited to five pounds, but as he had over a hundred contacts, he was able to place at least £500 on, without the money going back to the course. I was interested in what he told me, but as I always had four-figure bets on horses through Johnny Foy, I did not think I would avail myself of his offer at that time.

However, as I was not having a lot of money on Gloaming I felt that this would be a good moment to put his method to the test. I rang Idris and asked him to put £650 on the horse. Then I went off to Ascot. At the course I was so immersed in the races that I forgot about Gloaming at Worcester. Lee Byrne, who had a pub in Stoke, approached me by the stands.

'Guess what Alex?'

'What?'

'Your horse Gloaming has just won at 20–1.'

Poor Lee. He was the kindest and most willing man I had ever met, but he occasionally made mistakes.

'I can't believe that,' I said. 'You've made a colossal blunder.'

We walked through the Members Enclosure to see the starting price displayed on a big board near the paddock. Passing the Tote office, it confirmed that Gloaming had won and the dividend was twenty shillings and one penny. They had written it as 20–1. 'You've done it again,' I told Lee. 'It was only 9–1. Don't you see, 9–1 to a two shillings stake would bring in twenty shillings and one penny.' Nevertheless, we continued on our way to the board. I stood looking up at it in amazement. Sure enough, the horse had won. And the price was 20–1. I immediately wondered how Idris had got on. Had he backed the wrong horse? I did tell him Gloaming, didn't I?

I telephoned the canny chemist from the course.

'Idris, it's Alex. Did you get that money on Gloaming for me?'

'Of course,' he chuckled.

I had won £13,000.

I reflected that I had not told Evelyn the horse was running, but it did not matter, I reasoned. After all, she had lost interest in Gloaming. On the plane journey home I thought of Johnny Foy and felt a pang of remorse. It was the first time I had not confided in him when I had a horse running. That night at home, I broke the good news about the horse to my wife, over dinner. 'You might have let me know he was running,' she said angrily. 'I could have told the other people at the health clinic.'

'Yes darling, and you would probably have told Stanley Leif.'

Stanley was the boss of the clinic. He was a lovable man, but he had lost a fortune over the years backing horses. He could have told everyone that Gloaming's owner was a current guest, and they would have rushed to back the horse, affecting the price. Still Evelyn would not forgive me. Later she was to sell the horse and buy herself a new Daimler car as a constant reminder to me that I had done her wrong.

The following day Johnny rang. The conversation slowly came around to Gloaming, and he said:

'Tell Evelyn I was very pleased for her.'

The way he said it revealed the deep disappointment he felt. He never referred to the matter again, but I had got the message. From that day until betting tax was introduced in 1966, Idris was to win on balance £200,000 for me. In addition he worked successfully with Johnny. They built up a marvellous relationship and there was never a discrepancy or difference of opinion between them. 'Johnny is the straightest man I have ever met,' said Idris. 'The game is so full of sharks and liars that he shines like a light as an honest person.' That I should hurt a man like Johnny is still hard for me to bear.

There was another occasion too, when I must have hurt him deeply. As I have said before, Johnny placed millions of pounds in bets for me and I had complete trust in him. Sometimes he would tell me after a race that he had not put all the money on. Sometimes he had put more on. I always accepted what Johnny said without question. Then a few months after the Gloaming race Johnny rang and asked me to lend him money to tide him over a temporarily difficult situation. The request came shortly after I had promised my wife that I would never lend money again. 'I'm sorry Johnny, I'm afraid I can't,' I said. The words came hard and I felt acutely embarrassed.

I didn't tell Evelyn that I had turned him down until later. 'But darling, it is different with someone like Johnny,' Evelyn said. I could have kicked myself. I supposed it says a great deal that those two incidents did not affect the relationship between Johnny and I. We continued doing business over the next twenty years.

One of the most genuine horses I owned was Precious Heather. I bought him from Peggy Gosden for £1,500 at the end of his three-year-old days. Although he had only won over five and six furlongs, I felt that, ridden with patience, he would get a mile – and I had my eyes on the Lincoln. First, however, I entered him for the Ayr Gold Cup on 21, September, 1956. I had deep affection for the Scottish courses because I had always been impressed with the friendliness shown to me by everyone from the Clerk of the Course, to the bookmakers. Once when I ran four horses at Ayr, the Clerk sent for me. I was wary after my previous experiences in England, but when I entered his office, he greeted me warmly, welcoming my party to Scotland. Then he offered us drinks in his private bar and gave us badges for the day's racing. That was in stark contrast to the treatment I had received on less happy occasions in England.

Towser too could not believe the amount of co-operation he received from the Scottish racing authorities.

'I can't get over it,' he once said. 'They have let me put my horses at Bogside, so that I can gallop them. It's like having my own training ground.' Towser put these facilities to good use.

The betting market at Ayr was very strong. I backed Precious Heather to win £10,000 seconds before the off with Harry Miller, a tough Scottish bookmaker from Glasgow. At a vantage point my party watched the race and there was great jubilation as my horse, ridden by Edward Hide, won by a length and a half from Roman Vale, ridden by Jimmy Etherington.

Precious Heather was well named, for he ran many times in Scotland, and was never beaten.

On the Saturday following the Ayr Gold Cup, I ran my horse Ornithology at Bogside in the Stanecastle Handicap. The horse had a good deal in hand on a wonderful handicap and Edward was riding him. I put £6,000 on the horse and considered the race a formality. I discussed tactics with Towser and Edward in the paddock. 'You've got plenty in hand. If you can win cleverly, we will score again with a penalty and should run away with three or four races off this handicap mark,' I told my jockey.

Towser was not pleased. 'You should not say that Alex, you

make them over confident,' he argued. How right he was. Edward set out full of confidence from his victory the day before on Precious Heather. I felt confident too as I rated him as a man of excellent judgement. Towser, his wife Peggy, my nine-year-old son Laurence and I watched the race together. Coming into the last furlong Edward was tracking Raytona, ridden by Walter Bentley. The only other danger was Cobbler's Gold, ridden by Alec Russell, completely hemmed in on the rails. Edward made his move and set sail for home, going easily, sitting motionless. However, as he eased Ornithology past the pacemaker, Cobbler's Gold extricated himself from his pocket and switched to Edward's blind side on the left, beating him half a length on the post. Edward could have won by at least ten lengths had I not given him such bad advice. It was a day he and I would much rather forget.

'What a wonderful race,' said Peggy. Laurence looked at her and replied very quietly: 'Was it?' He had backed Precious Heather in the Ayr Gold Cup and had invested another pound from his pocket money on Ornithology.

I still felt that Precious Heather would win the Lincoln, but to make sure he could get the mile, Towser and I arranged a trial at Lingfield Park on 26 November, 1956, nine days after the finish of the flat season. I chartered a plane from Ringway and flew down with Billy Carter, Norman Baxter and Eddie Hide. It was a windy day and five very fit horses took part, each ridden by a senior jockey. There was my own Ayr Gold Cup winner Orthopaedic, ridden by Eddie; Tommy Degg's Pecan, ridden by Jack Crowhurst; Greenbatt with Stan Clayton on top and Audros partnered by Jimmy Lindley. Joe Mercer was on Precious Heather. Pecan, a good five-furlong horse, made the early running to ensure a strong gallop from the start. I clocked the race with Billy: Greenbatt, in receipt of a lot of weight, won, with Precious Heather a hard-held second. After the gallop Towser and I took the jockeys for lunch at a nearby hotel. Over a brandy, I pulled Joe aside and told him that Precious Heather would win the Lincoln, if ridden with the patience he showed that day. 'But keep it quiet and there will be a very good present for you,' I said.

When the bookmakers opened the market on the Lincoln in late February 1957, the average price for the horse was 40–1. One bookie even went to 50–1, but within days the odds fell to 12–1 and I was furious. I had planned to back Precious Heather, then a five-year-old, to win £100,000 and I had been biding my time, for I did not see any need to rush in. There had been no significant money from the general public, so it could only mean one thing. A commission agent had been backing the horse in London. I rang Johnny Foy and he made some enquiries. He discovered that was the case. My anger grew and I rang Towser to tell him I would probably take the horse out of the race, because I felt I was entitled to the pickings of the market. Within days the newspapers ran the story of the horse being a doubtful runner. Then bookmaker Maxie Parker rang Johnny. 'Please tell Mr Bird that a man who has had a big bet on Precious Heather is prepared to give him 16–1 about the horse, if he leaves him in the race.' That did it. When Johnny told me, I became even more determined. Knowing that the man must have averaged 25–1 or 33–1 on my horse, I took him out of the Lincoln. Towser rang me at home and implored me to let the horse take his chance. He even asked Billy Carter to plead with me, but Billy told him: 'Not on your life – he will think I have stolen his market.' It was a business agreement that Towser always reversed the charges on his calls to Billy and me. That Monday he rang Billy four times and was so upset that he paid for the calls himself. The following weekend, I arranged to meet Joe Mercer at the Compleat Angler in Marlow where I was staying for a London meeting. When he entered the bar, I came straight to the point. 'Joe, did you tell anyone about Precious Heather? I know that you were involved so please tell me the truth.' Joe was terribly upset, almost in tears.

'I was in the South of France, Mr Bird,' he explained, apologetically. 'I went to a casino, not to play, but just to watch. This man was losing all his money see, so I told him not to worry, he could get it back on Precious Heather in the Lincoln.'

That man was bookmaker Chummy Gaventa.

'Truthfully, I had no idea he was a big gambler, I'm terribly sorry,' Joe added.

Young Alex in the yard of his home, the converted inn the Travellers' Rest

Alex's sister May

Alex, wife Evelyn and son Harvey proudly display the Ayr Gold Cup at the Turnberry hotel

Alex's horse Vatellus wins the Ayr Gold Cup in 1952, with jockey Herbert Jones. The second, third and fourth placed horses followed his risky tactic of going down the stands side, and from that day the stands side was called 'Alex Bird's side' in the jockey's room.

Willie Carson brings in an unhappy Gorytus after finishing fourth and last in the William Hill Dewhurst Stakes at Newmarket on 15 October, 1982

William Hill, arguably the greatest bookmaker of all time.

Cyril Stein

He swore he would never make the same mistake and I believed him. When he asked if he could ride my horses again, I agreed, but there was no going back on my decision about Precious Heather for the Lincoln.

The race was won by Babur, ridden by Edgar Britt, the quiet-style Australian jockey, but I am sure my horse would have had the beating of him. Some months later I ran into Chummy at the Colony Restaurant in London. I had never met him before and he introduced himself to me. We discussed the Lincoln and he admitted: 'The truth is that I would have given you the whole of my commission, and I mean all of it, at about 50–1, 40–1 and downwards, because the bets were no good to me. I may as well have put my ante-post vouchers in the wastepaper basket!'

'But Chummy, Maxie only offered me 100–6 on your behalf!'

Chummy was astounded and his reply was unprintable. He had not restricted Maxie to those odds. Maxie had just wanted the profit on the difference. Chummy and I became good friends after that and he executed large commissions for me.

A few weeks later I called at the hardware shop in my village and as the girl who was serving wrapped up my six lengths of clothes line, she must have been thinking that I had a very large family to have so much washing to dry. I packed the rope in the boot of my car and drove to Haydock Park, where I had arranged to meet Towser. The shop girl would never have guessed that the clothes lines she sold for a few shillings were really worth thousands of pounds to me. I had always believed that on a round course there could be an advantage in not hugging the inside rails, if there was better going on the stand side. Most people felt that the shortest way home was the best, but I was convinced this was not always true, particularly when the going was soft. When I telephoned Towser, telling him I intended to test my theory with Orthopaedic at Haydock, he was sceptical. 'It's ridiculous, the horse will lose all of six lengths,' he said. 'No he won't. If the jockey crosses the track on a diagonal line, taking say one hundred yards to do so, he will only lose about a length and a quarter, and he will make that up on better going!'

Towser still did not agree and we arranged to meet at the course on the morning of the race, so that I could demonstrate my theory.

The bookies were still eating breakfast at their hotels when Towser and I strolled across the soft Haydock turf. We tied the lengths of clothes line together then used the rope to measure a line from the bend, to a point on the inside rail, about one hundred yards down the straight. Then, from the bend, we measured a line to a point one hundred yards across the track to the stands rail. Although this technique was not accurate to the inch, Towser had to agree that the tactic would only cost a length and a quarter. Jimmy Lindley was riding Orthopaedic for me in the Matthew Peacock Handicap over a mile. Before the race, we walked down the track together, and I pointed out where I wanted him to make his move. 'I understand, Mr Bird,' he said. Jimmy went off to the jockeys' room and I went to the rails where my agents put £2,000 on Orthopaedic to win £6,000. Jimmy carried out my instructions to the letter, coming wide on the bend. Orthopaedic won by a neck from Damask, ridden by Doug Smith. His victory was the start of tactics that were later to pay dividends.

The importance of the draw in a race cannot be overemphasised, and I have studied the effects that heavy rain can have on the going at different courses. These two factors have played a vital part in my success. Some say that I have a guardian angel watching over me. If I have, then she never lets me have a bet until all the omens are right. Every investment I make has been carefully considered. My mind becomes a computer in to which details about the horse, the draw, the going and the time of previous races, are fed. Only when these facts have been analysed do I decide whether or not to have a bet. Owning horses gave me the opportunity to experiment with these tactics and over the years they paid off – literally.

7

ON 4 JULY, American Independence Day, 1958 I was staying at the Hyde Park Hotel in London when the head porter approached me. 'Excuse me Mr Bird, but an American gentleman would like to know how to get to Lingfield races.'

'Tell him I'm just about to go there and he is welcome to come along. I'll be taking a taxi to Victoria Station in five minutes.'

The American joined me and we caught a Southern Railways train. We shared the table in a luxury carriage and popped a bottle of champagne. 'You're in luck today,' I said. 'My horse Precious Heather is running and I've got a spare complimentary badge that will get you in the Members Enclosure.' The American was greatly impressed with my hospitality. I showed him around the paddock like a tour guide and introduced him to several racing personalities and friends. We had more champagne, then strolled in the sunshine across the Members Lawn and there, sitting alone on a shooting stick, with his head bowed in thought under a wide-brimmed trilby hat, was Sir Winston Churchill. The American could not believe his eyes. 'Gee is that really *Him*?'

'It certainly is.'

A few yards from Sir Winston were two security men, but that did not stop my friend. He marched up to the stationary figure, clouded in cigar smoke and announced: 'Gee sir, it's nice to meet you. I'm an American.' The great man looked up momentarily. Then he let out a single grunt of greeting. My friend returned to my side, still unable to contain his excitement at meeting Britain's war time Prime Minister. 'They'll never believe me back home,' he said. As we walked away, he kept looking back over his shoulder to see if the figure on the shooting stick was real. He did not realise that on a British racecourse people did not make a fuss or appear to notice famous personalities. The only time I have ever felt odd about seeing anyone was at an Ascot Heath meeting when behind the stand I almost bumped into the Queen and the Duke of Norfolk. I wondered if I should acknowledge her, but I thought better of it and we strolled on to our respective destinations.

At Lingfield Precious Heather, ridden by Jimmy Lindley was running in the next race, the East Grinstead Handicap over six furlongs. He was second favourite at 5–2, and after I had put £1,000 on him, I told the American that he was worth backing.

My horse won by a length and the American made a nice little profit on his exceptional day. Then I decided to make it even more memorable for him by tipping Tintinnabulum, in the last race, the Croydon Handicap. The horse was from Towser's stable. 'I'm sorry but I can't possibly back him,' said the American stubbornly.

'Why not?'

'Because Sir Winston's horse Le Pretendant is running in the race. So I'll have to put my money on him.'

Sadly for the American, but happily for Towser, Tintinnabulum won. As Towser left the paddock later in the day, he passed Sir Winston, standing quietly in a corner. Towser had never spoken to him before, and to his knowledge, the statesman had no idea who he was. Suddenly, Sir Winston looked up and said: 'Oh no, not you again!' With that he walked off. The fact was that Tintinnabulum and Le Pretendant had opposed each other on at least six occasions, and every time, Towser's horse had come out on top. Sir Winston was obviously an avid student of the form book. I bade farewell to the American at my hotel, declining his kind offer to dine with him, as I had another engagement. 'Here's my card,' he said. 'Whenever you come to America, my Cadillac will be waiting to collect you at the dock gates. Then I'll treat you to a time you'll never forget, just like the time you have given me.' Whether his family and friends believed his story about meeting Sir Winston I do not know, but if they ever read my story, they will realise it was true.

On Tuesday 10 February, 1959, at Leicester, my commissioner

Teddy Hayes was approached by bookmaker Max Parker* who had heard I wanted to back Roddy Owen for a four figure sum to win the Cheltenham Gold Cup, to be run nearly four weeks later on 5 March. Max had just taken over Ladbrokes. I had only managed to get £250 on the horse at 5–1, with Tattersalls bookmaker Fred Binns, at Hurst Park, on 5 February.

'I believe Alex Bird cannot get the bet he wants on Roddy Owen,' said Max. 'Ask him how much he wants on at 5–1.'

I had £1,000 on and later Teddy reported back: 'You've got £5,000 to £1,000 on Roddy Owen. Now Max wants to know if you would like any more.' When I got offers like that from a bookmaker I was always suspicious that something was wrong so I decided that £5,000 to £1,000 was enough.

Bunny Cox, the top amateur rider, had ridden Roddy Owen in all his races and was set to partner him at Cheltenham, but two weeks after placing the bet with Max, Johnny Foy rang me at home. 'You've done your money at Cheltenham, Alex,' he said.

'Why?'

'Bunny Cox has refused to ride the horse because he has become dodgy.'

I put the phone down. Did Maxie know Bunny's sentiments when he laid me the bet? I wrote my wager off.

Sometime later at Sandown Park, I saw a horse that impressed

---

* Max Parker was one of four sons of European immigrants, the others being Jack, Isaac and Harry. Harry was known as 'Snouty' Parker, because his nose was a little on the large side. In his younger days, Snouty was a starting price bookmaker in the East End of London, but he blossomed out on the rails, betting in vast sums in the early 1930s. Soon he dominated the ring at Southern and Midland race courses.

Snouty knew the East End well and was king of the knock-out technique. He would pay a fleet of boys on bicycles to go around the illegal betting pitches, putting small amounts of money on a fancied horse. By the time he got to the course, he would have anything up to £4,000 on. Then he would shout out his prices for the horse at extended odds, hoping the reporters would return them at his price, which they nearly always did. If people tried to bet with him, he would ignore them by turning the other way. By manipulating the odds on his own bets that way, he won a great deal of money. In 1941 Snouty was warned off for allegedly bribing jockeys and he died in 1945, aged only fifty.

me tremendously. He was Pas Seul and even though he fell while
leading in the two-horse Grand International Handicap, I was
certain he would go well in the Cheltenham Gold Cup. So I put
£2,400 on him through Johnny to win £30,000. The horse trained
by Bob Turnell at Marlborough, was being ridden by Bill Rees. I
watched the Gold Cup from the stands and felt confident as Pas
Seul, full of running, took the lead approaching the last fence.
There he blundered and fell, interfering with Linwell, ridden by
the great Fred Winter, and Lochroe, partnered by Arthur
Freeman – almost bringing them down. I was so busy watching the
bumping that I scarcely noticed the green and white colours of
Harry Beasley on Roddy Owen, making his way through. 'Come on
Roddy,' I shouted, suddenly remembering my bets with Maxie and
Fred Binns. Roddy Owen won by three lengths and I picked up
£6,250. I had lost £2,400 on Pas Seul, so I made £3,850 profit on the
race. Roddy Owen may well have been 'dodgy' as Bunny had said,
but because of the calamity at the last fence, things had gone my
way. It was that guardian angel looking over me again. Although
my bet was struck with Max, the voucher and winning cheque were
made out by Ladbrokes, so from then on I was a client of theirs.
William Hill, Ladbrokes' arch rival, told me when I met him on
holiday in Jamaica that Max had bought the firm on the instalment
system. Whether they regretted my opening an account with them
I do not know.

In the late 1940s I did not think about opening an account with
Ladbrokes. Their form was in a different league to the rest of the
bookmaking world. They were not involved in the competitiveness
of the ring. Their clients were mainly members of the aristocracy
and without calling out the odds, Ladbrokes representatives like
Mrs Verney, a grey-haired dignified woman who looked about
seventy if she were a day, were merely there to accept bets for very
large amounts, without any fuss. Mrs Verney stood by the rails at
Newmarket and no one would ever have guessed that in the hurly
burly of the race track, she was taking bets. While other
bookmakers shouted out their odds she hardly ever spoke.

Over the years I have been well in the black with Ladbrokes.

The firm always operated a limit for my bets however, never permitting me to have the full amount on. They invariably halved or even quartered my intended amount, and on some occasions I did not get a bet at all. When Max died, his nephew, Cyril Stein, took over the chairmanship.

At the Newmarket sales Towser bought a yearling for me. His name was Gambetto, by Golden Cloud out of Queen's Gambit. Gambetto matured early and showed signs of great promise. I watched him on gallops at Lewes and liked what I saw. We gave him his first outing on Saturday 21 March, 1959 at the end of the first week of the Flat. It was over five furlongs at Hurst Park but as it was Grand National Day I was at Aintree watching Oxo win the big race so I did not think much about my own horse. That evening, however, Towser rang me at home.

'Good news Alex. Gambetto wasn't in the first four, but he ran with great promise,' he said. 'He's a future winner.'

There were forty two runners, and Gambetto, ridden by Jimmy Lindley, was prominent from the start. We agreed to run him next at Kempton Park on 30 March, again over five furlongs. When I arrived at the track, I was not surprised to see Gambetto open as low as 7–2, as his early pace had been noted by more than one expert on his first outing. It was the best price I could get and I backed him to win £6,000. The last price I took was 2–1 and he finished 13–8.

Gambetto, ridden by Jimmy Lindley, made all the running and won by a convincing length and a half. Towser, Billy Carter and I went to the bar to celebrate, but when we arrived there was an announcement over the tannoy.

'Will Mr Gosden come to the Weighing Room, please.'

Towser and I looked at each other ominously as this could only mean one thing: a steward's inquiry. Towser left and I stood wondering what could be amiss. When he returned he looked dismayed.

'The stewards grilled Jimmy and I about the improvement in Gambetto since his last race,' Towser said solemnly. 'They seem to think that Gambetto was not doing his best at Hurst Park. They

135

were not content with our explanations and have referred the matter to the Stewards of the Jockey Club. They want you to attend the hearing in London.'

That was unusual. Normally only the trainer and the jockey had to attend such hearings at the stewards headquarters in Portman Square. Since the day I bought my first horse Quags I felt some of the stewards had a vendetta against me. The power of the Jockey Club was unchallengeable, even in a court of law. At that time the accused was not allowed the benefit of legal support and nothing he said in his defence seemed to make the slightest difference. The verdict seemed a formality and he faced being warned off. That was a fate worse than death for someone like me. To be banned from every racecourse in the world would be untenable. I would have to leave the country. Racing was my life. My boys were at public school and I knew how cruel youngsters could be. Over the following few weeks I was approached by trainers at every meeting I went to. They wanted to know if there had been a change in the unwritten rules. For it was accepted practice for a two-year-old to have an introductory race.

In those anxious days between the race and the date of the hearing, I began to collate the evidence I needed. Painstakingly, I built up facts from my valuable records. Then I rang Towser. He told me that Scobie Breasley wanted to give evidence on my behalf. Apparently, Scobie's mount Cunning had impeded Gambetto during the race. As Cunning weakened, after being in the lead from the start, he fell back, baulking my horse. A few mornings later I arrived at the stewards headquarters. I was met by Jimmy Lindley, Scobie Breasley, Towser and the racing press. We were summoned into a large room and for a moment I was stunned by the appearance of the five stewards who sat before us. They were expressionless. Even the most carefree personality would have been subdued by the atmosphere. I sat down next to Towser placing my briefcase beside my chair. Jimmy and Scobie sat behind us. Out of the corner of my eye I saw Lord Rosebery on my right. I told the stewards that on the day of Gambetto's first race, I was at Liverpool and later that evening heard from my trainer that the horse had run with promise and would win a future race.

'As far as I am concerned gentlemen, the horse did its best,' I added.

Then Scobie told how his horse had hampered Gambetto and that in his opinion, my horse was going all out. There was no reaction on the faces of the stewards.

However, I thought things were going my way when the Hurst Park Stipendiary Steward was called and he told the hearing he had seen nothing untoward that day. His judgement had to be respected because he was the only professional steward at the meeting. There was silence for about a minute, then one of the officials looked across at Towser and I.

'How was it then that Gambetto was listed at 16–1 in the morning press yet finished at 13–8?' he asked.

Before I could reply, Towser stepped in.

'Gentlemen, I do not know if you are aware of the fact that the person responsible for putting those prices in the papers on Mondays is probably the office boy. The only thing I believe in newspapers is the date at the top of the page!'

Then I opened my briefcase and produced the names of sixty two-year-old horses which had run unplaced first time out and won on the next occasion, when they were well backed. Turning to catch Lord Rosebery's steely glare, I said: 'As a matter of fact my Lord, one of your horses is listed here.'

He looked shocked.

'Ah yes, it was Bass Rock,' I continued. 'He ran at Liverpool on 19 March, and was ridden by Manny Mercer. He opened at about 6–1, finished at 10–1, and ran extremely badly, beaten by PC, ridden by Frankie Durr.'

I paused for a moment then went on:

'Twelve days later on 31 March Bass Rock, again ridden by Manny, ran at Birmingham, where he was backed down from 8–1 to 9–2. He won easily, beating Frankie Durr on PC, the combination that had the measure of him on the last occasion. The turnround in form on those two races was twelve lengths!'

'But I did not back him!' Lord Rosebery said suddenly.

'My Lord, I am not suggesting that you did. I am only saying that this is a parallel case to mine.'

The look on Rosebery's face was a picture. There was nothing more to say. We filed out of the room and awaited the outcome. Less than an hour later we were summoned back.

'Mr Bird, it has been decided that there is no case to answer, and we are completely satisfied with your explanation,' said the head steward. We filed out past Rosebery. In that same race at Hurst Park, his own horse Calypso, which was well backed from 10–1 to 13–2 finished fourth. The stewards later published their findings in The Racing Calendar.

A few weeks later in the Members Enclosure on the July Course at Newmarket, I was approached by one of the greatest amateur riders of all time, John Hislop. Today he is a senior disciplinary officer for the Jockey Club.

'Alex, that inquiry should never have taken place,' he said. 'I was delighted to hear the outcome. I have never seen an explanation worded in that way by the stewards. It was an unreserved apology!'

The Gambetto inquiry made racing history and there were some people in high places, who did not approve of the outcome. However the fierceness of the vendetta against me came to light a few years later. Some stewards never believed I could be so successful without being crooked. They thought that I owned horses for one reason only – to make money. In fact I made a loss at owning horses. I enjoyed having my own runners but it was simply my way of putting something back into the racing game, that had given me such a wonderful lifestyle.

Once I was under the impression that the Jockey Club system was the fairest in the world. When it was founded in 1750, few people could have anticipated what profound influence the club would have on racing in future years. By the end of 1773, the Club had made new betting rules and regulations, and later into its ranks came many outstanding men, senior officials like Charles James Fox and Lord George Cavendish-Bentinohk, who was a leading figure in the investigations into the scandalous 1844 Derby. The

Epsom classic was won by a ringer, a four-year-old horse named Maccabeus, posing as the three-year-old Running Rein. Another steward, Admiral Rous, was the epitome of the upright stern victorian. He stamped out many dubious practices involving bribery and corruption and was the originator of the weight for age scale. His motto used to be: 'Keep yourself in the best company, your horses in the worst.' From these beginnings of promise, the Jockey Club grew to become all powerful and at times hypocritical.

One of the bad cases that still saddens me today was the treatment of a trainer in the 1950s. He had won three races at a top class meeting. The horses were all well backed, and the stable won a fortune. From that day, however, the trainer was a doomed man. The Jockey Club Stewards could not accept that he could win three races at that meeting without being crooked. Within months he was warned off.

A worse case concerned trainer Cecil Ray when I was a boy. Phil Bull, the owner and editor of *Timeform*, who is universally acclaimed as the most talented and intellectual man in the modern racing world, told me the story. He had horses with Ray and was close to the facts. It appeared that one of Ray's horses was diagnosed as having been doped. The trainer was completely innocent but he was summoned before the Stewards of the Jockey Club. It was a case of 'off with his head'. Ray was warned off and returned home a broken man. But he was determined to discover the truth about the doping. He and Phil worked together. They held their own inquiry at the stables, interviewing everyone, going over every minor detail. After weeks of painstaking investigations, they found the culprit. The stewards were informed and the trainer waited for them to reverse their decision, but he waited in vain. The stewards were inflexible. They would not bend the rules, even in the light of new conclusive evidence. It was true Ray liked to have a bit of a gamble now and then and they just could not remove this from their minds. Not long after, Ray died, as a direct result of the terrible stress he suffered over the disgrace and loss of his livelihood. On his deathbed Ray made Phil promise to expose this disgraceful story. Phil, who felt he himself was deemed guilty by association with Ray, said: 'It was a chilling tale of the abuse of power.'

The proof that Phil became a victim of the Ray inquiry was in the fact that a man like him, with such an extensive technical knowledge of racing, was never invited to become a member of the Jockey Club. His qualities of honesty and integrity would have proved invaluable. Few individuals had more influence on post-war racing than Phil. The son of a Yorkshire miner, he won a scholarship to Leeds University where he obtained a BSc degree. He became a schoolmaster but the life was too tame for him. Then just before the war he ran the Temple Time Test, which he advertised in the sporting press under the name William K. Temple BSc. The idea was to issue a list of horses to clients each week based on time performance. It was a successful operation and punters who backed the horses on a level stake made a substantial profit over the year. In fact the system paid so well that William Hill closed the accounts of many of Bull's clients.

Phil and Hill met on the issue and had a heated discussion. But the outcome was that the two became very good friends and joined forces. Phil became the bookmaker's personal assistant, going to races with him during the war. He even ran Hill's advertising and organised the ante-post prices.

In 1941 Phil went into ownership, buying the filly Lady Electra, although the horse was unnamed when he first saw her run. From that day he went from strength to strength.

In later years, Phil made a provocative speech to the North West Racing Club. He referred to the Jockey Club's reputation for integrity and honesty, a reputation that spanned two centuries, he said. But everyone was stunned when he added: 'However, in the 1940s it stank!' He went on to tell an interesting tale of a certain well-known Steward of the Jockey Club, whose horses did not try, with his full knowledge. No names were mentioned, but I have often wondered if it was the same man a jockey once told me about. The jockey said: 'I was in the paddock at Ayr discussing the preliminaries with his Lordship. He told me the connections of the horse that was the obvious danger, should be hanged for what happened in the south last time. I replied: "But if they face being hanged sir, then we are already dead!"'

In May 1959, I met Peter O'Sullevan at Newmarket and we discussed the forthcoming Derby. 'Look Peter, you know I think the English three-year-olds are sub-standard this year. I firmly believe that a French horse will win the race,' I said. Because of his connections I asked him if he would enquire whether there were any French horses for sale that would be likely Derby candidates. 'Leave it to me Alex,' he said, 'I'll get back to you.' A few days later he rang me at home and put me on the trail of Amourrou. He was a fine three-year-old, trained by John Cunnington Jnr. at Chantilly. The horse had run well in the Prix Hocquart at Longchamps, finishing fifth, beaten five lengths by Harbanger who was to win the French Derby five weeks later.

Within a week Towser, accompanied by a vet, was on his way across the English Channel. I bought Amourrou for £14,000 in a private sale and I phoned Manny Mercer at York to ask him to take the mount for the Derby. Manny, previously booked for Agricola, struck out of the race because of injury, immediately accepted. I put £500 on Amourrou at 25–1, just enough to pay for presents. To win the Derby would have been enough. A king's ransom would have been small in comparison. The race coincided with my annual tone-up at the Tring health farm, Champneys, and my main worry as the day drew near was whether I would be right in breaking my fast to celebrate winning the Derby with a bottle or two of champagne and a decent meal. Even though I always watched what I ate, I went each year to the health clinic for two weeks. For the first ten days I would have nothing but water followed by two days on salads. Harvey Wild accompanied me on these visits – but he was not on such a strict diet. On our daily walk through the countryside he would eat the blackberries from the hedgerows. Then, with a wicked twinkle in his eye, he would offer me the biggest one he could find. 'Just taste that, they're beautiful,' he would say. However, I always declined, and that amazed him. For years he told friends: 'He wouldn't eat a single blackberry, but by the following weekend you could hardly count the champagne corks.' I broke off the carrot juice and lettuce leaves to go to Epsom for the big day on 3 June.

As Mercer approached me in the paddock for the pre-race preliminaries I said to him:

'Well Manny?'

'Well sir,' he said in his broad North Country accent, 'It'd be very 'andy!' It was the understatement of the year!

It was a fine day and I watched the race from my usual place at the top of the stands. Amourrou was in a good position at Tattenham Corner, with Manny sitting as still as a mouse in about eighth position. I saw the leading jockey go for the whip. Then the other horses came under pressure. My glasses began to shake uncontrollably, something that had never happened to me before, I had to put them down. I watched the race from that point with the naked eye. I saw Amourrou drop back as Harry Carr pushed Parthia into the lead. When Manny realised that he could not win or be placed, he dropped his hands and crossed the line in seventh place. Parthia, owned by Sir Humphrey De Trafford and trained by Captain Cecil Boyd Rochford, won. The only other French horses in the race, Shantung and subsequent Arc de Triomphe winner, Saint Crespin, were third and fourth. By the unsaddling enclosure Manny said: 'I could have finished closer but there was no point in giving him a hard race.' I went back to the lettuce leaves.

On 20 June I wanted Manny to ride Amourrou in the Churchill Stakes at Ascot, but he could not do the weight so I engaged Peter Robinson to ride. I was hopeful of my horse's chances, for I liked to see good three-year-olds run against older horses. That day I backed Amourrou to win £15,000. Before the race I spoke to Peter in the paddock.

'I don't know what you are going to do,' I said. 'Lester Piggott on Primera is bound to sit on your tail and challenge in the last furlong, Primera has got to be ridden that way. He likes a last-second challenge.'

'Leave it to me Mr Bird, I have a plan.'

It was one of the most brilliant races I have ever seen. Peter led into the straight from the good Irish three-year-old Shackleton, followed by Blue Net, the only other French horse in the field. Lester was sitting with his bottom in the air poised to pounce with a quarter of a mile to go. Peter took a pull at my horse, and Lester found himself where he did not want to be, in front. Then Peter came again and took Primera on the line to win by a head. I had recovered the purchase price of my horse.

Some time later I was to entertain two students, one of them Richard Salm, son of my friend businessman Bob Salm, at the Garden House Hotel in Cambridge. I noticed Peter Robinson sitting at a table in the far corner and pointed him out to them. Then I told the boys about the great race he rode on Amourrou. When Peter left, he passed our table.

'Peter, I've just been telling these lads about your brilliant ride in the Churchill Stakes on my horse,' I said.

He smiled and replied: 'Ah yes, but there was something traumatic about that day I have never told you Mr Bird. It will have to keep until another time.'

Peter obviously did not want the boys to know and it was not until he rode for me again that the mystery was solved. He told me in the paddock that someone had offered him £1,000 not to try in the race. My mind started working overtime. I remembered how easy the horse was in the market. My initial bet had been 7–4 and my last bet was at 9–4. I am sure if the race had been delayed another five minutes it would have drifted to 3–1. I wondered if a bookie had known about the bribery plan. Had Peter falsely agreed to the bribe, and word had got around that he would not be trying?

Sometime later I was in the BBC box at Aintree with the chairman of a top Lancashire rugby league club, a great friend of Peter Robinson. He always stayed with Peter when he went to Newmarket. We chatted about Peter's ride on Amourrou, but I did not mention the bribe. 'Ah,' he said. 'That was the day Peter was offered £1,000 to throw the race.'

Amourrou was Manny Mercer's last Derby mount. He was killed in a tragic fall on his way to the post on Priddy Fair at Ascot on 25 September, 1959. The course was stunned. The Duke of Norfolk announced that the last race, the Swinley Forest Handicap would be abandoned. As I passed the first aid tent following the tragedy, Joe Mercer, Manny's brother, came out sobbing.

That year my horse Precious Heather was in the twilight of his racing career and not so well handicapped. He came second in the Lincoln and Joe rode him that day. A month later he ran in the Newbury Cup. I engaged Sir Jack Jarvis's young apprentice, Johnny Limb, to ride, as I thought he showed great promise. I gave him his instructions by the paddock well before the race.

'You must wait with this horse,' I said. 'I don't want to see you up front, until just before the post.' I took him to the course and pointed out a set of hurdles, conveniently placed alongside the flat, about one hundred yards from the finish.

'When you reach those hurdles, I want you to be a length behind the leaders, then make your move and you will win,' I said.

It was not a big betting race and there was no ante-post market. I backed Precious Heather to win £10,000. Johnny rode a perfect race, and when he was approaching the hurdles, he looked left, made his move and won nicely by half a length from Doctor Tadgh, ridden by David East. The following Monday the *Sporting Life* carried the front page headline: 'Johnny Limb, apprentice find of the season.'

In 1959 at Bogside I was to have a fracas with bookmaker Harry Miller. Handicaps were not computerised then, and each handicapper had to form his own opinion. As I had entered my horses for seven races on the Scottish circuit, I had to find out the best handicapped. I had entered my horse No Myth, ridden by Bobby Elliott, in the Doura Selling Nursery Handicap, over five furlongs. The difference between the best and worst handicap was 32lbs. Harry had laid my bet on Precious Heather in the Ayr Gold Cup without batting an eyelid, so I decided to wait until the last minute. When the horses were almost at the post, Harry went even money and I shouted: 'I'll have an even £5,000.'

'Alex, this is no Ayr,' he said rolling his r's in a broad Scottish accent and staring hard at me.

'All right, what will you lay me?'

'Nothing!'

I did my best to persuade him, but Harry was a man of many moods and must have still been smarting from my previous win with him. He just would not lay me a bet. Everyone could hear what was going on and the word went around like wildfire what was happening. Within seconds No Myth was odds on, and I had not struck a bet. I was so annoyed when the horse won by three lengths that I was not prepared to buy him in. He was knocked down to Alex Boyd, acting for Mrs Tosh, who had lost her horse in a selling race the day before.

By 1960 I was really backing to big money and had prepared myself for the largest bet of my life, but this was one time when horses were not in the reckoning. The contest was Conservative versus Labour. I considered it a formality that the Tories would win the General Election in a canter. The bookmakers agreed and the betting was 4–1 on for a Conservative victory. I paid a visit to Laurie Brown in his office at Manchester. Laurie, who had several horses in training, was an astute businessman who loved racing. We chatted about the forthcoming election and I told him of my intention to back the Tories at 4–1 on. Laurie, however, had a better idea.

'Rather than lay such prohibitive odds, you would fare better by buying steel shares,' he said.

He explained that in view of Labour's intention to nationalise the shares were depressed, but if the Tories gained a majority, they would greatly increase in value. Unfortunately I did not tell him how much I planned to invest, otherwise he would have explained a few important pointers to me. I suppose I could have been called a mug punter for not clarifying the transaction with him. Back home I made my decision. I would buy 40,000 steel shares for £60,000, as the one pound shares on average stood at one pound fifty. Had I told my broker, Walter Stansby, head of Arnold, Stansby & Co., who did the deal, that I was prepared to lose £60,000 in the event of a Labour victory, he would have told me that in the event of the steel industry being nationalised, the government would have had to pay shareholders one pound back for every share purchased. So I could only lose £20,000 as I would receive £40,000 compensation. However, I did not take him into my confidence – otherwise I would have invested £180,000 and bought 120,000 shares.

The Tories won by a big majority and within hours the shares soared to two pounds. I sold at that price and made £20,000, but I should have shown a profit of £60,000. To think that I have always said about racing: 'LEAVE IT TO THE PROFESSIONALS.'

(Postscript: Apparently I was not the only person who saw the merit of this investment. I later heard rumours that a Labour Minister also bought a large amount of steel shares as a hedge against a Tory victory.)

That year I entered Gambetto in a selling race at Doncaster. He was beaten by an Irish horse named Sir Gatric, trained by Paddy Prendergast. I timed the horses with my Omega stopwatch from the top of the stand and I realised that Sir Gatric had broken the course record for five furlongs. The official time had not been made public as I headed for the paddock, and I was probably the only person on the course to know. As Paddy told me that he was not buying his horse in, I bought him for 900 guineas. When it was officially known that Sir Gatric had indeed broken the five-furlong track record, Don Cox, the manager of the course, asked me as the owner of the horse, if I would donate a stopwatch to the winning trainer for a newly-formed race, The Sir Gatric Stakes. The name of the race has now been changed to the Scarborough Stakes and I still present the watch to this day, as it is the principal five-furlong race of the St Leger meeting.

In September work on new stands at Ascot meant the meeting was switched to Newbury and I went there with Harvey Wild.

In the early days I did not profess to be a judge of what horse would win in running, i.e., to see a jockey sitting with a double handful at the furlong marker. However, standing as I usually did by my friend Billy Carter, I learned a great deal as he was in a class of his own at that stage of a race.

'X horse for evens,' he would call, or perhaps 'X for a monkey (£500).'

There was no running commentary in those days and if X should be a good result for the bookmakers, he would invariably be accommodated. I personally did not win a fortune by jumping on the band wagon, though at Newbury I stepped in and won a tidy sum before people realised what was happening.

Before the Princess Royal Stakes Harvey wanted to have ten pounds on a horse called Green Opal, ridden by Lester Piggott. I dissuaded him because I did not fancy the horse over a mile and a half. The race started officially, but it was a complete farce as the horses crawled away from the gate and I wondered if it was a false start. After three furlongs the pace did not quicken at all. The bookmakers were still betting in running, offering virtually the same odds as before the race started. I heard one of them call '3–1 Green Opal'. So I took three monkeys . . £1,500 to £500, once, twice and tried a third time, but they would only take £250.

Green Opal won after leading in the final furlong and Harvey, a good loser, was puzzled. He said: 'But I thought you didn't fancy the horse over a mile and a half?'

'I didn't,' I chuckled. 'But you saw what happened. At the most it was a mile race, possibly less, discounting the first three furlongs. So I stepped in.' Until then Harvey had treated racing as an amusing diversion from his business interests, but from that day I think he gained a more healthy respect for my knowledge of the sport.

On Wednesday 8 March, 1961, at Cheltenham, I met trainer Fred Rimell by the paddock and congratulated him after Nicolaus Silver, ridden by amateur jockey Mr W Tellwright, won the Kim Muir Memorial Challenge Cup. Fred was with his beautiful wife Mercy, who, following his death some years later, was to carry on as a successful trainer in her own right. 'By the way Alex,' said Fred. 'Nicolaus Silver will very nearly win the National.' Taking note of his confidence and what I had already seen of the horse, I telephoned a well known bookmakers on Thursday 23 March, to back the grey for Aintree the following Saturday.

The firm had listed Nicolaus Silver, ridden by Harry Beasley, at 40–1 – a much bigger price than any of their competitors. The nearest odds were 28–1. I asked for £10,000 to £250. To my surprise I got the bet without delay and there was no restriction. Nicolaus Silver did win the National by five lengths from Merryman II, trained by Neville Crump and ridden by D. Ancil. To show my appreciation I sent a case of champagne to Fred after the race, but some weeks later I was to discover how fortunate I had been. I met Fred at Ludlow on Wednesday, 19 April. He was in a buoyant mood after two of his horses, ridden by that great jockey Stan Mellor, had won. Fred thanked me for the champagne and added: 'You don't know how lucky you were.'

'What do you mean?'

'Only two days before the National, my head man told me that Nicolaus Silver had a swollen leg.'

'How did that happen?'

'He had been shod that day and a nail had gone close to the quick.'

The stable was at panic stations. The vet had given up on the horse, saying it would not run that weekend, but Fred and his father, Tom, were not beaten. They cut away the infected area and injected penicillin.

'When we had done all we could,' said Fred, 'we went into the house and got drunk. It seemed that only a miracle would get the horse to Aintree.'

Nicolaus Silver was finally taken to Liverpool, not very sound but declared fit to run just a few hours before the race. Sometime later I read Fred and Mercy's autobiography *Aintree Iron*, and was shocked to discover what else had been going on in the run up to the big race. A French woman, claiming to be a magazine journalist, called at Fred's stables in Kinnersley, Worcestershire, asking to see his National entry. She was shown to Nicolaus Silver's box and left shortly after, but Fred was not happy. He told Mercy: 'I don't like the look of this. I'm sure I've seen that girl at Stratford races with some shady characters.' That evening Fred put another grey in Nicolaus Silver's box. One morning, later in the week, the substitute horse was found doped.

The firm that took my bet of course, were as much in the dark about all these incidents as I was, but they may have heard that the blacksmith had accidentally pricked the horse.

As I owned horses, it soon became obvious that they would be a target for the dopers, because there was nearly always a lot of money riding on them.

On Derby Day, Wednesday 30 May, 1961, I arrived at Epsom to be bombarded by trainers and backers, eager to squeeze information out of me. They wanted to know about the chances of my filly, Silver Span, running in the Nickelham Selling Plate at Epsom, two days later. I did not think anyone would give the horse a second thought, especially on such a colourful occasion as the Derby, with its carnival atmosphere. I was intrigued at their interest. The Epsom trainers were seldom involved in the big race. Their horses were not quite Derby class, so they continued with business as usual, and two-year-old Silver Span had obviously caught their interest because she was a decent horse, competing in a selling race. I was confident of the chances of Silver Span (by The Pelican out of Silver Yew), but as usual, I was cagey when asked about her. Each time I replied that the horse was no great shakes. I even invented plausible excuses for her.

'It's a six furlong race and Silver Span will have to tackle Tattenham Corner, so I just do not know how she will react,' I told one trainer.

How naïve I was in my early days as an owner. I was soon to learn that it would have been better to have said that my horse was a certainty to win. Then nobody would have believed me.

Arctic Prince, ridden by Charlie Spares, won the Derby in a canter by six lengths that Wednesday. The horse was trained by Willie Stephenson who also had a Grand National winner in Oxo.

The next day I found myself the target for the same enquiries about Silver Span. Trainers would start off by casually talking about the weather, and then bring the conversation round to my horse, as if they had only a small, passing interest in her.

Herbert Jones had ridden Silver Span in her previous race, a non-seller. She ran well, finishing third in a big field, but Herbert's weight was seven stone two. In this race, Silver Span was set to carry seven stone thirteen, so I engaged Tommy Lowrey to ride. He knew Epsom well, having won the Derby on Airborne after the war, but on Friday morning, a few hours before I was due to set off for the Surrey track, Tommy rang.

'Alex, some bad news. I can't do less than eight stone two and so I will have to put up 3 lbs overweight,' he said.

I was tempted to tell him it did not matter. It was only a question of a length, and I believed he had a few in hand. I paused for a few seconds, collecting my thoughts, knowing that as I was to have a big bet on the horse I could not leave anything to chance.

'Perhaps it would be better if I got someone who could do the weight, but I promise that you will get the same big present you would have done if the horse wins.'

Tommy was only too happy to accept my offer and I immediately set about the task of finding another jockey.

I booked Lester Piggott, who I had earmarked as a very promising rider. On the course the whole world seemed to know that my horse was expected to win and she opened up a hot favourite. I sent Herbert Howarth in to put £8,000 on Silver Span, and my colleagues had a further £5,500 on. I was pleased when Herbert reported that all bets were placed, but a suspicion that all was not well crept into my mind when he returned to my side in the stand.

'Surprise, surprise,' he said. 'The last £2,400 of your stake was with X and you know how canny he is. Normally he would halve me, but this time he didn't.'

X, a prominent bookmaker on the rails, had refused to lay me a bet at Newmarket during the Royal Alligator coup in July 1950. His reason then was that he did not bet big on selling races for two-year-olds. I listened with interest as Herbert continued.

'He laid me what I requested, £1,300 to £800. Then, as I was walking away, he again shouted "13–8 Silver Span." So I went back and told him that I would have it again. "You've got it," he said to my surprise. As I was jotting the bet down, X asked if I would like another £1,300 to £800. I just could not believe it. Again I accepted his offer. In my opinion Alex, X must know something we don't.'

Herbert, who was very intuitive, walked away, leaving me to reflect on X's unusual generosity. My trainer Jack Pearce joined me to watch the race. Within seconds of the off we were both stunned into silence as Silver Span ran the worst race of her life. She was beaten by many lengths and Lester could offer no explanation.

'What on earth do you think happened?' I asked Jack by the unsaddling enclosure. He was bewildered. We were both sure Silver Span had been doped, and so was Lester. The horse just could not have run as badly as she did.

'We must get her dope tested,' I said. Jack was taken aback.

'OK Alex, but we will have to wait until I get the horse away from the course, because if the test proves positive I shall be warned off.'

I was angry but I knew Jack was right. He would automatically be held responsible. I decided to let the matter drop. The one thing that played on my mind after that fateful day, was the readiness of X to bet so boldly in view of his admitted reluctance to bet on two-year-olds in selling races. It was not until some time later when I met him in a London hotel, that I spoke of my suspicions. X was standing by the bar when I approached him. Soon we were talking about the ill-fated performance of Silver Span. 'You must have known something that day X,' I said. I was not suggesting that he was party to any dirty work that went on, but X had a way of sniffing things out. He knew most things that went on in the racing world, good or bad. X put down his drink and looked me straight in the eye. 'Alex, on my mother's grave, I swear to you that I knew nothing about any funny business.' That was good enough for me. I let the matter drop. When a person made an oath like that, I had to believe them. It was not until I related the incident to Harvey Wild over dinner at my home, that I was to find out something about X's remark. Harvey said: 'So X made an oath and swore on his mother's grave did he? Well, that means nothing.'

'What do you mean Harvey? Speak plainly.'

'His mother was dead of course. Had she been alive *then* you could have believed him.'

Jack Pearce continued to train horses at Malton, although Silver Span was the last for me. I did not charge the trainer rent and when he died a few years later I sold the place.

8

THE RAIN WAS pouring down. I looked out of the lounge window at the black clouds hanging low over the moat and wondered if they were a bad omen. It was Grand National day in 1962 and Evelyn and I were about to leave for Aintree. I had backed the 7–1 favourite Frenchman's Cove at an average price of 23–1 to win £35,000. That same day Manchester United, who I had backed at odds of 20–1 to win £20,000 in the FA Cup, were playing Tottenham Hotspur in the Semi-Final and were now 2–1, so I had a wonderful value bet for the day.

Frenchman's Cove was a great slashing chestnut with a white blaze. He was a superb jumper and I had earmarked him as a potential National winner in his novice days. As we drove to the course, wrapped up in overcoats on that cold blustery morning, Evelyn and I laughed when I had to admit that I probably would not have become interested in the horse if I had not known why he had been named. Wealthy racehorse owner Mr Stanhope Joel, had named Frenchman's Cove after one of the most beautiful places in the world. Everytime I thought of that little slice of paradise, I was filled with a longing to return. Not long before that Evelyn and I were on holiday at Montego Bay in Jamaica, staying at the Sunset Lodge Hotel. 'Your time here will not be complete without a raft trip up the Rio Grande,' the hotel barman revealed to us one evening. So we arranged to go. We flew out in a small plane, piloted by a weather-beaten American with years of experience of life in the Pacific.

As we approached Port Antonio, he banked the aircraft to give us a better view of the idyllic beach below. The pilot told us that during the war he had been all over the Pacific and seen many wonderful places. 'But that is the most beautiful place on earth,' he assured us. Evelyn and I stared down in awe at Frenchman's Cove, a paradise of tropical trees, cliffs, blue water and sand. We landed at the Errol Flynn airstrip near the cove, named after the Hollywood star who spent so much of his time in Port Antonio. Then we went on to the Rio Grande, where we enjoyed our rafting trip. However, we longed to return to the idyllic beach we had seen from high above the clouds. So before we went back to Montego Bay, we arranged to call at Frenchman's Cove, the impressive estate owned by Canadian multi-millionaire, Mr Garfield Weston. A limited number of guests were accepted on a privileged basis and we were able to book a holiday there. It turned out to be unforgettable.

Mr Garfield's couriers showed us to our accommodation, a magnificent stone-built house on the top of the cliffs, overlooking the beach. There was a maid and butler tending exclusively to us. When Evelyn tried to buy some cosmetics locally, she was told to make a list of her needs. Then a driver went to Kingston for them. When she tried to pay for her sizeable order, she was told it was all in the price of the holiday.

To our surprise there were other luxuries in store for us too, such as a bar fully stocked with drinks of every kind, including a case of champagne. Should any special item be needed it was ordered from America and sent by plane the following day. If we wanted a car to go out of the estate, we only had to go to the garage, where every kind of vehicle from an American Cadillac to a British sports car was there for the asking. Not even a signature was asked for – one simply got into it and drove off. 'How do you keep track of the cars?' I asked Grainger Weston, the son of the estate's owner, 'Don't you ask anyone where they are going?'

'We don't like to inconvenience our guests,' he said.

No cars were allowed on the estate, however. Electric carts were provided. It was our idea of heaven, sitting on that beautiful beach watching the big waves roll in. Behind us a river flowed from the mountains into a fresh-water lagoon, where there were tropical fish of every colour. It was a delight to dive into the fresh blue water

ALEX BIRD

---

after swimming in the sea. At mid-day a chef would arrive in an electric cart to take the orders for dinner. There was no menu. Whatever we wanted, no matter how exotic, was provided. We could either dine at the Great House, a magnificent south country, American-style residence, or at home, waited on by our butler and maid. Most evenings we dined at the Great House, where we could enjoy a drink with fellow guests.

The highlight of the holiday was moonlight rafting on the Rio Grande. Such a venture could only happen one day each month, when there was a full moon. With other guests, we were taken by car to the top of a mountain, where a fleet of thirty, forty foot long rafts were assembled. Each raft carried two guests and a man to paddle it. Three rafts were reserved for a band playing calypso music. Up high on the banks as we floated idyllically by, were hundreds of local village people, singing their hearts out. The moonlight shone on their faces and I have never seen people so happy. 'This must indeed be paradise,' I said to Evelyn. I wondered what she was smiling at as she looked over my shoulder. I turned round and there was our butler, Fred, immaculate as ever in black trousers, white shirt and black bow tie, sweeping up beside us in a raft. In faultless style, he offered us a glass of champagne from the perfectly-balanced tray, his spotless white napkin draped over one arm and his other hand behind his back in the customary manner. Jeeves would have been hard-pressed to emulate him. Whenever the river broadened sufficiently to allow two rafts to run abreast, he was there with the iced champagne. Grainger Weston became a particular friend, always thoughtful and courteous. One day I asked him if guests ever took advantage of his lavish hospitality. 'There was one person who we will never allow to stay again,' he said. She was a famous Hollywood star.

'She chartered a plane to Montego Bay, where she bought £800 worth of goods,' he went on. The actress, of course, never paid. Although everything was settled without demur, it was felt she was taking things just a little too far.

Butler Fred did his best to make sure our last night at Frenchman's Cove was a memorable occasion. He placed hundreds of candles around the house and sixteen guests arrived for cocktails with us. Then we all set off for the Great House, serenaded by a calypso band. Tipping the staff was strictly forbidden. So I gave Fred several volumes of P.G. Wodehouse's famous books which feature the immortal Jeeves. He loved them.

After I returned to England I followed the career of the horse Frenchman's Cove with considerable interest. When I saw that he was entered for the 1962 National, I started to back him at long prices. He was to be ridden by the top-flight National Hunt jockey Stan Mellor, now a successful trainer. Coupled with my bet on Manchester United I felt that I had made a very good investment.

It was still raining that day when we arrived at Aintree. As usual, we had our box and private dining room and were waited on by Beard. 'I hope Frenchman's Cove wins the race for you Mr Bird,' he said. As he was a Londoner and lived in a house near the Spur's ground, he showed less enthusiasm about my bet on Manchester United.

United were beaten and Frenchman's Cove fell when brought down at the nineteenth. The race was won by Kilmore, ridden by the great Fred Winter, with Wyndburg second and the Irish Mr What third. Stan later told me: 'Frenchman's Cove was going well on the second circuit and I thought he was in with a chance, Mr Bird.'

Tracked by Team Spirit, the horses approached the nineteenth and disaster struck.

'Team Spirit swerved left into my horse's hindquarters,' Stan went on. 'His legs were knocked from under him and we had no chance.'

Kerforo, the Irish mare, ridden by that great horseman Pat Taafe, fell at the next fence and Kilmore stole the show.

The next day Bill and Nancy Thornton came to see us. Bill and I played tennis, while Nancy and Evelyn enjoyed a chat over coffee.

'Well, I am sure you cheered yourselves up with a lovely dinner at the Bridge Hotel last night,' said Nancy.

'I'm afraid not,' I replied. 'We were so exhausted we called in for some fish and chips on our way home through the village.'

156

'I knew things must have been bad – but not that bad!' she quipped.

A few days later, Nancy sent me this little ode.

> *On the pitfalls of gambling we've all of us heard,*
> *But listen to the story of poor Alex Bird,*
> *To Aintree he journeyed along with his wife,*
> *To have what he hoped, the day of his life.*
> *United for Wembley and its Treasure Trove,*
> *The National a cinch for that Frenchman's Cove.*
> *It was cold there at Aintree, and how it kept raining,*
> *But the Frenchman and Alex, they weren't complaining.*
>
> *The champagne was flowing in Alex Bird's room,*
> *With never a hint of the impending doom,*
> *But fate can be cruel, and by quarter to four,*
> *The Reds were in trouble – and the horse on the floor.*
> *To Beard in the box the news was relayed,*
> *And tho' in his heart he was hardly dismayed,*
> *As a very good servant his duty was plain,*
> *He got out in the passage to flog the champagne.*
>
> *As he saw Alex's face he cried: 'Sir please cheer up,*
> *I'll buy the damn lot if Spurs win the Cup.'*
> *As Alex and Evelyn made their way home,*
> *Each of them busy with thoughts of their own.*
> *They were tired and hungry and felt badly done to,*
> *But sixpence-worth of chips was all they would run to.*
> *So when you go gambling, think on these words,*
> *Or you'll end in the chip shop like poor Alex Bird!'*

Things don't always turn out the way one hopes and Frenchman's Cove, the horse, remains a disappointment. How nice it would have been to have that wonderful double up, a holiday in paradise and a Grand National winner to seal the memory.

When I saw him fall at the nineteenth in the race my feelings were with Stan Mellor while he lay for a minute curled into a ball on the turf as the field streamed over him. It is an accepted fact that National Hunt jockeys must be either crazy or supremely courageous. Every year when I walked the National course before the race, I would look at the daunting fences and say to myself: 'Each one of those jockeys deserves the George Cross.'

One of the most horrific falls I have ever seen was when Tim Brookshaw, a hard tough, courageous National Hunt jockey was thrown from his horse in a race at Liverpool in the 1960s. Among other injuries, he broke his back. Against all the odds, Tim left his bed within months and amazed us all by arriving in a wheel chair at the prestigious Bollinger Dinner at the Grosvenor House Hotel, London. He was the happiest person there that night and a tonic and inspiration to everyone. He had a perpetual smile and his wisecracks kept everyone in stitches. When the last guests were vanishing well past midnight, four jockeys wheeled Tim down Park Lane, but he insisted on showing them how he could ride the chair on one wheel. Then he shouted:

'Don't bother about a taxi home lads, I'll take you. Jump aboard!'

With that the four other jockeys mounted the chair, one of them on the shoulders of another, and off they went careering down Park Lane as Tim shouted with delight.

The following year, Tim appeared at the dinner again. By that time he was able to walk – just about. I joined him by the bar and he proudly told me how well he could stand without his sticks. He was not very steady and was balancing himself on his heels. As he raised his champagne glass to his mouth, he swayed backwards and I just managed to catch him. I shudder to think of what further injury he might have caused himself if I had not saved him from hitting the floor. Every time I saw Tim after that he would smile and say to everyone:

'Meet Alex Bird who saved my life!'

Sadly Tim was to die in a fall while riding a horse at his home a few years later.

If National Hunt jockeys were asked to vote on the most

enjoyable social occasion in their calendar, I am sure the Bollinger Dinner would win by twelve lengths going away. It is an occasion to make awards to the previous season's champion riders, professional and amateur. The jockeys are, of course, the most important guests. However, everyone who is someone in the racing world attends. Every department is represented from the Stewards of the Jockey Club to the Chairman of the Levy Board. Every racing journalist worth his salt is there along with breeders, bookmakers and one professional backer: Alex Bird!

I never really knew why I was invited. I must have attended more than fifteen of those dinners. Until recent years there were no women in attendance, apart from that gracious lady from the French champagne family, Madame Bollinger. Now with the female revolution, there is more than a fair sprinkling of ladies. Only at the Bollinger Dinner did I feel that I could speak freely with jockeys and enjoy myself without onlookers thinking I must have an ulterior motive connected with backing horses.

Some of the dinner speeches still make me laugh when I recall them. One should be recorded for posterity. It was the time when that lovable character Lord Oaksey, [John Lawrence] of TV fame, who jokingly says he can never tip a winner, took to the floor. His description of withdrawing a champagne cork was very near the mark.

'It should be done in a careful, caressing way and the sound should hardly be audible, like a contented woman after making love!' he said.

The only lady present at the time was Madame Bollinger sitting next to him, who laughed. Obviously her English was pretty good.

On another occasion John ensured future Bollinger invitations for himself by referring to a rival champagne as the lavatory detergent Harpic.

I laugh too, when I recall a remark made to me by that marvellous trainer Bob Turnell as Terry Biddlecombe was making his speech as Champion Jockey. 'He couldn't ride for me you know, not with that long hair!' he said.

When you are an owner people are wary of your tips, and especially if you are a backer as well. I was to discover this on Derby Day, 1962. Before the big event, my horse Vatellus was running in an eight-runner race. I knew he was a solid each way bet. Backers could not lose. So I told everyone I met that Vatellus would be a wonderful each way investment for them. I did not care about the price coming down – I just felt that it would be a great honour to win a race on Derby Day. Much to my surprise Vatellus opened at 6–1 and finished at $12\frac{1}{2}$–1. He won easily. Everyone I had told about the horse was stunned: they honestly believed that Alex Bird would not have told them his horse would win, if he really expected it to.

A few weeks later on the evening of 27 July, the phone rang at my home. 'We're all set for the morning Alex,' said Stanley Platt. Like the captain of a cricket team changing his bowlers to confuse the opposition, so I changed my agents and betting methods to confuse the bookmakers. Betting shops had been legal for nearly a year and I had designed a new, foolproof method of backing a horse, using twelve men and six cars. One of those men was Stanley, who had worked out a route, taking in more than 350 betting shops in Lancashire and Cheshire. Another was Albert Aspinall, who owned a baker's shop in Stockport. 'Do you know Alex, I employed this lad to make some scones for me to sell at tuppence each, but they were so big I told him to cut them in half and I still sold them for tuppence!'

The betting shops, which were owned by big companies, were under instructions to phone headquarters when accepting bets of five pounds and over. My team planned to put £2,000 on my own horse, Bewildroom, running in The Ripon Rowels over a mile, in bets of about £4.15s.0d each, and each man had a target of nearly seventy shops. On the morning of the twenty-horse race at Ripon, the campaign started the moment the door of the first betting shop opened. I did not go to the course that day, for if I had been seen it would have been taken by the bookies to mean I had confidence in my horse. All went well – for a while. The horse was on the drift at 14–1 and would probably have gone to 20–1, but as the race drew

Alex Bird, bane of the bookies

Alex punts around the moat of his Cheshire home

Alex studies form in the peace of his lounge

Alex Bird, Derby Day 1983

nearer, the odds suddenly shortened and finished at 10–1. I wondered what was going on. Had my scheme been discovered? Unhappily, Bewildroom, ridden by Derek Morris, was beaten into second place by a length and a half, by Miss D, partnered by Frankie Durr. Later I discovered why the odds had shortened so quickly. It was because of a few careless words that so often undid many hours of careful planning.

Jockey Derek had met Jabez Barker by the paddock before the race. Nicknamed 'Gypsy Jabez', because of his dark looks, he lived in the Newmarket area and owned several horses, but he also liked to bet. Derek told him that he should put a few pounds on Bewildroom and Jabez put seventy on the horse to win £1,000. It was only a small amount, but it was sufficient to alarm the bookies because Jabez did not throw his money around. If the horse had won, I would have made £20,000, but without Derek's careless words, the figure would have been about £40,000. I lost on the day all round, for apart from my £2,000 stake, I had to finance the whole operation, including payments to helpers and petrol costs.

Bewildroom was a good class horse with a strange temperament. I bought him out of a selling race at Birmingham. He was trained by Peter Nelson who told Billy Ball he had no intention of buying him back. Billy passed the message on to Billy Carter and me, and so we felt free to bid for the horse. We were very pleased with ourselves when we bought Bewildroom and sent him off to Towser in a horse box. That night, however, my trainer rang Billy Carter. 'What the bloody hell are you and Alex doing buying a horse like that?' he asked. 'It nearly kicked its way through the front of the box and almost ended up sitting next to the driver!'

The Bewildroom operation was a one-off. We knew we could not do it again. The bookies would have rumbled us by close of business on that day. Their network is so good they would have added the bets together, and come up with Alex Bird. Then they would have realised what a narrow escape they had had and worked out a way of protecting themselves from then on. Today such a bet would be worth around £500,000.

Later that year I received a letter from Towser, and I could not believe the words in front of me. It simply asked me to take my horses away from his stables. There was no explanation. He merely said: 'Don't ask me why Alex.' I stood reading the letter over and over again in the lounge of my home. What could I have done wrong? We had been great friends, hadn't we? For days I wrestled with his words. I was not to find out what had caused Towser to end our relationship so abruptly until some years later.

When the ties were finally broken with Towser I did have a bet on one of Tommy Degg's horses. It was at Haydock Park and the horse won. Tommy was furious. He accused Billy Carter of telling me the horse was fancied, but that was not true.

I fancied the runner on the form book, and felt free to back him. Tommy never forgave me. Billy however, understood completely.

By this time another part of my life was ending too. I was beginning to discover that I was not alone in judging a photo finish. Bookmakers, tired of my one-way traffic, put their own men on the line. They were photo finish experts at greyhound racing, where decisions were more difficult to make than in horse racing. They had learned the hard way and knew the importance of keeping one's head still. The betting market weakened from then on and as I was not prepared to bet for coppers, I called it a day. It was the end of a fantastic era. In all that time I had only lost in a big way once on the photo. It was at Epsom the day after a very heavy party. I put £3,200 on the horse running on the near side. It lost by the shortest of short heads. Luckily, that was at the height of my success. If it had happened in the early months of my photo finish bets I would have lost the confidence to go on.

At this time I was always on the lookout for habitual losers who would have no trouble backing horses for me, and it is a shame I did not make more of my meeting with Hollywood film star Omar Sharif. I was in Deauville, France, with Irish trainer Charlie Rogers and racegoer Bill Hall from Manchester. We went to an hotel to dine and spotted the handsome Egyptian actor having brandy with Australian jockey Bill Pyers. We joined them and talked about racing for nearly two hours. I found Omar a most charming man. I will never forget the look of amusement on his face when Bill told us the story of Lester Piggott on a visit to France. Bill had told Lester how the starter's assistant would give special privileges, like tightening the girths and other formalities. 'I suggested to Lester that if he gave the man ten quid he would get similar treatment himself,' Bill said. Lester showed great interest in the idea and asked if Bill, who spoke fluent French, would handle the arrangement for him. 'I fell for it,' said Bill. 'Just before the race I gave the starter a tenner and he fussed around Lester, but I've never seen the colour of his money since!'

After I returned to England and told my friends that I had met Omar, the ladies almost fainted. They wanted to know every sentence of my conversation with him, and what he was really like. When I think of how much Omar has lost gambling in his lifetime, it makes me shudder to think how much we could have won together. The bookies would have rushed to accept his bets, not knowing that he was backing for me. We could have worked out some way of communicating with each other and we could have been partners on a 50–50 basis. He would have ended up a much wealthier man than he is today, even though his royalties from box office hits like *Lawrence of Arabia* and *Dr Zhivago*, must have been phenomenal.

A few weeks before the 1963 Grand National I took Evelyn on an exotic holiday to Jamaica, but before I left I invited twenty four guests to join me in my private room on the day of the big race. When I returned a few days before the event, however, I received a telephone call from Stanley Platt.

'Some bad news I'm afraid Alex.'

I stared out of the lounge window at the moat that surrounded my new home, The Old Hall, in the shadow of a Cheshire village. Stanley was not the sort of man to take things lightly. If he said bad news, he meant bad news.

'I've received a letter from Mirabel Topham cancelling your dining room at Aintree this year!'

Eighteen stone Mirabel was a very formidable woman who

fought tooth and nail against racing authorities, local councils, TV stations and bookmakers to keep personal control of the National, the race dearest to her heart. Aintree was her domain and she ruled it with a rod of iron.

I was flabbergasted at the cancellation of the room. Nothing like this had ever happened before. I thought of all the invitations that had been sent out. I knew that Mirabel and I had not seen eye to eye over my dining room for some time. For years I had the best private dining room on the course. It was just up the stairs from the paddock and unsaddling enclosure. My guests there were the stars of stage and screen, including John Gregson, Margaret Lockwood, Margaret Leighton, Sir Laurence Olivier and the writer Terence Rattigan.

Trouble started because I had taken pity on the doorman who stood guard in all weathers at the entrance to the row of private rooms. He looked so cold I would send Beard to give him a whisky to perk him up. This angered Mirabel who thought I was bribing him to let unauthorised guests in.

I listened intently as Stanley explained the reason behind the cancellation. It was the inaugural year of the Schweppes Gold Trophy at Liverpool and Mirabel wanted my room for executives from Schh you know who. Legally I could not argue. Having the room was just a tradition, a gentleman's agreement, as were my bets. I was angry; I knew how Mirabel operated. She once said: 'If people don't do what I jolly well want, I jolly well let them know it!'

I rang her at her Paddock Lodge home on the Aintree course.

'Alex here, Mirabel.'

'What can I do for you Mr Bird?' her voice was cold.

I explained how I had invited guests to dine with me on the day of the National, how it was an unwritten contract that I had the room.

'Anyway Mirabel, you've cancelled it just a few days before the race, I don't think it's fair to do that! Do you?'

'Mr Bird, I rule here and the National is my race. I can do anything!'

I switched my tactics. I knew that Mirabel was a great friend of

Tommy Appleby. He always reserved her the same seat at the Manchester Opera House and got her tickets for the big shows in the West End of London.

'Now look Mirabel, you always go to Tommy's theatre for the opera. How would you feel if you arrived with guests one night to find no seats available for you?'

'Mr Bird, I'm afraid the dining room is not available for you this year.' With that she put the phone down.

If it were not for the fact that I had invited so many guests, I would have told her just what to do with her private room. However there was nothing for it. I could not be humiliated in front of my wife and friends. I rang Tommy for help. This amazing man managed to negotiate a compromise with Mirabel. That year I sat down to a meal served by my waiter Beard in an old storeroom with no windows or ventilation, that had been hastily cleared for my visit. The lunch went without a hitch, but I refrained from smoking too many Havanas, respecting the lungs of the ladies. I never again took a private dining room at the course although one was offered to me many times. The Schweppes Gold Trophy was switched to Newbury the following year.

Mirabel Topham loved the stage. Born Mirabel Hillier, her father was the manager of London's Haymarket Theatre. Her burning ambition was to be a big star but it was not long before she was on her way to fame and fortune of another kind.

In 1922 she joined the cast of Quality Street at the theatre her father ran. There she met Arthur Ronald Topham, whose family had controlled Aintree racecourse since 1849. Mirabel was spellbound by Arthur and gave up her glittering career to marry him. Before long however she had made her presence felt on the Topham company board and in 1938, the year I backed Battleship in the National, she won control of it. From then on she ruled Aintree.

She was always headline news. She once said: 'I've got all my own teeth and I can bite like hell!' She could too. Mirabel lost only one battle. It was with the blower men who relayed betting information from the course. She demanded £5,000 a year rent for their telephones, but the bookies and news agency reporters who needed the lines had the last word. They hired telephones in nearby houses and relayed their information by reading the signs of the tic-tac men from the bedroom windows.

Apart from my battle with her over the dining room, our relationship was friendly.

Once we watched a race together in the private Aintree box that used to belong to Lord Sefton, former owner of the famous course. I passed my binoculars to her and she peered through the glasses down the course to the horses hugging the inside rails after clearing the fourteenth fence.

'Here they come Alex!' she shouted, jumping from her seat. The thunder of the hooves grew louder, as the field on the first day of the Liverpool meeting, raced down to the Chair jump, an open, six foot wide ditch. As the horses streamed over it one of them did a fly jump, strangely flicking his legs to the side in mid-air.

'Did you see that?' former chorus girl Mirabel screamed almost dropping the binoculars. 'He danced just like I did when I was on the stage.'

Before I could say Havana, heavyweight Mirabel hoisted her dress, revealing her plump legs, took a strenuous leap in the air and kicked her feet to the side, almost knocking over a bottle of champagne.

I burst out laughing, completely forgetting about the race and the horse I had backed. The field thundered towards the water jump and past the winning post on the first circuit, as I stared with watering eyes at the red face of the puffing First Lady of the Grand National, the race that has had more farewell appearances than Frank Sinatra.

Mirabel who once claimed that the only way to cure arthritis was to drink cabbage water, died aged eighty eight at her Paddock Lodge home. When she was eighty, weighing eighteen stone, she said her biggest ambition was to be nineteen stone and ninety. She almost made it. I heard about her death in a radio news broadcast as I breakfasted and I could not help thinking that the race that was her life had played a big part in my life too.

Bookies were forever trying to restrict my bets, and an example of this came in 1964.

I phoned Ladbrokes and asked for a bet on Manchester United to win the F.A. Cup. They were listed at 20–1 with all the advertising bookmakers and I wanted £20,000 to £1,000, but the clerk said: 'Mr Bird, you can have £500 at 20–1 and £500 at 18–1.' That meant odds of 19–1.

'This is not a race horse that has done secret gallops,' I protested. 'I'm backing a football club that everybody lists at 20–1.'

He would not budge. It was the firm's only offer to me.

'I'll just take £500 at 20–1 then.'

Johnny Foy put the other £500 on at 20–1 with another bookmaker without any difficulty. Unhappily for me Manchester United were beaten in the semi-final.

At Ascot around that time I was backing a horse at 7–4. As I made my way down the rails I had £1,400 to £800 with four bookmakers. I arrived at the Ladbroke pitch, to find Dickie Gaskell representing the firm. He was an elegant gentleman, who had been a director of another bookmaking firm that had been taken over by Ladbrokes. I asked him for the same bet at 7–4. 'You can have half that Alex,' he replied. There was quite a crowd around the rails and I protested as loudly as I could.

'I have just had this same bet several times over with your competitors and yet you are halving me! Why?' Dickie seemed very uncomfortable. People were looking our way. He had obviously been instructed to cut my bet.

'Right Alex, you've got £1,400 to £800.' He must have cursed himself when the horse won.

Some time later Evelyn and I were invited to a luncheon party at the home of trainer John Sutcliffe senior in Epsom. We had been looking forward to it, as he had a reputation for being a superb host. The food and drink was always the very best.

John and I respected each other. Years before I had claimed his horse, Blue Baby, out of a selling race, and he claimed the horse back next time he ran. This was not the 'done thing' but it did not bother us. When we became good friends later the subject was never mentioned. Evelyn and I were early and as we stood sipping champagne in the lounge, I asked John who the other guests were. 'Cyril Stein and his wife and daughter,' he said. His reply took the wind out of my sails.

'Bloody hell,' I blurted out.

'What have I done? Are you enemies?'

'Well no, we're not enemies exactly . . .'

What could I say? For John's sake the luncheon had to be a success. I had never met the formidable Ladbrokes' chairman before, but we were well aware of each other. Cyril arrived with his family, and the usual introductions were made. It was a most delightful lunch and Evelyn was surprised. 'Anyone would have thought you and Cyril had been friends for years,' she whispered to me in the corner of the lounge. 'There you were, chatting away to each other, how two-faced can you both be?' We were all due to go to Epsom races, but Cyril had come by taxi and looking at me pointedly, he asked:

'Who's going to give me a lift to the course then?'

'I'm very sorry, Cyril. I can give your wife and daughter a lift, but there's no way I can take you,' I said. 'If you are seen getting out of my car, the racegoers will think the world has come to an end.'

Cyril made his own way to the course and his wife and daughter travelled with me. Now we are friends. We have a good working relationship and a healthy respect for each other. Had I been in his position though, I should not have allowed Alex Bird to open an account with the firm.

I could not be seen with Cyril and I could not be seen with jockeys either. As I have already said because of my fantastic success, I became a marked man by some stewards at the Jockey Club, so there was a lurking suspicion at the back of my mind that for a jockey to be seen talking to me could cause problems for him. Because of this, I made quite sure that the only contact I had with jockeys was in the parade ring, when my horses were being saddled, or when I was due to give a rider a present for winning a race. Then I would go to the weighing room in full view of everybody, and ask an official to inform my jockey that I wanted to see him. 'Thank you for winning on my horse,' I would say loudly, 'I hope you will ride again for me and here is your present.' That was all.

Once a top jockey rang me at home. He and another leading rider were arriving at Manchester Airport en route for Chester races. They wanted me to collect them and take them to the course. I apologised and explained that I had a business meeting in the morning and was not certain to get to Chester in time for the first race. Really I would have enjoyed the journey to and from Chester with them, but could imagine only too well the furore which would follow should either of them have the misfortune to be beaten on a hot favourite, gossip that it was a fix would spread through the ring like wildfire, if they had been spotted getting out of my car before a race.

William Hill stopped me by the paddock at Goodwood in July 1966. 'Good God Alex, I never thought I would see you on a racecourse again,' said the greatest bookmaker of the last fifty years. After the introduction of betting tax, Hill had told his board that the careers of men like Alex Bird were over. It was true that when the Chancellor dropped his bombshell, there was a funereal atmosphere at courses like Kempton Park, Newbury and even Cheltenham. If an undertaker had been fortunate enough to get a pitch on the rails, he would have done more business than the leading bookmakers. The days of the professional backer seemed numbered and with his demise the market became less of a true estimation. For the professional backer bets to figures, and if those figures cut down on his profit margin, it was no good him beating his head against a wall. He might just as well get out.

Hill first started making a book in his teens at the BSA works in Birmingham, during the First World War. He started racing in the 1920s, but did not come to prominence on the rails until the early days of World War Two. From then until 1955, when he retired from the ring, he was the undisputed king of the bookies, well

169

ahead of other legendary figures such as Willie Preston, Percy Thompson and Laurie Wallis.

He had a wealth of colourful stories to tell – and one of them concerned the Aly Khan. Hill claimed that if the Aly had a losing week he would not settle his account immediately but let it run for nearly a month before he was on the right side. Then he would send someone round to the unhappy bookmaker for a cheque. Over three or more years, he took nearly £100,000 off various layers, while making only one or two derisory payments himself. Hill was one bookmaker who felt that that tactic had to be stopped. One day, following a winning week, one of the Aly's men arrived at his office and requested a settlement of about £9,000. Hill gave the emissary a letter telling the Aly that he would put the £9,000 to his credit and add a further £5,000, making a total of £14,000 for him to bet up to. Hill felt that at last, this was a way of beating the Aly. However, the Aly went a full season without having a bet with Hill and at the end of it, the bookmaker sent him a cheque for the £9,000 and closed his account.

Hill was a great percentage man. A bookmaker has to be, but there were very few punters like me who were that way inclined. The first betting tax was two and a half percent. At the time I reckoned my profit on a £2 million a year turnover, after deductions for generous expenses, was one point eighty three percent. So I was obviously in trouble.

I consulted my records, which dated back to before the war, and by itemising a lot of my previous betting I was able to discover where my profits were the best.

I seldom bet on handicaps, but I used to bet on three-year-old maiden races. By going into it deeply, I discovered I was losing on them, especially three-year-old fillies' races. So I knocked them on the head. Finally, by being selective I found that I could still make the game pay.

I sometimes describe bookmakers as My Friends The Enemy, but I have had very few real enemies in their ranks. In the main they were colourful, humorous men.

However, some of their operating tactics I despise. One such operation is what I call the knock-in technique. If an office bookmaker has taken a lot of money for a horse, and wishes to reduce the price to cut his liabilities, I have no objection. If he backs a horse in a strong market, his price is only reduced marginally, and the prices of the opposition will be extended marginally. That is a fair business transaction. But it is unfair when a bookmaking firm shortens the price of a horse in the closing seconds, and this can be done without investing a substantial sum of money. Course bookmakers virtually close their books in the last minute, and are not prepared to lay a large bet. One big starting price bookmaker, knowing this, will tell his representatives to bulldoze their way through the ring, asking for impossible bets.

What happens is that if the price offered in the closing minutes is 2–1, the firm's representatives rush around asking for £4,000 to £2,000, or bets of similar magnitude. On-course bookmakers then offer a 'keep-off' price, not wanting to lay. The odds would be reduced in seconds from 2–1 to 7–4 to 6–4 and at the off, probably even money. Then the SP returners from the *Sporting Chronicle* and *Sporting Life*, have no alternative but to return the horse at the artificially short price.

Some of the big betting chains have as many as 1,000 shops. If on average each shop has one hundred pounds for a 2–1 chance, it would normally be returned at that price without manipulation. If it is returned at even money, the saving would be £100,000 should the horse win.

That method is the equivalent of putting a hand in the punter's pocket. The computerised percentage of profit to the bookmaker on the starting price would now be in the region of forty percent, there being no time to adjust the prices for the second and third favourites.

No doubt anyone who carries out this practice considers that it is just business – and I suppose it is.

In 1966, during an autumn meeting at Chester, I saw that colourful Scottish bookmaker John Banks betting on the rails, after an absence of several months.

'What on earth are you doing back here?' I asked.

He knew that a bookmaking firm was shortening the price of favourites in the last few seconds. So when the massive bets were asked for by the company's representative in the closing minutes, he would stand up on the rails and lay them fully, much to their dismay.

'Alex, I cannot lose at this,' he said. 'I am laying a horse at even money and 5–4 against, whereas the correct price should be 2–1.'

John proved to be a thorn in the flesh of the firm's management, but the fearless bookie did not bat an eyelid. He would laugh it all off, for he loved a joke.

I wrote a letter to a newspaper protesting against the practice of artificially shortening starting prices. It never appeared. Three days later, on Sunday morning before lunch, I received a telephone call from the bookmaking firm's chairman. He asked me why I was making a point of opposing his company and condemning their method of shortening prices.

As my letter had not been printed, I wondered where he had got his information from, and I told him that I had not mentioned his firm by name.

'Yes, but you did mean us, didn't you Alex?' he replied.

'If the cap fits, you have no alternative but to wear it,' I said.

He must have been on the phone to me for half an hour, asking me to be reasonable and co-operate with them. He even promised that they would execute my commissions for me on very good terms. He finished up by saying he did not believe my accusation that they were being unfair was true. Then I startled him. I told him that I had in my possession a document, which was a directive to the company's course representatives which would prove my case. The letter was sent by a director of the firm. The Chairman did not believe it. 'I'll confirm that with him personally and ring back,' he said. I waited by the telephone for the next hour, but the call never came.

The Editor of the newspaper concerned told me that he could not allow an accusation of that kind to be published, when he was accepting big advertisements from the firm. Then he said he had no idea how my letter had got into the bookmaker's hands. Some weeks later I had another telephone call, from journalist and TV personality Brough Scott. He wanted to see me about my claim over the manipulation of starting prices. Brough spent the day at my house working on the story for his paper the *Sunday Times*. It was never printed, and when I asked him why he revealed that the paper's legal department had killed it.

My conclusion is that the only way to stop the interference with the starting prices market, is to allow betting on a racecourse, which represents five percent of the gambling, to be tax free. The starting price punter would then be reassured that he was getting a fair crack of the whip. Then the ninety five percent return on gambling off-course, which the Chancellor of the Exchequer receives, would be safe-guarded for the nation.

When Lord Rothschild was the chairman on the Royal Commission on Gambling, I believe I was the only professional backer invited to give my views. In his palatial boardroom in the City of London, his secretary told me how involved Lord Rothschild was with the Report, but he thought he could spare ten minutes of his valuable time to listen to what I had to say. However, after more than half an hour we had to conclude the meeting. I had explained to him how a certain bookmaking firm had been manipulating the odds, but when I went on to say how they, not being satisfied with this manoeuvre, went a step further, he was most interested. Let me explain:

If a horse is withdrawn without coming under starter's orders, there is a fixed scale for adjusting the starting price of the winner.

If the withdrawn horse is over 10–1 there is no deduction.

If the withdrawn horse is less than 10–1 there is a varying scale of deductions.

What this firm of bookmakers did was to reduce the price of a horse which was obviously about to be withdrawn for various reasons, like lameness, or having bolted, from a big price to a price under 10–1.

Their bets would be void, but the fact that the horse was then priced at less than 10–1, would enable SP bookmakers to deduct ten percent from the winner's price. Though Lord Rothschild was not a racing man I think he fully understood that this was a form of daylight robbery. As we passed through the doors of that magnificent board room, I felt sure that he was musing over what had been said. He stood aside and switched off the lights. I could not help but notice that he was saving electricity and I remarked: 'Now I know why you have got a lot of money, my Lord.' He smiled.

The night before the Vernons Gold Cup at Haydock, in November 1966, Peter O'Sullevan rang me at home. His horse, Be Friendly, was being ridden by Colin Williams in the big race.

'Alex, as you understand all this business about the draw, would you instruct my jockey what to do?'

'I would be glad to Peter.'

At lunchtime on Gold Cup day, Peter, Colin and I met at the weighing room, and then walked to the bend at the entrance to the straight. I gave the young jockey precise instructions, and even pulled a pen from my pocket, marking the spot on the rails where he should make his move. 'Now Colin, if you come in with paint on your boots, really hugging the outside rail, there will be a double present for you!' Of course, he would never be able to see my mark from a horse travelling at speed, but he got the message. The going for the six furlong race was dead, and I felt certain that if Be Friendly went over to the better going he would steal the race, so I backed him to win £10,000. Peter did the TV commentary and when Be Friendly came wide on the bend, he described the manoeuvre in detail to viewers. He sometimes gets excited when describing a race, but on this occasion he was as cool as a cucumber. He might have been talking about someone else's horse with only a passing interest. Colin followed my instructions to the letter, and Be Friendly won by two lengths, from Green Park, ridden by Russ Maddock. When Christmas arrived, the biggest bottle of whisky I had ever seen in my life, was delivered to my home. It came 'With the compliments of Be Friendly'.

1966 cannot be passed by without a mention of the World Cup.

Shortly before the competition I drove professional backer Leslie Wood, Billy Ball and Billy Carter to Newmarket. Leslie told me he favoured England for the World Cup. Every match they played would be at Wembley and he estimated that gave them a goal advantage each time.

Leslie had a reliable system for formulating soccer odds. In international matches he always favoured the host country. For example, European sides always found it difficult to win in South America or vice versa. Only Brazil were the exception to that rule. So he always gave the home teams an advantage.

I backed England to win £5,000 and every Great Briton must know the result. If they do not, suffice it to say that my bank balance rose by £5,000 after one historic afternoon on the Wembley turf. That day must have been the greatest moment of their lives for captain Bobby Moore and his men.

The following year my good friend Charles Turriff entered a horse he bought for his wife Georgina in the Grand National, the race they both loved. But the day held painful memories. The horse was called Popham Down and proved to be aptly named because he created the most ghastly pile-up at the fence after Becher's, second time round. Popham Down jumped across the twenty third and brought down or impeded the rest of the field. With one exception all the horses still in the race were brought to a halt. Only the moderate Foinavon jumped the fence unimpeded and was left out on his own. He eventually won by fifteen lengths from Honey End, who cleared the fence at the second attempt. Poor Charles and Georgina.

In the following November Scobie Breasley rode Be Friendly in the Vernons Gold Cup and Peter again asked me to give advice on tactics. I arrived at noon as arranged, but Peter and Scobie were already on the track. I walked to the bend and met them coming back. 'Now Scobie,' I started, ready to divulge my precious information.

'It's all right Alex, I know exactly what to do,' he said, and I could not persuade him to return. Being the true professional he was Scobie carried out the manoeuvre perfectly. Be Friendly won, but only by the shortest of short heads, from Mountain Call, ridden by Russ Maddock, who had partnered the runner-up the year before. For by now Russ knew the drill about going over to the stands side, and he followed Be Friendly's move. I won £5,000 that day and after the race, Scobie told me: 'As I swung wide, Russ hesitated for a split second, and I only just beat him to the stand rails. If he had not hesitated he would have beaten us.'

The only jockey who worked out such manoeuvres for himself was Edward Hide. He probably calculated his tactics on his way to the post, though I always believed he made an inspection of the going before the afternoon's races. It takes courage for a jockey to carry out unusual instructions, such as going wide, when the rest of the field remain on the inside. If a jockey does this on his own initiative, without the owner and trainer's knowledge, and the horse is not good enough and gets beaten, they will never forgive him. Meanwhile, I have known jockeys, having been given their orders, to swing wide, come half way across the track, remain there for a couple of strides, think better of it, and tack back on to the others. I could almost see them changing their minds through my binoculars.

I am always on the lookout for a two-year-old which has done a fast time over seven furlongs or a mile as a prospect for the Derby. Once such horse was Ribofilio, owned by American Charles Englehard and trained by Fulke Johnson-Houghton.

I first saw Ribofilio run on 20 June, 1968, in the six-furlong Chesham Stakes at Royal Ascot. It was a good class race and the horse, ridden by Lester Piggott, won easily at odds of 7–2. Then, on 10 September, I went to Doncaster to see Ribofilio run in the seven-furlong Champagne Stakes. As there was no electric timing on the course in those days, I stood at the top of the stands with my stopwatch, for I could not rely on the newspaper clockers to give me an accurate record of the race. As an added check, I enlisted the help of Billy Carter, who had experience of greyhound racing and therefore had lightning reactions. From the off, Ribofilio went like a rocket and crossed the line an easy winner. I looked at my watch in disbelief. Billy too was puzzled, but before he could speak, I told him: 'Keep it quiet. Ribofilio must be a certainty for next year's Derby!'

Already my mind was calculating a series of bets for the classics, and later that day, I backed Ribofilio to win £10,000 in the Derby with William Hill.

Meanwhile I had heard that athlete Derek Ibbotson had been called in to help train Manchester City and my betting interests were aroused in that direction too. They were tough, back-breaking sessions and he even had captain Tony Book and his men, including their star player Francis Lee, running around the pitch on their usual Monday morning off. 'Professional footballers don't know what fitness is, compared with top class international runners,' Ibbotson would say.

Manchester City's previous season had been a bit of a disaster and their price for winning the League was 40–1. Ibbotson was supposed to be a flash of inspiration to them, and with all the revolutionary training I felt the side had to be worth a small bet. I rang Johnny Foy and told him to put £250 on City to win £10,000. As the season progressed, the team's rigorous training programme paid off, and they hit a winning streak. I asked Johnny to increase my bets and he got me odds of 20–1 and 16–1.

On Monday 11 November, I went to Laurel Park in America, with journalist Richard Baerlein. We sat in John Schapiro's private box overlooking the course and as the winner of the first race passed the window it seemed almost an intrusion on our private thoughts. We had come to Baltimore for one reason: to see Lester Piggott ride Sir Ivor in the big event, the £37,190 Washington DC International. John owned the course. Richard had given the millionaire American a lot of publicity in his early days and for that he was eternally grateful. So we were treated like royalty. Sir Ivor's owner, Raymond Guest, was with us in the box, and we all felt that this would be our day. I was confident that I had made a wise investment, for Johnny Foy had backed the horse for me in England to win £17,000.

Ten minutes before the eight-horse race, Richard and I climbed the scaffolding above the stands, and sat on some struts so that we had a Bird's eye view of the track. From the off, Lester rode his normal, super-confident race. The course was compact, like a dog track and the run-in was very short. Lester came into the straight, head down and bottom in the air, in his inimitable style. When Lester is riding there is no need to consult the racecard to distinguish the colours.

Then Richard and I nearly fell off our perches when Sir Ivor suddenly checked in the straight. Seconds later, however, Lester eased him through the field and he won hard held by three quarters of a length from Czar Alexander, ridden by J. Velasquez. Later, in Schapiro's box for the celebrations, Richard and I were still bemused by what had happened on the run-in and when Lester came in I seized my chance. 'Well done Lester,' I said, patting him on the back. 'But what the hell were you doing checking him in the straight?' He gave me a quizzical look. 'I saw a bit of soft ground so I eased him over it. Then I won easily.'

'You might have won but you knocked ten years off my life!' I said.

When Richard and I arrived at Baltimore Airport to board the plane home I bought every American newspaper on display. I could have used a porter to carry them, because they were about five times the size of our Fleet Street editions. Richard found the racing reports fascinating, and we laughed when we saw they referred to Lester as a 'bum jockey'.

The American journalists just did not seem to understand his brilliant riding technique, but Lester was to get his chance to prove himself to them later.

By the end of the 1968–69 soccer season I stood to win more than £20,000 if Manchester City nabbed the League title. Finally, I was a match away from success. City only had to win their final game at Newcastle. That day I went to see Manchester United play Sunderland at home. If City lost their match, United could snatch the title by winning their game. I had been fortunate to secure a private box right on the half way line at Old Trafford, with my neighbour Eric Ingham, who ran an engineering company. For years we enjoyed a ring side seat at all the big games. I had a telephone and a TV installed in the box and normally I would arrive a few hours before a match, and watch the racing first. The day of the City game Bill Thornton had arranged to ring me at Old Trafford, with the up to the minute score which was being broadcast from Newcastle. 'City are winning 4–1' was his first message, as I watched the United forwards race towards the Sunderland goal. I thought my money was as good as in the bank. 'Newcastle have just scored, it's 4–2,' Bill said in his second call. The first doubt set in. Then he rang again. 'Sorry Alex, it's 4–3.' I spent the next thirty minutes thinking that his call about an equaliser would come at any second. It did not, City won.

Just to show my appreciation, I bought every member of the City team a watch. Francis Lee still has it to this day. He told me later: 'The training under Ibbotson was so hard that many players were thinking of asking for a transfer, because they were so exhausted.' Now Francis is involved in racing in a big way. He has a private stud at Wilmslow, Cheshire, and a large number of horses in training.

United's chairman, Louis Edwards, and I had flown to Europe together to see United play in European Cup matches and were great friends. However, he was so upset when he heard that I had backed City to win the League, he did not speak to me for nearly a year. I was told he felt I was being disloyal to the team, but Matt Busby said: 'Good luck to you Alex!'

The former United manager seems to have been around all my life. Once at a cocktail party in my house, I was standing nearby as Evelyn said to him. 'How are Manchester City doing these days?' I shuddered. Evelyn used to watch Matt play for City in his younger days, and that is where she had got a little confused.

Matt put his arm around her and said: 'Evelyn love, I don't think we'll talk about football any more.'

Not long after that night came the tragic Munich air crash, in which so many of those talented Busby Babes were killed. Matt of course was lucky to escape with his life, and the first time he went in a plane after that was with me. Johnny Foy and I persuaded him to fly with us to Ayr in my charter plane from Ringway, to see my horse Precious Heather run. Matt sat next to me, joking during the flight and never showed the slightest twitch of apprehension. That is the kind of man he is. Nothing ever seems to bother him.

By now my thoughts were firmly on the Derby and Ribofilio. His first race in 1969 as a three-year-old had been the 2,000 Guineas Trial Stakes on 11 April, at Ascot. This time Joe Mercer rode him. He led from a furlong out and won the three-horse race in a canter. Three weeks later on 30 April Ribofilio was at Newmarket for the 2,000 Guineas. I did not back him that day, as I had it in my mind that staying was his game. The race was like a bad dream that will remain in my mind forever.

Ribofilio, 15–8 favourite, ridden by Lester Piggott, did not go well from the start. I saw him fall further and further behind at the halfway mark. Eventually Lester, knowing that something was radically wrong, almost pulled the horse up. Spectators watched in amazement as Ribofilio walked past the post like he was drunk. As he was led away, he looked distressed and exhausted. At that time, the doping menace was at its height, and there was no doubt in everyone's minds that Ribofilio had been got at, but dope tests proved negative. After the race poor Ribofilio lost stones in weight, and it looked as though it was the end of his racing days. However, blessed with a strong constitution, the horse began to pick up. His owner Englehard breathed a sigh of relief, and trainer Johnson-Houghton was able to turn his mind to the Derby again. But time was not on his side. The race was just a few weeks away. Nevertheless, Ribofilio continued to thrive, and his owner decided that people should not merely take his trainer's word that the horse had recovered. He ordered a public trial at Sandown Park on 27 May, eight days before the big race. I arrived with Billy Carter to see Lester ride the horse in the gallop and was amazed to find a crowd of about 1,000 people. I had never seen so many racegoers at Sandown Park before noon. Billy and I stood ready with our stop watches. To ensure a good gallop, several useful runners were in the trial, and another horse was put into the race at the final bend, with about half a mile to go.

It was a daunting task for Ribofilio, taking on a fresh horse when he had the measure of his galloping companions. He did not quite get up and when Lester saw he could not win, he did not drive Ribofilio too hard. As the horses passed the post, I realised that the time was fantastic. I checked with Billy. He had timed the runners from jumping off, and I had clocked them as they were passing the starting gate. There were no stalls in operation so it was a flying start. By adding the two times together and dividing them we got as near as possible to a correct time. It was two minutes eight seconds, just one and a half seconds outside the course record, held by St Paddy, when he won the Eclipse Stakes at that track on 8 July, 1961. His jockey then was Lester, who also won the Derby on him the year before. On the day of Ribofilio's trial it was raining hard and had the going been good, he would have broken St Paddy's record. Billy and I joined bookmaker William Hill for lunch in the club dining room, where we discussed the gallop. I felt sure that Billy and I were the only ones to know of Ribofilio's time.

'I am confident the horse will go very close for the Derby,' I told Hill.

However, I was surprised when the game bookmaker replied:

'Well then, I will lay you 4–1 for the race – and you can have it with a run.'

I immediately accepted the offer and took £8,000 to £2,000. The concession with a run was important, for up to then, Ribofilio was considered to be a doubtful starter. As I was leaving the dining room, I met David McCall, manager of the Engelhard horses.

'I was very impressed with Ribofilio today,' I said. His face lit up. I told him about the horse's time and that I had just taken another bet with William Hill.

'That's very interesting,' he said. 'I'm about to ring Mr Engelhard in America. He's waiting to hear the result of the gallop. Lester wasn't impressed with Ribofilio, but I'll tell the owner, what you have said and the bet you have taken.'

Engelhard decided to run Ribofilio in the Derby. 'If Alex Bird is confident, that's good enough for me,' he was reported to have said. As the day of the big race drew near, my confidence in the horse grew. At the Derby dinner in London's Savoy Hotel, I saw Lester talking to trainer Johnson-Houghton. The jockey had a long face and something was obviously troubling him. When he was alone, I went over.

'Come on Lester, why the bloody hell are you going about with such a long face?' I asked. 'You will win the Derby this week, I can see your name in the record books now.'

'Do you really think so Alex?'

'Of course I do. Didn't you realise how good that gallop was?'

I told him that the time was only one and a half seconds outside the record.

'Do you know what horse holds that record?'

'No.'

'St Paddy, and you were riding him on that occasion!'

No one knew that horse better than the top jockey. It was impossible to tell from his face what he thought about my revelation, although I did detect a small crumb of interest.

'Now look Lester, put the doubts out of your mind and go home after the dinner. Don't go nightclubbing!' I told him.

Lester smiled. 'All right Alex, and I promise to look up Raceform to check what you have told me.'

Nevertheless I do not think Lester was convinced about Ribofilio's chances, and neither was Lord Oaksey. He wrote in the *Sunday Telegraph*: 'Alex Bird must be a braver and wealthier person than me to back Ribofilio!'

I wrote to John, telling him of my reasons for backing the horse. I explained that unknown to me trainer Harry Wragg, that great exponent of times, was at the gallop with his stop watch and had later confirmed my times. He told me that he wished he'd trained a horse which had done such a fantastic gallop. I was not to get a reply from Lord Oaksey until after the big race.

I watched the Derby with Billy Carter, a supreme judge of horses in running.

'Come on Lester,' we cried simultaneously, as Ribofilio cruised up to the leaders at the distance pole. Lester was sitting with a double handful. Then suddenly he must have felt the petrol running out. Ribofilio fell back and was unplaced. It was all over. Blakeney, ridden by Ernie Johnson, was the winner. Lester would never give a horse a hard race if he felt he could not win. Winning is what matters to him. I felt he probably had in mind Ribofilio's chances in the Irish Derby at the Curragh three weeks later. A few days before the Irish Derby I received a phone call at home. It was Lester. How he got my number I do not know. He has never rung me before or since.

'Just a quick word to let you know that Ribofilio will win in Ireland!' he told me. The call confirmed my belief during the English Derby that Lester was keeping something up his sleeve. I immediately backed the horse to win £15,000 and on Saturday 28 June, went to the Curragh to watch Lester ride the 2–1 favourite. I stood half a dozen steps up the grandstand, and was confident that Lester had the race in the bag, when he came with a telling run and took the lead at the distance. While Lester was in front, I hurried down to the horse's manager McCall just below me, taking my eyes off the race for a few seconds.

'Well done David, you've done it!' I said. The crowd suddenly roared and I looked up just in time to see the 7–2 joint second favourite, Prince Regent, ridden by Geoff Lewis, flash past the post, catching Ribofilio in the last few strides to win by a length. Blakeney, ridden by Ernie Johnson, was five lengths away third. A few days later I received Lord Oaksey's reply to my letter. He wrote:

'If I had thought a bit harder I would have realised that you were far too old a hand to make any mistake about the flying start. In any case, Ribofilio has since proved that his Sandown time, was in fact, a really good one. I am only sorry that he wasn't quite ready at Epsom to win your money. He certainly would have, if he had shown his Irish Derby form. I still think you are braver and richer than me, and I hope Ribofilio gets the chance to repay anything he may owe you before the season ends!'

On 10 September, Ribofilio and Lester were unluckily beaten $1\frac{1}{2}$ lengths in the St Leger, by Intermezzo, ridden by Ron Hutchinson. With hindsight, I believe that the brave attempt to run Ribofilio in the Derby, with all the fast work that entailed for a very sick horse, proved his undoing. The trial probably took too much out of him. Who knows? However, there is, after all, only one Derby, and I think Engelhard's decision to let his horse take his chance was a fair one.

Ribofilio was a great horse, ruined by the dirty deeds of the dopers, and that is what Lester thought too. A few months later he sat with Richard Baerlein on a flight back from racing in France and told the top journalist that he was certain the horse had been got at. Ribofilio's staggering weight loss after his tragic run in the 2,000 Guineas, had made him even more sure.

That year I found out that some stewards were behind Towser telling me to withdraw my horses from his yard.

I was at Goodwood with Billy Carter. We were enjoying a drink by my car in the car park in the centre of the course, when he said: 'I suppose you're still wondering why Towser did not want your horses at his stables?' Billy went on: 'It was because of something Sir Harold Wernher told him.' I listened in amazement.

Sir Harold owned several good horses that were trained by Towser.

'Apparently Sir Harold said that the stewards of the Jockey Club were against you and that in order to get at you they would warn Towser off. Then you, who they believed was the mastermind behind the operation, would be warned off at the same time.'

I could not believe what I was hearing. It was the first time I had ever heard of an owner being warned off, because it was normally only the trainer who was held responsible.

'Don't judge Towser too harshly,' said Billy. 'When Sir Harold first warned him, he did nothing. For twelve months it was constantly on his mind. Then Sir Harold brought the matter up again, this time more forcibly.'

I was terribly sad over what Billy had told me but I felt no malice against Towser. He had a wife and children and was doing what was best for them. Racing was his livelihood and he risked losing it. Sir Harold Wernher had the best connections. What he said had to be true. He was even friendly with the Queen and was often a guest at Windsor.

I remember being told a story of how Sir Harold sat on the Royal lawns with Her Majesty. A footman appeared carrying an official-looking black box.

'Oh no, Ma'am, surely you're not working on affairs of state on such a lovely day?' he said.

'Of course not,' replied the Queen, with a smile, as she pulled out copies of the *Sporting Life* and Racing Calendar.

After Billy told me what had happened over Towser I began to discover that other close friends knew about it too, but had never told me. One of them was Richard Baerlein. Some months later in the paddock at Epsom, he said: 'It wasn't an easy decision for Towser, Alex. When Wernher first warned him he came to your defence, and told him about your three-year-old horse Sapphire.'

Sapphire ran in a race at Lewes over a mile and a half. Towser fancied the horse's chances because it had been going well at home, but I refused to back him because his form was not good enough. I was proved right. Sapphire ran badly in the race and finished tailed off. Towser felt he had been made to look a fool. After the race, he left the course without speaking to anyone. I had never seen him so upset. He was determined to prove that he was right about the horse and over the next few weeks worked Sapphire with a recent winner proving that he really did have some ability. He then told me that Sapphire had a chance in his next race and I could probably get 20–1 about him.

'No Towser, I stand by what I said, I don't want to back him without any form at all,' I told him.

'Let the horse run in a better class race, so that the public can have a look at him.'

We ran Sapphire in the competitive, fourteen-runner Southwell Handicap at Nottingham a few weeks later. He finished fifth. It was a very promising run, so we entered him in the Dunchurch

Handicap at Warwick the following week. That day he was ridden by Josh Gifford,* the now famous trainer, then a 5 lb claiming apprentice.

I put £1,000 on Sapphire at Nottingham and he won by a neck at 4–1.

Richard continued his story: 'So Towser finished by telling Wernher that there could not be a fairer and more honest man than Alex Bird. He could have put the horse in a lower class race, got odds of about 20–1 and easily won a lot of money.'

Wernher was not impressed. He repeated his warning to Towser about me and left the trainer wondering what to do.

* I have always admired Josh Gifford, especially for standing by his jockey Bob Champion, when he had cancer. At that time almost everyone, including owners in the stable, would have preferred to substitute another jockey, as sorry as they were for Champion. Fortunately for brave Champion, the owners of Aldaniti were not among the doubters, and when Bob won the 1981 National for them on the horse they and Josh were more than rewarded for their faith.

9

On 13 May 1970, I went to York races with Harvey Wild.

I planned to put £2,000 on a horse called Capistrano, ridden by Greville Starkey in The Scarborough Stakes. I had seen him run his first race at Newmarket a month before, when Lester Piggott rode him gently, finishing third. The time was very fast and I had earmarked him as a future winner. On the day of the York meeting, Lester was riding a horse called Fireside Chat at Salisbury. Fireside Chat also run in a twenty seven-runner race at Newmarket, winning by four lengths in a very fast time. I could imagine Lester's feelings as he journeyed to Salisbury. He had no option but to ride Fireside Chat, because the horse, owned by Charles Engelhard, was trained by Fulke Johnson-Houghton, who retained him as the stable jockey.

'I think it would be better to put my £2,000 on a double today,' I told Harvey. 'Capistrano and Fireside Chat.'

'In that case put £100 on for me,' he said.

It was a fast race at York and Capistrano won by half a length from the favourite Protam, ridden by Greville Sexton. The price was 7–2. I stood in the stands feeling very pleased with myself. On a quick reckoning, I estimated that my dividend of £9,000 going on Fireside Chat, would yield me about 20 per cent – not bad for one hour's investment. It was better than putting my money in stocks and shares. An hour later the smile had gone from my face. I was shaken to discover that an unknown and unfancied horse had beaten my investment, by an impressive four lengths in The Salisbury Stakes. His name was Mill Reef, owned by American banker Paul Mellon. He was ridden by Geoff Lewis; this was a partnership that would make racing history.

'That serves you right for being greedy,' I said to myself as I stood staring at the result board near the Tote.

The following day, after I saw the time of the race in the *Sporting Life*, one minute four point thirty three seconds, I met Harvey and said to him:

'Never mind about your loss yesterday – we'll get our money back on Mill Reef in next year's Derby.'

Why I said the Derby and not the 2,000 Guineas I don't know, as the race at Salisbury was over the minimum distance, five furlongs.

I had learned from an early age that, if a horse has a sufficiently stout pedigree to win a Derby, he still had to have speed to make him a great horse. However, there was a mystery over Mill Reef: why did the bookmakers allow him to start at 8–1 at Salisbury? I discovered that there had been a pre-race gallop on 9 May. Ian Balding and his head man, Bill Palmer, had decided they would let the horse stretch his legs. His galloping companion was a useful runner called Red Reef. Mill Reef, ridden by work rider John Hallom, won by thirty lengths, without being extended. The only way Ian could have known for certain that this was a great performance would have been to have clocked the gallop, but as it was only a preliminary spin, he did not. The horse therefore went to Salisbury with more hope than confidence behind him.

Even with their brilliant information network the bookmakers must have been in the dark about the gallop. It was the first time I had ever known them to be unaware of such a fantastic run. Perhaps they had heard about it, but like Ian could hardly believe it. The only people who backed Mill Reef, were the boys in the stable, and Ian's mother, who doubtless did not risk more than a tenner.

Mill Reef's next outing was the Coventry Stakes at Royal Ascot, on 16 June, 1970. Again ridden by Geoff, he was 11–4 on favourite and won in a canter eight lengths from Brian Taylor on Cromwell.

Four days later Mill Reef went to France for the Prix Robert Papin at Maisons Lafitte. That day I could not back him as English bookmakers did not bet on the race. To my surprise he was beaten the shortest of short heads by My Swallow, ridden by Lester

Piggott and trained at Newmarket by Paul Davey. The horse looked a shadow of his former self. He had travelled badly and refused to eat for two days. He had lost stones in weight and did not have the best of luck in running.

The following month I went to Chester races expecting to see Eli Rose, the fearless bookie from Manchester. I was disappointed to discover that he was not on the course as I would have placed my bets with him. His firm was represented, but they were only taking small stakes and so I placed my money elsewhere. There were five bets and they all won, bringing me a profit of £18,000. Within six days of the meeting, I learned that Eli had defaulted and fled to Australia. He had cashed losing punters' cheques by special clearance and sent unsigned cheques to the winners. Later in Australia he was to buy himself some race horses, one of which was the top class Lancashire Lad. When Tattersalls Committee heard he was operating Down Under he was debarred from racing there and had to sell his horses. I despise such people. They blacken the name of racing. I do not know how much money was involved or how many backers he defaulted on, but I do know that Phil Bull suffered for many thousands of pounds. He came back to England later and offered Phil twelve and a half percent in full and final settlement. Phil told him exactly what to do with such a paltry offer.

At this time my mind was still on Mill Reef and a few weeks later, on 20 August, I went to York with Harvey Wild, determined to have my maximum bet on the horse for the Gimcrack Stakes.

It was a tortuous drive over the Pennine Chain, that mountainous backbone of England. The rain was cascading down and we wondered if the meeting would be called off. There was no let up in the bad weather when we arrived at the course and my heart sank. I had an inflexible rule never to back a horse in heavy ground, unless he proved himself capable of going through the mud. My confidence in Mill Reef diminished with every drop of rain. The track was like a quagmire. Mill Reef's owner, Paul Mellon, trainer Ian and jockey Geoff, were in a dilemma. They deliberated at length whether to let the horse run. Finally, Paul made the decision. Mill Reef was to take his chance. Still the rain kept pouring down. Finally, as I stood in the stands with Harvey, I recalled Johnny Hughes's advice to me.

'Never back a horse on heavy ground, especially at York. You must button up your pocket.'

They were wise words and I decided to follow them.

What a race! Mill Reef, 5–4 on favourite, pulled his way to the front at the two-furlong marker, and won in a canter from Frankie Durr on Green God. Had Geoff not restrained him he would have won by twenty lengths, instead of ten. I stood in awe of the horse's performance, recalling the great Ribot. I had seen him win three races outside his native Italy, at Ascot and Longchamps; they too were on heavy ground – but I could not remember him winning on firm ground. Yet here was a horse who broke the clock on races run in firm going and had just won the Gimcrack in thick mud. I knew then that Mill Reef was a superhorse. Until that moment I had held the view that horses with big feet, commonly called soup plates, were better in this kind of ground, because they did not penetrate the surface very deeply. However, Mill Reef, a small horse, had proved me wrong. Timeform boss Phil Bull had been right. He once told me that a small horse with small feet could skip over soft ground better than a horse with big feet. That was backed up by Ian Balding, who some time later walked the ground where Mill Reef and his other horse Aldi had run.

The ground was very soft and he discovered that Aldi had made an imprint of several inches. Mill Reef, however, had scarcely made an impression. 'It was as though a ghost had galloped by,' he said. Mill Reef ended his career as a two-year-old by winning the Imperial Stakes at Kempton on 19 September, 1970 and the Dewhurst Stakes at Newmarket on 16 October. At Kempton he won by a length from Hecla, ridden by John Gorton, the quietly spoken South African jockey. But the odds were so prohibitive I did not back him. However, when he won the Dewhurst by four lengths from Wenceslas, I cleaned up with my biggest bet of the year. I had £20,000 on him at odds of 6–4 and 7–4 on, his starting price.

On Tuesday 11 November, Lester Piggott was booked to ride Karabas in the Washington DC International at Laurel Park. The horse was owned by Rory More O'Ferrall and trained by Bernard Van Cutsem. I knew that bookmakers in England, having suffered a big loss on Sir Ivor on an earlier occasion, would be on their guard against taking a beating with Karabas. I had no alternative – I would have to disarm them, and the way to do it was to make Karabas the short-priced favourite. I flew to America and invested £5,000 on the horse in the preliminary betting at the course on Saturday, two days before the race. America is a Tote-monopolised country, and as there was very little betting on the race on that day I knew the horse would quickly be relayed by the Press Association to England as 5–4 favourite. Finding the money to put on Karabas in America was tricky. Currency restrictions were tight at the time, but I managed to raise the cash through a willing aunt who lived in the country.

When English bookmakers saw the odds relayed to them from the course they were prepared to take more money for the horse. If it had been reported at 4–1 or 3–1, they would have imposed betting limits. Johnny Foy was with me at Laurel Park and I instructed him to put a further £5,000 on Karabas in England. He made one phone call, and the money was spread throughout the country via his brilliant network of agents. But it was not long before the English bookmakers smelt danger. Johnny always used the same helpers, and soon the bookies, realising that Bird money was going on, feared the snowball. Although I only bet £5,000 each helper in turn often added his own money, and by the time the bet was finally placed with dozens of bookmakers, the stake could be as much as £50,000.

I had already told several English journalists covering the race meeting about my plan on condition that they did not break the story. On Sunday morning at my motel near the course, I sat drinking coffee with Karabas's trainer, Bernard Van Cutsem. He was worried because he heard that I had placed £5,000 on the Tote. He also backed his horse in England at Tote price and naturally thought my bet would have an adverse effect on the odds.

However, when I told him the story, he completely approved of it. The whole 15,000 dollars already in the pool would only be a fraction of the total amount, normally reaching half a million dollars. Apart from disarming the British bookmakers, the American racegoer would read his morning papers, and decide the horse was not worth backing at the price. Little did I know then that one well-known bookmaker was determined not to be taken for a ride over Karabas.

A few hours before the race Johnny and I were sitting in the Laurel Park administrative office, drinking coffee and looking forward to a successful day, when a racecourse official answered the phone. 'Who? Mr Who from where? Ladbrokes in England? You want to put how many thousands of dollars on Karabas?'

Johnny, realising what was going on, quickly stepped in. He grabbed the official by the arm and, putting his hand over the receiver, said: 'Tell him NO! Currency restrictions won't allow it!'

'I'm sorry, but we can't accommodate you because of the very tight currency restrictions between our two countries.'

There were more protestations from the other side of the Atlantic and the official was having a hard time.

'For the last time tell him NO!' said Johnny firmly.

The official followed the instructions to the letter and put the phone down. If only the bookmaker had known that on the other end of the line were the very men he was out to beat. Nevertheless, full marks to him – he did not give up easily. The phone rang a second time and we all played the game again: he never got his money on. He must have kicked himself when Lester rode a magnificent race on Karabas, winning easily by one and three quarter lengths from Hawaii, ridden by J. Velasquez. Czar Alexander, the horse Valasquez was runner up on when Sir Ivor won in 1968, was beaten into third place by half a length. The American press men clamoured around Lester when he went into the jockey's room.

After a shower Lester relaxed and talked briefly to reporters. When they asked him at what stage he thought he was going to win the race, he said: 'A week last Thursday!' That evening Britain's top jockey attended a party given by John Schapiro. Then he flew to New York en route for Japan.

Under the heading: 'Piggott silences the critics with Karabas,' the *Washington Post* said his performance was 'a masterful ride'. The *Baltimore Sun* said: 'A jockey of considerable talent. He rides extremely high in the saddle, so high you can spot him in the middle of a cavalry charge.' I won £18,000 on Karabas and celebrated my win at the Jockey Club Restaurant in Washington. I was privileged to buy the wine for Mr O'Ferrell and his guests. It was a memorable evening. There was only one thing that spoilt the whole thing for me. One journalist *did* break the story of my coup, which I had revealed to him off the record. Tim FitzGeorge-Parker, filing from Laurel on Thursday 13 November, wrote in the *Daily Mail*:

'Alex Bird, last of the big time punters, landed the betting coup of the year on Karabas in the Washington International. The enthusiastic Cheshire gambler revealed details of the operation that netted him £18,000 in America and England . . .'

I did not speak to him for eight years, but we are friends again now.

The following year at Sandown, as I stood with professional backer Leslie Wood by the paddock discussing the day's racing, he said: 'I think Derby County are a coming side. They could be worth a bet for the League Championship next year.'

Leslie placed my racecourse commissions with great expertise, but as I discovered during the World Cup in 1966, he had another string to his bow. The former head waiter of the Embassy Club in London was possibly the best judge of football results I knew. Leslie would leave the Embassy at around 4.00am and after a few hours sleep go to the races. How he did it I will never know. He must have had the constitution of an ox. He first became successful putting bets on for Billy Carter and adding something extra for himself.

Leslie was impressed with the half-back line that Derby County had for the new season. It had been reinforced by their new acquisition from Sunderland, Colin Todd. They had other players who impressed him too, like Roy MacFarland, Martin Hennessey and of course Francis Lee. Manager Brian Clough's team looked like a good long-term investment. Leslie had brought the matter up at the right time, for I was looking for a League Championship interest.

There were pitfalls in such a bet, however. After all, it was a long season, with plenty of time to think, be hopeful, confident, doubtful and despondent. There were forty two ninety-minute games – almost like living through hundreds of Grand Nationals. I put £200 on Derby at 28–1 with Chummy Gaventa, but the following day I saw in the *Sporting Life* that bookmakers Heathorn were offering 40–1. So I pressed my bet, putting on another one hundred pounds with the firm. Then I put the investment out of my mind and went back to racing.

After winning the Greenham Stakes at Newbury as a three-year-old on 17 April, 1971, Mill Reef went for the 2,000 Guineas on 1 May. I did not have a big bet on him that day. I just put £2,000 on, possibly because I had bad memories of Ribofilio's shock performance in the Guineas, or it could have been because I had a fixation about the Derby. On the walk to the member's enclosure from the car park at Newmarket, I met John Hislop. 'What do you think will win the Guineas, Alex?' he asked.

'Well, My Swallow is a good horse, but Mill Reef will beat him,' I said.

It was not until we went our separate ways that I realised John's own horse, Brigadier Gerard, ridden by Joe Mercer, was third favourite in the race. There was no excuse for being so rude. I could have made some favourable comment about his horse. After all, he won four races as a two-year-old. John and Jean Hislop had been offered £250,000 for the Brigadier and had turned it down. I thought they were crazy. I had never been particularly impressed by the Brigadier. In each of his races Joe Mercer did not sit still like Lester, but had to push and push the horse. Joe, however, was very deceptive, and when he was apparently scrubbing, he could have two stone in hand. I wondered if the Hislops' vision was clouded by looking through rose-coloured glasses, making their goose into a swan. They had bred the Brigadier after all. How wrong can you be? It was a great race. My Swallow, ridden by Frankie Durr, made the early running. Mill Reef, the 6–4 favourite, joined him after a furlong. Brigadier Gerard, challenged at the bushes – and went away to win by three lengths. When the horses crossed the line my disappointment was eased by knowing that the race could not have gone to a greater sporting couple than the Hislops. There were excuses for Mill Reef's defeat. One was that he and My Swallow took each other on in the early stages, and Joe was able to challenge and come with a telling run in the last furlong. Another excuse was that he did not look well and was bad tempered before the race. However in my opinion he was beaten on merit, by possibly the greatest miler in the past few decades. After all, Mill Reef finished three lengths in front of My Swallow. All in all 1971 was an exceptional year in producing three horses of their calibre.

I have watched and analysed thirty five Guineas since the war and each one of those horses would have won any of them, and I am not forgetting winners Sir Ivor and Nijinsky.

Part of my success at this time was due to my dedication to timing horses in running. In all weathers, as I have said, I would stand with the professional watch holders at the top of the stands, opposite the finishing lines with my stopwatch. I would spend the whole afternoon meticulously noting the time of each horse and comparing my notes with the other clockers.

I had bought one of the first video recording systems in Britain from BBC commentator David Coleman for around £1,500, and was probably the first person to use it as a means of analysing races. When I told Phil Bull about it he came to my home with his right hand man Reg Griffin to look at the equipment. He was so impressed he ordered one for his Timeform organisation. Stanley Platt and I would run through the video recordings together. We knew that a competent, professional watch holder could get within two fifths of a second of the official electrical time. Using the video and re-running the races time and again, we could confirm which horses had been non-triers and check for luck in running. I had always doubted the accuracy of the Watesta electrical timings, and now with the video I was certain I was right.

The Watesta times were recorded by Racecourse Technical Services and they were supposedly beyond reproach. I did not always believe that the times, which were not televised, were absolutely correct because approximately three races out of ten were timed to one tenth of a second. However, the average should be one race in ten, and I knew from the number of races where the RTS had issued no times because of breakdowns, that they were having teething troubles with the equipment. I sent letters to the sporting press, criticising RTS for their failures. On one occasion I even likened them to Fred Karno's Circus, and in another letter, published in the *Sporting Life*, I said that the peace-loving Swiss people would be forced into military action, if they had just a small percentage of such electronic breakdowns in their winter sports events. I could tolerate a small number of malfunctions but there were too many, and a professional backer like myself needed complete accuracy. When my letters first appeared in the press, Lord Wigg, who as Head of the Levy Board was responsible for RTS, shot my theories down. He confirmed that the Watesta times were one hundred percent correct, but I continued with my criticisms. Finally, Wigg stopped replying to me on the pages of the *Sporting Life*. Now the letters were signed by RTS chief, Lieutenant Colonel Aveline. This proud and very upright gentleman again said the timings were one hundred percent correct.

'The Watesta timer is a good instrument, based on well-tried electronic techniques,' he stressed.

A few weeks later at Epsom, I bumped into Lord Wigg in the Members Enclosure: 'You crafty old fox, you're passing the buck to Aveline on those electrical timers,' I said. He looked at me with a twinkle in his eye and walked away laughing.

Meanwhile my thoughts were on Mill Reef and the Derby. I had backed him to win £38,000, and Harvey Wild also had a good bet.

I smiled when I heard that the Earl of Rosebery, aged eighty nine, was reported as saying it was the worst Derby field he had ever seen. Little did he know he was about to see a great horse. For twenty three years the journey by taxi from the Mayfair Hotel in

London to the course had never taken more than one hour and I never set out before 12.30, allowing the majority of people to arrive and the traffic to ease. That day, because I had so much at stake, I left the Mayfair at 11.00, expecting to arrive at Epsom by 12.30. However, things never quite work out the way you expect them to, and I found myself stuck in a giant traffic jam. A new tunnel had recently been constructed under the racecourse, which should have eased the congestion. Something had gone badly wrong. Cars for miles around the course were stationary and the journey finally took me three and a half hours.

'Bloody hell, I could have travelled from Manchester to Epsom in less time,' I told the car park attendant.

I arrived in the stands a few minutes before the big race, a short head in front of Ian Balding, who arrived redfaced and hatless. Puffing and blowing, he told how he had abandoned his car and run three miles to the course. Luckily, he had a stout pedigree for such an ordeal, being a fine athlete, a former Cambridge Rugger Blue, amateur jockey and cricketer. Even so, it must have been a gruelling run in a morning suit. Minutes later the race was under way. Mill Reef, the 100–30 favourite, was well placed coming round Tattenham Corner and entered the straight about fourth. I smiled to myself as he took the lead a furlong out, and won by an easy two lengths from Linden Tree, ridden by D. Keith, and A. Gibert on Irish Ball. As I put my binoculars down, I felt happy that my prophecy to Harvey thirteen months earlier had come true. Paul Mellon was richer by £61,652.25p. He said after the race: 'I need every penny of it! I have a big tax problem in America.' That was a joke of course. His Philadelphia-based family ranks as one of the wealthiest in the world. 'I've owned horses since 1930 but winning the Derby has been my happiest moment,' he said. 'It's always been my greatest ambition.'

For me there was some personal satisfaction too. I had backed seven Derby winners in eight years.

Mill Reef was to win his next five races before going to stud in 1972. In two of them the odds were so prohibitive that I would not back him. In the other three I was to go in heavily to pick up

---

£85,000. Mill Reef's career was to finally earn me around £123,000. They say that horses are not machines, otherwise there would be no bookmakers. Mill Reef was nearer to being a machine than any horse I have ever seen. On two occasions he was not firing on all plugs, otherwise he would have been unbeaten.

A few days before the Oaks in June 1971, Lieutenant Colonel Aveline took me on a personal inspection of the Watesta system at Epsom, proudly showing me all the RTS equipment. I was still not convinced. Finally things came to a head over the timing of Altesse Royale's victory in the big event. The official electrically-recorded RTS time was two minutes, thirty six point ninety five seconds, a new record for the race. Jockey Geoff Lewis was very pleased, but along with other experienced watch holders I contested the verdict. I timed the race on my video recorder and I knew I was right.

Over the next few weeks I continued to bombard the *Sporting Life* with letters protesting about the timing of the Oaks. Lieutenant Colonel Aveline replied in their pages saying that a thorough investigation of the equipment had taken place and I was wrong. He wrote: 'A malfunction of the Watesta timing system can virtually be ruled out!' He stood by his times and stressed that the National Physical Laboratory had analysed the system. The bickering went on for so long I thought we must have been boring the readers. In my final letter to the *Sporting Life* I said that RTS must be wishing I would get run over by a bus as I had not heard from them for so long. This must have spurred RTS into action because a few days later, Aveline wrote to me saying: 'Come down to my offices and I will demonstrate once and for all that I am correct over my timing of the Oaks.' I rang Stanley and told him. Then I invited Richard Baerlein to the meeting. That day, armed with our stopwatches, Stanley and I arrived at the RTS offices with Richard, just off London's Kingston by-pass. We were ushered into a waiting room where half a dozen dignified looking men were sitting in silence. They were obviously RTS directors, and it is unlikely that any of them carried a rank lower than colonel. Stanley and I sat down opposite them, waiting to be shown into the room where the RTS recording would be shown. The minutes dragged on and we wondered how much longer we would have to wait. Stanley pulled out his five pound stopwatch and the directors eyed him disdainfully as if to say, 'how dare these men challenge our electronic equipment worth thousands of pounds, with their cheap timepieces?'

Aveline came into the room and signalled to us all to stay in our seats.

'Gentlemen, my technical staff have just told me that the time in question was a hand time, as the electronic equipment had broken down on that occasion,' he said.

His words were greeted with silence. The officials left and he came over to me.

'Now that you are here, would you like to see our equipment?' he asked. It was just a matter of courtesy, and we declined. I felt sorry for Aveline. He had been let down by his own staff, who he had nobly backed, and I felt even sadder when I read on the front page of the *Sporting Life* the following day, that he had resigned. As captain of the ship he had no alternative. The paper went on that I had been right in my conviction that the Oaks time was incorrect. The hand time to a non-professional watchholder, was approximately one second faster than the electronic time, the equivalent of five lengths. Apparently the Watesta apparatus failed to start electrically and was turned on by hand by one man, an RTS employee. He kept the fact secret, not even owning up when the battle of the letters began. It was not until the eleventh hour that he stepped forward. Unfortunately the casualty was to be Aveline.

By now the soccer season was well underway and my confidence in Derby County had grown. So I went in again and put £200 on at 18–1 for the league, and some weeks later another £350 at 14–1. The run-up to the end of the season was a nail biting time for me. Finally Derby played their last match on a Saturday, but the League Championship was still an open race. It depended on two games, to be played the following Monday evening. Leeds United had to play their last match against Wolverhampton Wanderers. If they won or drew, they would win the League. Liverpool were in with a chance too. If Leeds lost and they won their last match against Arsenal at Highbury, they would be champions. If both Leeds and Liverpool lost, Derby and I would be home and dry.

On the Monday morning I was amazed to learn that the book-makers were offering 6–1 against Derby. It is not often that they get their sums wrong and offer over the odds. They have computers to help them formulate the prices, but computers are not infallible as I was to discover many times in my career. If the information fed into them is wrong, the answer will be wrong. I spent a long time that morning reckoning the chances of a Wolverhampton victory and a Liverpool defeat. To me, there was no way that the odds were more than 3–1. I phoned Leslie Wood and he agreed that odds of 6–1 were most liberal. He computed that it was 2–1 against Wolves winning or drawing, and 2–1 against Arsenal winning. So the price for the double should have been 7–2.

I had read in a daily newspaper that Malcolm Allison, the controversial manager of Manchester City, favoured Derby's chances. So I telephoned him in his office at the Maine Road Ground. 'I could not agree with you more Alex, six to one is way over the odds,' he said. I told him I was about to ring the bookmakers and press my bet. 'Can you do me a favour then?'

'Of course.'

'Put fifty pounds on Derby for me.'

I did, and I put on a further £800 to win £5,000 for myself. In all, I stood to win more than £20,000 if Derby succeeded. On the evening of the matches Evelyn and I had arranged to play bridge at the home of our friend in Wilmslow, Kate Kerr. First we were to dine at our favourite Chinese restaurant, the Mandarin, in the small Cheshire town. As the Wolverhampton game was being broadcast I would have loved to cancel our bridge game, but there was no way we could possibly disappoint our hostess.

The big match started at 7.30 and the moment the ball was kicked off from the centre spot, we sat down to dinner. At the same time, the Derby County players, on a team holiday in Majorca, switched on their radios to listen in. Unknown to Evelyn, I had concealed a small transistor radio in the breast pocket of my jacket. When she saw me putting the tiny plug in my ear, she frowned across her pork spare ribs and mushrooms, but I managed to carry on my conversation, without much trouble. The meal took over an hour, and as we prepared to leave the restaurant, the game was into the second half.

Wolverhampton were winning by a goal when suddenly there was a flash that Arsenal were leading Liverpool. I kept my fingers crossed that the scores would remain that way. We drove to Kate's home in my car with the radio on. Kate was oblivious for she was a little hard of hearing, bless her. The Highbury game had ended and Arsenal had won. There was only one hurdle left. Wolves had to hang on to that precious advantage. Leeds were making a desperate attempt to draw level and the Wolves goal was under a furious bombardment. We arrived at Kate's house and I dashed in, making straight for the radio to the astonishment of the other guests. As I frantically turned the knob to tune in to the right station, Evelyn politely explained to everyone else what was going on. The last five minutes of the game turned out to be nearer twelve minutes, as the referee added extra time. They were the longest minutes of my life. The referee just would not blow his whistle. 'Bloody hell, there must be at least three broken legs and a broken collarbone for him to let play go on this long,' I announced. 'Either that or his watch must have stopped!'

Suddenly the Leeds forwards were racing towards the Wolves goal again. Surely they would break down the defence this time. Then, just as I had a vision of the ball going into the back of the net, the whistle went and there was a cheer from everyone in the room. 'Now let us get down to the really big gamble – a serious game of bridge,' I said. The stakes were high as usual, a penny a hundred.

Little did I know then that the vital Wolverhampton-Leeds match was to be the subject of a Football Association inquiry some years later. There were allegations that a bid was made to fix the match in favour of Leeds. The charges sparked a storm of controversy that made headline news for weeks.

For years after my win Leslie told people: 'That Alex Bird

backed Derby five times, when most people would have been hedging their bets in the final days. That proves he's a value backer and not a gambler.'

On 22 April, 1975, at Epsom, the rain had been pouring down all day, and the going was getting heavier by the minute. I decided that the last race of the day, the Evelyn Handicap, over seven furlongs eleven yards, would be ideal for trying out my tactic of coming across to the stands side, but although I searched through my racecard, I could not find an owner or trainer I knew well enough to ask. Then I spotted Greville Bayliss, a keen racegoer and husband of TV personality Katie Boyle, by the unsaddling enclosure and asked him if he knew of anyone who would co-operate. 'Trainer Peter Nelson is a great friend of mine, I'll have a word with him,' he said. Peter agreed, so we got to work. The horse was Velvella, ridden by Lester Piggott, and the tactic was explained to him in detail by the trainer.

Velvella opened at 7–1, and I backed him down to 3–1, to win £15,000, knowing the horse would get every assistance from the saddle. Peter, Greville and I watched the race from the stands. As the field came round Tattenham Corner into the straight there were two horses well clear of the rest, Velvella and Fastacre, ridden by Frankie Durr. Lester was on the outside of Frankie. 'Come on Lester, straight across,' I shouted in my excitement, but he did no such thing. He stayed on the far side with Frankie for a furious neck and neck duel up the straight. Velvella was beaten by three quarters of a length, and I could have cried with frustration. My theory was proved to be absolutely right the next day, for every single winner came across to the stand side on entering the straight and won by a big margin. A few weeks later, at Chester races, as I drank champagne with friends by my car, I spotted Lester crossing the car park, and offered him a drink. 'No thanks, I don't drink during racing,' he said, 'but I'll have one of those cigars.' He had spotted my Havanas on the car seat. I could not let him get away without asking him what had gone wrong in the race at Epsom.

'What the hell were you playing at Lester, I thought your

instructions were to come across the course?'

'Oh, the horse was hanging to the left.'

I could not resist pulling his leg.

'That's a great pity. As a matter of fact, you were on a £1,000 present from me, had you come across and won!'

The eyes in the poker face actually twinkled.

'Oh well, that would have been different,' he replied.

Johnny Foy was as near to a saint as a bookmaker could be. He was a great friend to me and to the Catholic Church. When he died in November 1975 he took a little piece of me with him.

Johnny was a deeply religious man. He was a bookmaker, because, like myself, he was born into the business, although in his case it was his mother who ran it.

I had seen him talking to ladies of easy virtue, but he was always trying to reform them. He would say: 'Here's a fiver love, now go home.' He was a great benefactor of the Alexian Nursing Home in Moston, a suburb of Manchester adjoining Newton Heath. The home is run by the 600-year-old nursing order of the Alexian Brothers, a religious congregation dedicated to caring for the mentally and physically retarded, regardless of race or denomination. Johnny would always say to me: 'Alex, when I have had a bad day at the office or I am feeling out of sorts with the world, I just go there and talk to the boys.' He was referring to the patients, some old, some young, who were terminally ill. 'After they go in there, Alex, they only come out feet first,' he would say.

'When I come out of there, I feel I am the most selfish man in the world ever to make the slightest grumble.'

Johnny's great friend was Canon Joe Lakin. One evening in 1978 he joined Johnny for dinner at my home. Later, as we sat talking in the lounge, the subject came round to life after death. I am not a believer and I told them the story of how I caught a pike in my moat. 'I usually kill them,' I said, 'because they attack my ducks, but when I looked at the face of this 30 lb monster, it reminded me so much of my grandmother that I threw it back. Do you think that we come back to earth in another form when we die?'

Canon Joe and Johnny looked at each other as if to say: 'Don't say anything. That Alex Bird will never understand.' That night as we bid them farewell on the drive, Johnny leaned out of Canon Joe's car and shouted: 'God bless you Evelyn, I've not had such a good evening for years.' Forty eight hours later Johnny suffered a massive heart attack, while on a visit to the Alexian Nursing Home. When we heard that he was in intensive care, I was shattered. Hearing the news of someone's illness has never affected me more. I just did not know what to say. Evelyn was equally upset. We could barely talk. 'Let's go for a walk,' I said.

We went out and strolled down the winding road near our home in silence, both of us reliving the years we had known Johnny. When we returned, Evelyn said: 'What are we doing here? Let's go and see him.'

'What can we do there darling? There's no way we can help him,' I replied, however I knew she was right. We had to go. While I was upstairs changing, the phone rang. Johnny was dead. I am not an emotional man; I do not believe in showing my feelings. Crying to me is a weakness, but I could not help shedding a tear or two at Johnny's funeral.

It was at the Catholic church in Middleton, Manchester. My three boys did not have to be asked to go; each of them dropped everything to attend. My sister May, who thought the world of Johnny came from Blackpool and her daughter Sheila from America. There was not a vacant seat in the church, and there were as many people outside as in. Most of the Manchester United team were there, and Sir Matt Busby, with Jean and their whole family. I looked across at Canon Joe and caught his eye. He was perfectly tranquil, as if to say: 'Don't worry, Johnny is where he wants to be.' I felt so emotional that I had to turn away. I recalled Johnny's words that I had heard so many times: 'Alex, if I thought I would not see my old mum when I died, I would not want to carry on.'

At least eight Catholic priests attended the service, taken by the Bishop of Middlesbrough. He told the congregation that if Johnny had not died so early in life, he would have received high honours from the Catholic church.

Johnny once had an audience with the Pope in Rome and was photographed with the Pontiff. He proudly showed me the picture and jokingly observed that someone had commented: 'Who's that with Johnny Foy?'

Johnny had a wing of the Alexian Brothers home named after him. Four years later, in December 1982, masked gunmen broke in. They punched administrator Brother Gerard in the face, stuffed a rag down his throat, bound his hands and feet to the desk and demanded the safe keys. They left with £5,300, much of it savings of the chronically sick residents. Johnny had been a founder member of the Charity Commandoes, a non-denominational group of Greater Manchester businessmen. The original committee included Sir Matt, Joe Mercer, the manager of Manchester City and Gus Demmy. In the past they raised £15,000 for a new extension to the home. The Charity Commandoes pledged to replace the stolen money, and they planned a sportsmen's cabaret night in Manchester on Friday 11 March, 1983. I received a letter from Maurice Brown, the Commandoes chairman. At the top was a printed verse dedicated to Johnny.

> '*He asked nothing, but wanted to give,*
> *Everything that Jews may live,*
> *All of our faith are forever in debt,*
> *To a human being we must never forget.*'

Contact had been made with a businessman who owned Fagin's, a large Manchester club. He kindly agreed to stage the show there. He even shut the club to his own members for the event. On behalf of the Commandoes and myself, I thank him. The event, on Tuesday 15 March, 1983 was a great success.

Johnny, give my regards to your mum.

Lester Piggott is the best jockey in the world, the best judge of the form book and the greatest judge of his own races. That is why I will never understand the view he apparently took over the capability of a classic horse, after just one bad race. What goes on in that calculating, index-linked brain of his, I will never know. On 8 September, 1976, Lester won the Laurent Perrier Champagne Stakes at Doncaster on J.O. Tobin, beating Durtal, ridden by Ernie Johnson, by an easy four lengths. When Lester returned to the unsaddling enclosure he must already have decided that J.O. Tobin would be his 2,000 Guineas and Derby mount the following year.

Durtal's owner Robert Sangster, and his trainer Barry Hills, were standing by the paddock. Robert, who once asked me to manage his horses in England, seemed dejected. 'Don't look so worried,' I told him. 'You have a top class filly in Durtal. She has just been beaten by the best horse I have ever clocked.'

'Thank you Alex, that is most comforting,' he said. Lester must have held the same view, for he partnered Durtal in all her subsequent races. It is as if he has a mini computer inside his head. Even when he is riding for his life, he is logging the ability of the other horses around him. I won £5,000 when he partnered Durtal in the William Hill Cheveley Park Stakes at Newmarket, on Wednesday 29 September, winning by an easy three lengths from the best two-year-old fillies in England.

J.O. Tobin was by the great American sire Never Bend out of Hill Shade, by Hillary, and was trained by Noel Murless (later to be knighted), at Newmarket. J.O. Tobin was a big horse, but well put together and very athletic. Rich dark brown, with a white star on his forehead, he was noticed as something out of the ordinary by his regular work rider, Chris Lines. His next race was the Grand Criterium at Longchamps on Sunday 10 October, where he was to meet Blushing Groom, the top French two-year-old. My friend Tony Kelly, head of the great building company Beldale Homes, and I wanted to put £10,000 on the horse. But that morning, before we flew to Paris for the race, Johnny Foy could only manage to get £4,000 each on for us with English bookmakers, at French Tote prices.

We chartered a plane from Manchester with four other friends and when we arrived in the French capital we had a wonderful meal at the world-famous Tour D'Argent, on the Left Bank of the Seine, with its breathtaking view of Paris. At Longchamps the champagne bar by the paddock was not too crowded, as it was a normal race meeting. I was about to sit down when I saw journalist Charles Benson of the *Daily Express*, at the next table with a handsome man in his early thirties. I went over and asked Charles if he thought J.O. Tobin was a certainty for the race. He seemed a bit uncomfortable and I could not understand why. Without really answering my question he turned and introduced me to his friend. I did not hear the gentleman's full name, but I caught the word Khan.

'Oh Mr Khan aren't you the Khan who has the stud in Sussex?'

'No, I am the Aga Khan,' he replied quietly.

The Aga owned Blushing Groom, the favourite for the race. No wonder Charles seemed a bit nonplussed over my question. Talk about putting both feet in it!

I suppose I could have been forgiven for not recognising the Aga. He was just embarking on his racing venture and his face was not familiar. (*The following June I met Sussex stud farm owner Rabbie Khan in the champagne bar at Epsom and told him of my clanger in France. 'Oh yes,' he joked. 'The Aga is just a poor relation!'*)

I returned to my table and told Tony what had just happened. Ever the opportunist, he said: 'Why don't you ask him if he will bet £10,000 that his horse finishes in front of J.O. Tobin?' I thought it was a good idea and felt the Aga would accommodate us. I called out to Charles and he came across. I did not want to make a direct approach to the Aga at this stage.

'Would the Aga be prepared to bet us £10,000 that Blushing Groom will beat J.O. Tobin,' I asked. 'I know his father, the Aly Khan, liked to back horses in a big way.'

'Sorry Alex, but the answer would be no,' said Charles. 'The Aga never bets.'

It seemed the father and son were like chalk and cheese. Aly was a heavy gambler who won and lost fortunes. He was a big spender who liked the company of pretty women and Hollywood stars, but his erratic lifestyle led the old Aga to pass him over, and leave the bulk of his wealth to his grandson, Karim, who took the title.

I cannot tell you of the absolute disappointment and humiliation felt in the English camp when J.O. Tobin was beaten easily into third place by Blushing Groom and the unconsidered Amyntor. The winning margin was four lengths. I had backed J.O. Tobin to win £25,000 in the 2,000 Guineas the following year, and so I was anxious to get the reaction of Noel Murless to the defeat. He had said that if the horse failed to win the Grand Criterium in convincing style, he would retire. The owner of J.O. Tobin, Noel's great friend Mr George Pope had declared that if that happened, the horse would return to America, where he was bred, to continue his career. Murless was passing the champagne bar after leaving the paddock, when I interrupted his thoughts.

'Good afternoon Mr Murless. That was a very disappointing result for you. What did Lester say?'

'He told me the horse would not stay the mile and I have made my decision to retire at the end of the season.'

'Mr Murless, it is not often I disagree with Lester, but for me there is no question the horse will get the mile for the Guineas and possibly a mile and a half for the Derby. Any horse that could win the Champagne Stakes as a two-year-old, over seven furlongs, in such a fast time, must be able to get the mile as a three-year-old.'

'It is no use Mr Bird. I have made up my mind and I will take Lester's advice.'

I still had faith in my timings, which indicated that J.O. Tobin was a great horse. So when he ran in America in the Preakness, the second leg of the American Triple Crown, I had a further £12,000 on him. However, he was easily beaten, and that was the decider for me: perhaps Lester was right after all. I decided never to back him again.

I told Richard Baerlein of my decision, and asked him to ring me with the result of the horse's next race. What happened then is best explained by his story in the *Observer* newspaper.

Richard wrote: 'When I heard the news that J.O. Tobin had won the Swaps Stakes at Hollywood Park, by eight lengths, in two fifths of a second off the course record, I dared not ring Alex Bird. Finally Alex rang me, wondering why I had not called, and I then broke the news to him that the horse had even left behind America's latest Triple Crown hero, Seattle Slew.'

So I was right about J.O. Tobin, and later I discovered the reason for his defeats in the Preakness and the Grand Criterium.

I already knew he was an excitable horse. Richard Baerlein had seen him when he re-entered the paddock after winning the Champagne Stakes. He was awash with sweat and looked more like a horse who had won the Cesarewitch by a short head on a hot day. Richard had mentioned this to trainer Bruce Hobbs, who told him: 'I don't normally pay attention to other people's horses, but when J.O. Tobin comes on to Newmarket Heath for his exercise, he is always in a lather.' That was confirmed by Chris Lines. He recalled that J.O. Tobin was extremely highly strung, as are many of Never Bend's progeny.

The horse was normally a good traveller, but when Chris went with him to France, things went wrong. A horse box was waiting when the plane landed, and J.O. Tobin was loaded up without incident. Unfortunately the other occupant, an excitable horse trained by Harry Wragg, was already distressed by a long wait and doing his best to kick the sides out of the box. This would upset most thoroughbreds, but for J.O. Tobin, it was the last straw. He sweated and fretted and the French customs officials were abominably slow. By the time the box left the airport after a delay of one and a half hours, he had thrown away any chance of winning the Grand Criterium the next day. At exercise on the morning of the race, he was listless and not himself. Chris told Lester about his fears over the horse, but J.O. Tobin did a token dance when the top jockey mounted him in the paddock, so he thought all was well.

There is no doubt the delay at the airport was a crucial factor in J.O. Tobin's defeat. He was not travelling in the last furlong at Longchamps. The long journey to America on top of all that smashed his chances in the Preakness.

10

28 SEPTEMBER 1978 is a date that will stay firmly in my mind, when I watched the racing from Ascot on TV. The fifth race on the card was The Clarence House Stakes over six furlongs for two-year-olds. It did not look a particularly hot event, but I decided to clock it as usual.

The race was won by a horse called Tromos, ridden by John 'Kipper' Lynch, and when I looked at my watch after their ten-length victory, I could not believe my eyes. I was measuring it against my great yardstick, the Diadem Stakes, a race for the older top class sprinters over the same distance run earlier in the day. I thought I must have got the time wrong as it was very, very fast. I rang Stanley Platt, who I knew would be clocking the race the same way. His telephone was engaged for a couple of minutes and when I got through I joked:

'You must be running up quite a phone bill.'

'I know, I've just clocked Tromos and his time was so fantastic, I had to check it with a friend to make sure I had got it correct.'

'And had you?'

'Yes.'

Stanley and I then checked our respective times and there was only a tenth of a second difference.

I put the phone down and as the horses were returning to the paddock, Peter O'Sullevan told viewers that the big bookmakers were offering 25–1 against Tromos for the 2,000 Guineas the following year. I immediately rang three bookmakers who were offering that price. I asked each one for £1,000 at 25–1. I wanted more but I knew I had to go in for a reasonable bet. Even then I did not get what I wanted on. 18–1 from the Tote was the last price I took, ten minutes later, and by late afternoon I had backed Tromos to win approximately £60,000. The following day the best price on offer was 10–1, which I still thought was very liberal.

I went to see Tromos, again ridden by Kipper, in the William Hill Dewhurst Stakes at Newmarket on 20 October. Kipper was unconvinced about Tromos. He had ridden him regularly since Ascot and told his friend Newmarket trainer Neville Callaghan that he was not the wonder-horse I had labelled him to be. Callaghan and I had a private bet on the race for a four-figure amount, and Kipper's doubts must have been relayed to the bookies because in spite of my own heavy bets on the course, the horse's price opened at 9–4 and drifted to 11–4. I pressed my bets and in total stood to win over £16,000. It was one of my biggest stakes that year. Tromos, never out of a canter, won by three lengths. The Guineas looked a formality. I did not stop talking about the horse the whole winter. By early spring, the world knew that I had gone for a very big win.

Tromos became an odds on chance for the Guineas and I decided it was a wise move to hedge my bets. So I had a private bet with Tony Kelly for an even £4,000. Having done so, I reckoned my average price on Tromos was 130–1. A lot of money was at stake, so I rang Richard Baerlein and asked him if he would suggest to trainer Bruce Hobbs that a twenty four-hour guard be put on the horse. 'Alex, the horse's owner Mr Cambanis is a wealthy man and every effort has been made to keep a watchful eye on Tromos,' he assured me.

When I went to Doncaster for the Lincoln in April, Peter O'Sullevan passed me as I stood by my car having a drink. I invited him to join me. His expression was glum. 'Alex, have you heard about Tromos?' he asked. My heart skipped a beat, and he added: 'The fact is . . . the horse is fine!' He broke into laughter, unable to keep a straight face any longer. I laughed too, but my happiness was short-lived. On 17 April, Tromos, ridden by Kipper, ran in the Ladbroke Craven Stakes over a mile at Newmarket. The ITV cameras were at the course and as commentator Brough Scott ran through the horses, he called me over and asked me to say a few words. They say there is nothing like race horses and women for making a man look like a fool, and I am afraid that I qualified as the idiot of the year. I stared into the cameras and told the great British public: 'Tromos will definitely win the Craven Stakes and I will be disappointed if he doesn't do so by at least three lengths going away!' The race, however, was won by Lyphards Wish, ridden by Joe Mercer with Tromos two and a half lengths away second. I stood stunned in the stands and could have kicked myself for making such a statement on TV. Nevertheless I felt the horse had not been ridden correctly. He was restrained instead of being allowed to go in front like previous races. His price drifted for the Guineas and he eased to 7–2. My confidence had taken a slight knock but I still thought Tromos would win. Over the following few weeks I heard reports that he was going exceptionally well at home. Then on 26 April at Epsom, I met a bookmaker that I knew in the champagne bar.

'Do you still fancy Tromos?' he asked.

My confidence was restored in the horse and I replied: 'Of course, but why do you ask?'

'I have just left a man who wants to lay Tromos at 5–1.'

'As you probably know, I have backed Tromos to win a lot of money, but if you can guarantee that this man will pay me, I will take the bet. How much does he want to lay?'

'£20,000 to £4,000.'

'That is a large bet – who is the man?'

'Oh, you know him, but I can't tell you at the moment. When I see him after the next race I will point him out to you.'

Before the bookmaker left I told him: 'If I have the bet with this man I will deposit £4,000 with you, provided you hold his £20,000.'

He agreed. 'We'll call him Mr X for now,' he said. 'He is not a bookmaker as such, but he is all right, he will pay.' The bookmaker did not see the man that afternoon, but assured me the mystery gambler would be on the course the following day. Mr X never appeared so there was no bet. I started to feel apprehensive. Was there something wrong with Tromos? The horse was a short-price and there had been many occasions when favourites had been got at for the classics. I wondered whether Mr X knew something I did not. That evening at my London hotel I rang Richard Baerlein and asked him to check with the horse's trainer Bruce. Richard rang back. 'Alex, I've been assured that the horse has never been better.'

My happiness was short-lived. Richard rang me at home on the following day. 'I'm sorry Alex I've got some bad news.'

'What do you mean?'

He paused for a few seconds and said: 'Tromos is coughing and has been withdrawn from the Guineas.'

I had lost my money just a furlong from home. My stake was not enormous, but the sum I stood to win was. The bookies must have been very happy indeed. Within half an hour the telephone rang again. It did not stop ringing all morning. Racing journalists from nearly every daily newspaper in Britain wanted my reaction. What could I say? I told them I was shattered. Finally, Evelyn and I were so fed up with the calls that we decided to go out for some fresh air. We picked up our grandsons Matthew and Mark and took them to Chester Zoo. I was glad to get away and enjoyed the drive there. Mark and Matthew loved the animals, and I tried to lose myself in the antics of the monkeys. As we strolled along, giving peanuts to the boys to throw into the cage, I spotted a familiar face. It was Len Bell, the editor of the *Sporting Chronicle*, who was with his wife. My first reaction was that he had followed me to the zoo, so I made the opening gambit about Tromos. 'It's such a shame he has been withdrawn from the Guineas,' I said.

'Has he?'

I was surprised and relieved when he revealed he had not heard the news.

After some small talk, Len and his wife moved on. I still felt as if I had a heavy weight on my mind. I stared hard at a giant chimpanzee, who was looking at me as he sat on a withered tree trunk in his cage.

'Doesn't he look sad,' I said.

'He certainly does,' said Evelyn gazing at the squashed pitiful look on his face.

'Do you think he knows I have just lost my money on a horse called Tromos?'

We both roared with laughter and I felt a lot better. After all, it was only money.

When Evelyn told Nancy about our zoo outing, she sent me this poem:

> One day last week you may have heard
> Luck ran out for Alex Bird.
> A fortune waiting in the offing
> On the morning Tromos started coughing.
>
> Said Alex: 'Whatever came over me
> To stick my neck out on TV?
> How could I know when I talked to Brough
> That the stupid horse would get the cough?'
>
> Alex was so shattered. He'd nothing to do,
> So he picked up his grandsons and went to the zoo,
> In a cage in a corner he happened to see
> A very disconsolate chimpanzee.
>
> The keeper explained: 'He's really distressed,
> He'd a monkey on Tromos that's gone west.'
>
> Now the chimp and Alex are full of remorse
> That they'd placed such faith in this wonder horse.
> And it grieves them to think that one so classy,
> Could well finish up in a tin of Lassie!

What was really wrong with Tromos I shall never really know. Bruce Hobbs told me the horse was recovering, but apparently he was so ill, it must have been more than just a cough. I am sure he was got at. He became another casualty in the long list of wonder horses that never ran again.

Some time later at Doncaster, I was in the champagne tent at the invitation of Richard Baerlein, when I met Bruce's charming wife,

Mrs Betty Hobbs. We were talking about Tromos's breeding and Stilvi, the dam who was in stud at Newmarket. Mrs Hobbs invited me to see her on my next visit South and said: 'It was such a shame about Tromos. You did know what happened when he went to America where he died?'

'I'm afraid not.'

Apparently an autopsy revealed that the horse's insides were badly seared. In my mind that was confirmation he had been doped.

Doping horses is something I have fought against all my life – and another of my campaigns has been the misuse of the whip. For me there is no sport in subjecting horses, or indeed any animals, to merciless beatings. My feelings can perhaps be summed up by my grandchildren.

One winter's afternoon as I sat talking to the two young boys Mark and Matthew by the fire in my lounge, I explained to them about my letters of protest to the *Sporting Life* over the misuse of the whip and how racing journalist and commentator Peter O'Sullevan felt the same.

'But Grumpy,' said Mark, who was only nine, 'why do they hit horses that are already trying their best?'

What is it they say about 'out of the mouths of babes'?

My first doubts about how sport can be cruel to animals came as long as thirty years ago at a bull fight in Palma, Majorca. I was sickened by the lances that pierced the taunted bulls and by the way the horses were gored in spite of their padding. I turned to Evelyn who sat beside me. She could hardly speak and tears were rolling down her cheeks. She managed to say two words: 'Let's go!'

As we walked away I tried to think of how we treated animals in Britain. Were we as cruel as the Spaniards seemed to be? My mind wandered to fox hunting. But at least the fox had a chance to escape just like the hare did in greyhound coursing. I thought of what I had been told of ponies, working in the depths of the coal mines all their lives, blinded because they had never seen the light of day. Were the British really lily white?

It was not until many years later that I began seriously to wonder about the use of the whip on race horses, and that was partly due to my trainer Towser Gosden. Towser's love for his horses was stronger than his appetite for success, as I was to find out. If there was one thing he could not stand, it was the misuse of the whip. After one of my horses had won a race at Newcastle, Towser looked at the animal in the unsaddling enclosure and gasped: 'Bloody hell, just look at that!' There were several deep whip marks on the horse's flank. Towser waited ten minutes for the well-known jockey to emerge from the weighing room, but he must have had his card marked because he disappeared through the back entrance. I began to feel the same as my trainer. Why should horses trained for the job and trying their hardest be beaten with a whip? What was wrong with hands and heels? From then on my doubts grew.

On 8 November, 1979, Peter O'Sullevan galvanised me into action on the issue.

In his *Daily Express* column headlined: 'You Can't Beat 'Em' he told how television viewers and racegoers were becoming increasingly dissatisfied with the use of the whip and invited readers to air their views. He also told how in Sweden the maximum total length of whip possible was fifty centimetres, which included a thirty centimetre shaft and two three-centimetre wide leather flaps.

'There is no restriction on the length of whip carried in England,' he wrote. 'A sixty-five centimetre to seventy-five centimetre fibreglass whip is normal and there is no restriction on its use except that excessive whipping is regarded as improper riding.'

In Norway the rules were even more protective, he added. There a rider could not remove his hands from the reins, other than to correct a horse who was hanging. On the following Monday, 12 November, he revealed how the readers felt about the issue under the headline: 'Merciful Mercer'.

Joe Mercer, Peter wrote, had been repeatedly commended in a massive response to the whipping debate. The jockey had been singled out for his 'sheer artistry and gentleness'. One fan expressed the hope that in view of the results the jockey had achieved without using the whip, other riders would follow his example.

By 14 November the controversy was in full gallop and Peter was avalanched with mail from readers calling for a special race in which whips were not carried. Soon I was to enter the debate. I felt I had no choice after watching TV coverage of the Irish Sweeps Handicap Hurdle at Leopardstown in late December of that year. I was so shocked at the handling of Deep Gale that I wrote to the *Sporting Life*.

The letter was published on 3 January, 1980. It said:

Dear Sir,

I have not met John McManus, the owner of Deep Gale, who I am told is a very nice man, or Tommy Carmody, whose quiet style of riding puts him for me, at the top of his profession.

I was therefore shocked at the exhibition of Carmody in the Irish Sweeps Handicap Hurdle. I cannot believe that John McManus, no matter how large a bet he had invested, would have wished his horse to be subjected to such a beating.

I can only hope that with Carmody it was a one-off exhibition, never to be repeated.

Peter O'Sullevan, in his campaign to have such excessive use of the whip stamped out, has the full support of all animal lovers and I can only hope that when Carmody has viewed the Leopardstown race on the video, he will accept my criticism as a just one, and revert to his quiet, effective style.

Peter had already referred to the race on 29 December. That day Carmody was riding Wayward Lad in the Panama Cigar Hurdle at Newbury. In his appraisal of the race Peter mentioned that the successful owner would receive a bonus from the sponsor of a case of 1966 claret and the rider a magnum of champagne.

But he added: 'In the event that it is Carmody he should forward his as a peace offering to his Sweeps Hurdle partner Deep Gale, who he subjected to an uncharacteristically hard race at Leopardstown.

'If the normally quiet and outstandingly effective Irish rider studies the video, he may agree that his use of the whip achieved little other than setting a poor example.'

Journalist Valentine Lamb, writing in the *Irish Field*, did not attack Peter O'Sullevan, but he described my letter in the *Life* as an 'uncalled-for slur on a leading National Hunt jockey.' He went on to write: 'Bird burnt his fingers badly in the ante-post market over the 2,000 Guineas favourite Tromos.'

This really had nothing to do with the controversy over the mis-use of the whip, and why he wrote such a thing I do not know to this day. I had backed Tromos at 20–1 and 16–1 to a lot of money and when the horse became odds on, I laid my bet off as I have revealed earlier. That was hardly burning my fingers.

Unfortunately Lamb did not stop there in his attack. He went back twenty years to 1950 and quoted my horse Gambetto who ran at Newbury in a nursery handicap. He wrote: 'Gambetto, after taking a walk in the market from 6–1 to 100–8, proceeded to lead all the way to win by a comfortable length. It was understood afterwards that even the exceptionally strong Jimmy Lindley was unable to restrain Gambetto and ride a waiting race as instructed.'

Richard Baerlein wrote in the *Observer*: 'I do not know what he was trying to get at, but most horses go badly in the market from a bad draw at Newbury, especially in a large field over five furlongs. There were no waiting instructions as Jimmy Lindley will confirm. Valentine Lamb is the only man not in step on this issue.'

Perhaps Lamb thought I criticised Carmody because he was an Irish jockey. I did suggest in a letter to the *Sporting Life* that in view of the fact that one Irish jockey was suspended for three months for excessive use of the whip, and another heavily fined, it might be a good idea to prohibit the use of the whip for the Cheltenham Gold Cup meeting. I realise now that this was an impracticable suggestion as the rules would have had to be changed and re-framed and it would take time. However, I still think this idea should be taken seriously by the Stewards of the Jockey Club. Even if it took two or three years to come to fruition, it would be worth it.

Today my hope is that good sense will prevail and that whips will be banned. There is no substitute for teaching an aspiring jockey to ride without a whip. All kinds of spurious arguments will no doubt be advanced in its support, such as the whip is a balancing pole, or that the horse is lazy.

Some wise words on the issue come from former top jockey Johnnie Gilbert, who became General Manager of the Apprentice School. He said: 'I always tell the youngsters that if they learn to wave a whip correctly they will get the same from a horse as they do when they try to hit him hard. The terrible thing one sees at Fontwell and jumping tracks in particular are ten stone men hitting horses down the stifle as they have never been taught where the whip should land.'

Before the Stewards of the Jockey Club issued their directive on the misuse of the whip, Lester Piggott had given Roberto the full treatment when he won the Derby in 1972. If that Derby were to be re-run tomorrow, I wonder what Lester's thoughts would be a furlong from home. Rheingold, ridden by Ernie Johnson, was in front and looked an assured winner, but he was hanging to the left towards the rails. Lester somehow squeezed Roberto through on the inside of him. Had the Jockey Club directive been in operation then, Lester might have wondered if the prize was worth giving the horse the full treatment. Knowing of Lester's determination and desire to win a Derby, I expect his decision would have been to pull out all the stops and go straight for the line, realising that he would face a ten day suspension. The Jockey Club would have been responsible for this by not handing out a longer suspension for an offence of this kind.

I always remember the career of Diadem, one of the greatest horses of all time. She ran thirty nine races, won twenty four and was placed eleven times. In his book, *Men and Horses I Have Known* the Hon George Lambton said:

'After Diadem's three-year-old career Steve Donoghue was associated with most of her triumphs, and a perfect combination they made. Stephen is a great lover of horses, but I am sure Diadem held first place in his affections and she thoroughly reciprocated it. I have seen her after a hard race as he unsaddled her turn round and rub her nose against his hands – more like a dog than a horse. Win or lose you could not have made Stephen hit her for anything in the world.'

Bernard Carslake, a great jockey of that era, said of Donoghue: 'Stephen can find out more about what is left in his horse with his little finger than most men with their legs and whip.'

When I talk to jockeys or trainers about the misuse of the whip I get mixed reactions. Some even look sympathetically at me as if to say 'what does he know about it?' Maybe they are right.

Finally, I have a great love for all creatures great and small, and this is probably at the root of my loathing for the whip.

In 1980 I was convinced that I had found another Derby winner. His name was Beldale Flutter and was owned by Tony Kelly in partnership with Lord Harrington.

As a two-year-old Beldale Flutter, trained by Michael Jarvis at Newmarket, was an unlucky loser of the Royal Lodge Stakes at Ascot on 27 September. Ridden by Taffy Thomas he came fourth, beaten a length and three quarters. The race was won by Robellino, ridden by John Matthias. A month later, on 25 October, Beldale Flutter was entered for the William Hill Futurity at Doncaster. Pat Eddery was riding him and was opposed by two horses who had finished just in front of him at Ascot – Robellino and Recitation. There was also a horse called Shergar, ridden by Lester Piggott. He had had only one race but was the short-priced favourite. Nevertheless, I backed Beldale to win £15,000. I watched the race with Tony and I have relived it many times in my mind. It looked like a telling run from Shergar, as Lester made his challenge at the distance, but Beldale Flutter drew away from him and won by two and a half lengths. Excuses were made for Recitation and Robellino, and also for Shergar who was considered green. Such excuses were ridiculous – Beldale Flutter won on merit. One journalist wrote in his weekly column that he would not take 50–1 about Beldale Flutter for the following year's 2,000 Guineas. I replied in a letter to the *Sporting Life*, that if he had any spare cash he could lay me the bet. If he did not have any cash, but owned a house, I would arrange a mortgage for him to do so!

Beldale Flutter was slow coming to hand as a three-year-old and in 1980 was beaten in races at Newbury and Newmarket. Both times French jockey, Yves St. Martin, partnered him, but the horse seemed to run better for Eddery than anyone. My confidence grew when I heard that Pat was available for Beldale Flutter's next race, the Mecca Dante Stakes at York on 13 May. It was a Group Two race, and considered the best Derby trial. The rain had softened the ground and as Beldale Flutter had been going well at home, I backed him to win £10,000. I went to the meeting with Tony and had a memorable day. Beldale Flutter won by three quarters of a length from Shotgun, ridden by John Bleasdale. Centurius and Robellino, first and second in the Ladbroke Blue Riband Trial Stakes at Epsom a few weeks before, were left toiling in the rear, and Kalaglow, winner of the 1982 King George and Queen Elizabeth Stakes at Ascot was beaten fifteen lengths. Eight days before the Derby on 3 June, Beldale Flutter took part in a mixed gallop at Newmarket, with two other Derby runners. Beldale Flutter won very easily on the bit. When Eddery dismounted he could not contain his excitement. Instead of the usual discreet talk about the horse's performance with the owner and trainer, he exclaimed: 'That's a flippin' good horse!' Or words very similar.

The following day at Brighton races, Eddery was told that he might have to ride a horse in the Derby trained by Vincent O'Brien, who retained him. The news spread around the course like wildfire. Within an hour Lester Piggott told Michael Jarvis that if Eddery was unavailable, he would take the ride. That was not a bad position for Tony Kelly to be in, having possibly the second best jockey in Britain, with the best jockey in the world standing by.

On 29 May, six days before the Derby, I rang Tony and told him: 'There's only one thing that will stop you winning this race – that's if there is no Derby.'

I stood by the phone watching the rain beating at my lounge window. It had been falling incessantly for days. The only hope of the Derby being run was that Epsom, like Newmarket, was a quick-draining track.

'Alex, I'm just off to morning Mass and I'll ring you when I get back,' said Tony.

I had backed Beldale Flutter to win £38,000 in the Epsom classic and I was reflecting on the other runners when the phone rang about an hour later. Tony was choking as he spoke to me.

'Alex, bad news. Beldale Flutter dislodged his jockey this morning and careered over Newmarket Heath, crashing into Moorestyle.' Moorestyle was a multi-million pound horse owned by Moors Furnishing Ltd. Tony paused for a moment to let me take it in then continued: 'Moorestyle was on the floor injured but Beldale Flutter galloped on until he reached the main road.' Tony paused again. 'He slipped and injured his leg so badly that the vet was brought in and fifty stitches were put in.'

I just could not believe it. For a second, I thought Tony might be pulling my leg, but I quickly realised he couldn't be. Some weeks later at York I met Michael Jarvis by the paddock and he told me the rest of the traumatic story.

The horse was in a state of shock, and so was everyone in the stable. The leading work rider, who had been dislodged, was in tears, and the rest of the boys, who had thought the horse a certainty for the Derby and put all their savings on him, were equally shaken.

'The worst thing was just to look at Beldale Flutter in his box,' said Michael. 'His ribs were badly injured, making it too painful for him to move very much. There was no way he could lie down, which of course was a good thing because it might have caused more damage.'

After twenty four hours in the box, Beldale Flutter was led out. It was thought that the horse would not run again that year. How his trainer got him onto the course at York three and a half months later to contest the Benson and Hedges Gold Cup is a mystery to me. It was a case of dedication, love and tenderness. Michael Jarvis and his staff must be congratulated on that wonderful effort. Before the race I said to Michael: 'He's looking very well.'

'Alex, the horse has been going very well at home and should give a good account of himself.'

However, there was no way I could back him. I went to the stands to watch the race, hoping and praying he would run well. Beldale Flutter, ridden by Pat Eddery, came back from the dead. He won by three quarters of a length from Lester Piggott on Kirtling, with Master Willie, ridden by Philip Waldron, another three quarters of a length away third.

What a marvellous feat of training. Beldale Flutter went on to run in the Arc de Triomphe in October, but the hurly-burly of the race was too much for him. It was understandable that he should have developed a nervous tendency after such a terrible accident. His last race was the Laurel Park International in America on 7 November. He was unplaced. It was a very short, crowded track and again, although he ran well, the close proximity of the other horses completely unnerved him. That was the end of his racing career. Now he is at stud in Newmarket. Whether he would have won the Derby remains an open question.

It was won by Shergar, ridden by Walter Swinburn. He won by ten lengths from Glint of Gold, partnered by John Matthias, with Geoff Baxter on Scintillating two lengths away in third. Tony and I watched the race together and as we walked down from the stands I said: 'Whatever happened, we would not have beaten that.' Some weeks later though I talked to Pat Eddery at Haydock Park. He had ridden Riberetto in the Epsom classic, the horse who had been well beaten in Beldale Flutter's wonderful gallop just before the accident. Eddery said: 'Apart from Shergar, the rest of the field were moderate, and I still think we would have won.'

In 1981, the *Sun* newspaper and Coral bookmakers staged a computerised race to find the best Derby winner since the war. Called the Computer Classic, the odds were given for each horse and readers could back their fancy with the bookmaker. Shortly before the event, the paper's racing editor, Terry Clark, rang me at home, and asked what my all-time Derby winner would be. I had no hesitation in telling him. The headlines the next morning read:

'Alex Bird, Britain's No. 1 professional punter, picks Mill Reef.'

However, the man compiling the odds for Corals did not share my view. He set Mill Reef's price at 20–1. Nevertheless the next day the headlines proclaimed: '*Sun* punters follow Alex Bird.' The horse had been backed down to 8–1.

The race was staged and Mill Reef, ridden by Geoff Lewis, won. Henbit, ridden by Greville Starkey was second and third was Lester Piggott on Nijinsky.

Not long after the *Sun* race I read an advertisement in the *Sporting Life*. It said: 'Are you a losing punter? If so, contact Terry Myers, professional backer and rails bookmaker, at this address.' Myers was flying high, but his success was short-lived, and at considerable cost to me.

The majority of my bets at starting price were placed away from the course, but it is important to explain how the system works, from the standpoint of the bookmaker. Long ago, racing consisted of matches: two horses running against each other. Such events were exclusive to the landed gentry who would wager against each other. Later, as the fields grew bigger, the first bookmakers appeared on the scene. Their reasoning was simple. If they thought all the horses in a five-runner race had equal chances, they went 3–1 against each of them. So by laying three units to one against each horse, they had a holding of five points. Whichever horse won meant they paid out four points. That left one point for them, representing a twenty percent profit. Betting, of course, does not always follow such an orderly pattern. Today, sometimes the 3–1 chance may be $3\frac{1}{2}$–1, maybe another horse becomes 2–1, and so on, but even so it averages out at 3–1 the field, and there is still a twenty percent profit for the bookmaker. Sometimes of course, the bookmakers lose heavily, but overall, if a bookmaker can maintain just a five percent profit on a bad spell, he is happy, and this is what they all aim for.

It does seem ironic, however, that bookmakers on a racecourse, who are responsible for a healthy betting market, are furnishing the returns for the bookmakers away from the track. It is like the tail wagging the dog, because the racecourse market constitutes just five percent of the whole of the betting. The other ninety five percent is away from the course, on credit accounts or in betting shops. So the on-course bookmakers have a lot of power, as small as their market might be. Two press representatives are responsible for returning the starting prices of the on-course bookmakers, one from the *Sporting Life* and the other from the *Sporting Chronicle*. These men are beyond reproach. Their job is difficult for they have to be fair, both to the bookmakers away from the track and the punters who bet with them. If some bookmakers are offering 3–1 on a horse at the finish, and others $2\frac{1}{2}$–1, the SP reporters compromise, and return the horse at $2\frac{3}{4}$–1. I have never known an SP reporter to stray from the straight and narrow, even though they must be a target for bribery by backers who want longer odds. On the other side of the coin, they could be the target for bookmakers who have heavy commitments away from the course, and want a horse returned at a shorter price.

I have revealed the story of bookmaker Harry 'Snouty' Parker's system of backing a horse off course, and then extending odds on course so that the price would be returned by the SP reporters. Myers was another exponent of this knock-out system, in the Midlands in 1982.

Because of the desirability of spreading his bets away from the track, and also to avoid paying tax on them, he put an advertisement in the *Life*. The idea was to recruit punters who would back horses for him through private accounts. They would invest his money and not charge him tax, and they would benefit by putting their own cash on his selections. Once a horse was backed he would extend the odds on the course. I met Myers at Wolverhampton races. The flamboyant card-playing bookie from Beeston near Nottingham, seemed an amiable chap. And his theory had merit. He was forty four and had a reputation for always being immaculately turned out. He first became famous as a dog layer at Derby and rose to the top rails position at Midland racecourses. He told me that he had hundreds of private punters and as he could bet with them without tax, he would accept my wagers, charging me just four percent. It seemed a good business proposition, against the ten percent tax on starting price business, and I took up his offer. Things went well for a time but then I saw a

225

warning light. Myers owed me almost £10,000 and his cheque was days overdue. I phoned him at his office and threatened to 'Put him in the rooms'. That meant report him to the Tattersalls Committee as a defaulter.

'I've been having cash problems but everything is all right now,' he said. 'I'll send you a cheque immediately.'

It arrived ten days after it was due.

I was still suspicious and asked the bank to find out quickly if the cheque would be honoured. My bank manager contacted Myer's bank. He was told that the cheque had been stopped that morning. Again I rang Myers's office. An assistant promised that another cheque would be sent. It arrived by recorded delivery the following morning, but it was postdated for fourteen days later. I had no alternative but to wait until I could cash it. Inevitably, that cheque was stopped too. So I reported Myers as a defaulter. I contacted the National Association of Bookmakers in Leeds, where the pitch committee sits. They are the officials who allocate pitches for the bookmakers on courses throughout Britain.

From that day Myers was stopped from betting on a racecourse. Then I put in my complaint to the Tattersalls Committee. A seven-day order to warn Myers off every racecourse in the world with which Tattersalls have an agreement was issued, but he had already fled his home. Myers still owes me the money to this day. The last I heard of him was that he had gone to Australia. He did return secretly for a few days I understand, but before I had time to issue a writ he had again flown the nest.

All in all 1982 was very eventful for me, but I remember it mostly because it was the year that another super horse entered my life. His name was Gorytus.

I first saw the son of Nijinsky run in the seven-furlong Acomb Stakes at York on 17 August, 1982. Trained by Dick Hern, and owned by Mrs Alice Mills, Gorytus was an unraced two-year-old and not particularly well fancied. I studied him in the paddock, and even with Willie Carson riding him was not particularly impressed. The horse who caught my attention was Salieri, the 2–1 on favourite, ridden by Lester Piggott and trained by Henry Cecil, the son-in-law of Sir Noel Murless. Salieri had won his two previous races by a distance, first at Newmarket and then at Goodwood. The general feeling around the paddock as the horses went to the start was that Lester was unbeatable.

The going was good and I watched the race from the top of the stands. Gorytus, at 5–1, left the stalls like a rocket and nothing could touch him. He crossed the line to win by seven lengths from Salieri. I was amazed along with everyone else, but I soon put the race from my mind, thinking that Salieri had just had an off day. When I saw the official time for the race later that day, however, I was startled out of my apathy. It was one minute twenty three point seventy three seconds, a course record; the previous best was one minute twenty four seconds. I was sure there had been a mistake, it was too fast. Racecourse Technical Services had ironed out their teething troubles, largely due to my battle with them in the early years, but I still thought the time listed on the board was a misprint.

'I just can't believe the time of Gorytus in the Acomb Stakes,' I told Richard Baerlein, when I met him by the rails bookmakers shortly before the fifth. 'Someone has slipped up.'

We decided to check it out and spent a hectic ten minutes dashing about the course trying to find out where the recorder was placed. John Sanderson, the racecourse manager, directed us to the RTS van outside the paddock and from there we went to a vantage point on the stand, where the machine operated. The official in charge double-checked the result. It was correct. We had missed the fifth race but it was worth it. Now I knew Gorytus offered an opportunity too good to miss.

'I'm going to back this horse for next year's 2,000 Guineas and Derby,' I told Richard. 'Nothing will beat him.'

'Why don't you place a bet with this new bookmaking firm Esal,' he replied. 'They're offering 33–1.'

Richard often placed ante-post bets for me so I asked him to get £100,000 to £3,000 for the Guineas. He agreed, and I returned home leaving him at York for the three-day meeting, with high hopes for my forthcoming investment. That evening Richard rang me from his hotel.

'There's good news and bad news,' he said.

'Give me the bad news first.'

'The Esal representative will not lay you the bet because you do not have an account. The good news is, he is arranging for you to open one immediately.' I was surprised, for it had not been necessary for me to open an account with a bookmaker for thirty years. Was something wrong? Or was it just my suspicious nature? I patiently waited to hear from Esal. A few days later I received an application form and lost no time in returning it duly completed. The following week, I opened Esal's reply over breakfast. Their letter was short and to the point. They refused to let me open an account. It was the first time a bookmaker had ever banned me from doing so.

There was no explanation; there never was in these matters. My credit was good and my reputation for honouring bets irrefutable. So what could be wrong? I found out a few weeks later from a friend, Colin Ingleby Mackenzie, the former England cricketer and captain of Hampshire who led his team to their first county championship in 1961. He told me that he was at Doncaster as a guest of Esal, who were sponsoring a race. Over lunch in the company's private box, Colin mentioned to one of the firm's top executives that I had not been allowed to open an account with them. The executive, who knew about it, said: 'I'm afraid we couldn't allow Mr Bird to bet with us because he's an habitual winner!'

Gorytus next ran in the top class Laurent Perrier Stakes over seven furlongs, at Doncaster on 10 September. In the past this race had proved to me that J.O. Tobin and Ribofilio were classics candidates. Gorytus, again ridden by Willie Carson, won by an impressive five lengths from Proclaim, ridden by Greville Starkey. There was no doubt in my mind that Gorytus was the best horse I had seen for ten years. Later that day I saw the William Hill representative on the course, and put £2,000 on him at 5–1 for the 1983 2,000 Guineas, and a further £1,600 on him to win £10,000 for the Derby.

On 15 October my wonder horse Gorytus ran in the £37,747 William Hill Dewhurst Stakes over seven furlongs at Newmarket, a top class race for classic two-year-olds.

Although he was opposed by another good Henry Cecil horse, Diesis, ridden by Lester Piggott, I was so confident of the outcome that I put £4,000 on him at a short price. That day I was too busy to fly to Newmarket, so I watched the race on TV. I clicked my watch on the instant the stalls opened, and for the first two furlongs I watched with approval as Carson held Gorytus up. When he made his move I could not believe my eyes. Gorytus began to stagger and rapidly lost ground. I stood up shaking my head in disbelief as Carson almost pulled him up, and he trailed in a pathetic last in the four-horse race. He was so far behind that the judge could not even record an official distance. Trainer Dick Hern and jockey Carson were summoned before the Newmarket stewards, but they could offer no explanation for the horse's dismal performance. Gorytus, staggering around, distressed and exhausted after the race, was given a dope test. A spokesman for the security service stated: 'It appears that no person tampered with Gorytus at his Berkshire stables, or at the Newmarket course, and that includes the time between the horse leaving the paddock and the start of the race.'

Eight days later the incredible Gorytus story began to unfold. On 23 October, at Doncaster, I met Snowy Chalmers by the rails bookmakers. Snowy, in his seventies, was a regular racegoer, well known and respected by trainers, owners, jockeys and bookmakers. He loved to back horses but was content with just a ten or twenty pounds bet. I had previously told him how impressed I had been with Gorytus, and he had a few pounds on the horse with me for the 1983 2,000 Guineas and Derby. That afternoon I mentioned the mysterious performance of Gorytus in the Dewhurst Stakes. Snowy had been at Newmarket and I was shocked over what he told me. Apparently five minutes before the start, he had been in the stand with trainers Denys Smith and Ryan Price when a Scandinavian vet, well known at Newmarket, approached them.

Snowy said: 'The vet asked what horse I had backed. I told him that I had not had a bet but that I fancied Gorytus, and had put a few quid on him for the Derby, with Alex Bird. Then he told me it was a good job I hadn't backed the horse that day because I would have lost my money!'

Snowy continued: 'He told me that Gorytus had fouled so much just before entering the paddock he didn't have a chance of winning. The vet had never seen so much excreta from one horse!'

My mind started working overtime. What Snowy was saying was matching a jigsaw of facts.

'After that pathetic run by Gorytus, the vet took me to the place where the horse had fouled and I was shocked,' said Snowy. 'Very few people had seen what had happened, because it was away from the paddock.'

I went over the events and I deeply regretted that I had not been able to go to Newmarket on that fateful day. If I had done, Snowy would have alerted me to the condition Gorytus was in and I would have reported my suspicions to the stewards immediately. The little bits of information I had acquired over the years added up to just one thing: Gorytus had been got at. Somehow someone had given him the strong purgative, croton oil, used by vets treating rhinos and elephants. Although the results of the dope tests had not yet been announced, I knew they would be negative. Croton oil is not a drug, and would not show up in the normal way.

One clue came from another friend of mine, businessman George Paul. He had just returned from a trip to Australia with an interesting little tale. He told me that he had met a man in a Sydney bar, who had just been released from jail in England, where he had served a sentence for horse doping. The case made headline news and now the man – I shall call him Johnny – was living it up.

'The more wine I gave him, the more he talked about Pinturischio,' said George.

On 13 April 1961, three-year-old Pinturischio, owned by Sir Victor Sassoon, and trained by Noel Murless, ran in the Wood Ditton Stakes at Newmarket over a mile. The horse, which never ran as a two-year-old, started at 5–2 on, and was ridden by Lester Piggott. He won in a canter. The horse's reputation spread, and he was rumoured to be the best horse Murless had ever trained. On 26 April 1961, Lester rode Pinturischio in the 2,000 Guineas. The 7–4 favourite was unluckily beaten by two lengths. The reason was that he was still green, but that did not deter the punters. The horse immediately became short-price favourite for the Derby.

'About six weeks before the Derby, Pinturischio was found doped in his stables, and it was the handiwork of my new acquaintance in Sydney, Johnny,' said George. 'His paymaster was a bookmaker!'

I raised my eyebrows when George told me the name of the man, for I knew him personally.

'The only trouble was that Pinturischio began to recover, much to Johnny's dismay – and the bookmaker's,' George added. 'The horse again became clear favourite for the race, but when Johnny tried to get his money for doping the horse his paymaster refused to pay up and told him to go back and do a proper job. The doper had no alternative but to return with his gang. The raiders arrived at the stables in the dead of night and were dismayed to see a watchman warming himself over a brazier outside Pinturischio's box. Apparently Murless had put a twenty four-hour guard on the horse, after being tipped off by William Hill that the horse would be doped again. One of Johnny's men crept round to the rear of the stables and hurled a brick onto the roof of the box. The watchman leapt to his feet, grabbed an iron bar, and went round the back of the building to investigate. As soon as he was out of sight, Johnny slipped into the box, and forced a capsule of the potent croton oil into Pinturischio's mouth. He left as quickly as he went in, and the watchman was none the wiser!'

The purgative was so strong it almost killed the horse, and he was withdrawn from the Derby. Some time later he did run again, but he was just a pathetic shadow of his former self. When I realised the similarity between the case of Pinturischio and Gorytus after seeing Snowy, I went immediately to the Jockey Club representative and told him of my suspicions. The following day, the telephone rang at my home. It was Bob Anderson, the chief Jockey Club Investigator.

'Alex, I have checked your claim about Pinturischio and you are correct, the horse was given croton oil and purged himself in the same way as Gorytus. We will follow up your claim and get back to you.'

I was not confident that we would discover the truth. It was too late. The horse's excreta should have been examined on that fateful day. A week later, Bob rang back. His investigations had solved nothing and the dope tests were negative, as I expected. Bob explained that the man in charge of Gorytus was elderly and one hundred percent trustworthy, and so it has remained a mystery to this day. The Jockey Club closed their files on the case and I felt foolish for alerting them to my suspicions.

I turned my mind to other matters. It was at this time that I began to grow concerned over the increasing fortunes of the bookmakers due to their trimming of the starting price returns. In my heart I could still not understand why punters kept flocking to the betting shops.

I had never personally had a bet in one. When I worked with my father, the average punter lost eight percent of his stake. Out of that, the bookmaker paid five percent in collecting fees to agents and overheads, making a net profit of three percent. Today, the average betting shop punter loses up to twenty two percent. Out of that, the bookmaker pays an eight percent tax and one percent levy, leaving thirteen percent profit. There are several reasons for the bookmakers' increase in profits. Firstly, the starting price returns have been pruned, allegedly for easy calculations when decimalisation was introduced. A horse returned in pre-tax days at 100–8, which was $12\frac{1}{2}$–1, is now priced at 12–1, and so it goes on along the line – 100–9, 100–7 etc.

All these prices have been trimmed to the detriment of the punter, and the place odds have also been cut. The pre-tax place odds were one quarter – now they are one fifth the odds. Races below a certain number of runners, used to be one third the odds, now they are one quarter. A new imposition came when one of the big four bookmakers, Corals, decided to charge a sixth of the odds a place, instead of one fifth in certain races. The other three members of BOLA waited to see the reaction from the punters. In November 1982 I protested against this tactic in letters to the *Sporting Life* and *Sporting Chronicle*. The *Sporting Chronicle* published my letter, but the editor of the *Life* declined to do so.

Who knows, if the *Sporting Life*, with its bigger circulation, had published my letter, the other three bookmakers, Hill, Ladbrokes and Mecca, might not have followed suit on the place odds, because when there was no public outcry, they jumped on the bandwagon too. Nevertheless I am glad to say that they are on their own in this and most of the other bookmakers are still betting at the old prices.

It was the top four bookmakers who made the first move in charging ten percent tax. It had previously been an eight percent tax, and one percent levy. The reason they gave was that overheads had increased so much, it was the only economical way to run their businesses.

I have never believed that. Their move did not affect me directly, for I never paid the nine percent. I hardly ever paid more than the four percent racecourse tax. The only exception was when attractive ante-post odds were being offered by bookmakers when I was not at the track; I would then bet with a ten percent deduction. For example, if I considered that the horse's chances were 10–1 and the bookmaker was offering 20–1, it was still good value even with an inflated tax deduction.

However, I felt I still had to protest about the new charges. I wrote to the *Sporting Life* saying that punters should not accept this new imposition. They should shop around to find bookmakers who charged less. I suggested that backers should form their own organisation, called the Punters Protection Association. To become a member, a punter could buy a bond worth, say, one hundred pounds. This would be the maximum value of his credit for betting purposes. Once he lost that he would have to renew his bond, but there would be no limit to the number of bonds a punter could buy. If he was a £1,000 backer, he could buy ten bonds. The money would be invested, and at the end of the year the punter would be entitled to a share in the dividend, or rather, the interest on the bond investment. Then, there would be no reason why the tax deduction should not be reduced to eight percent. So the punter would profit whatever happened. The *Sunday Times* was interested in my proposition and carried a leading article on the centre pages. Then the BBC tuned into my theory and the big bookmakers got really alarmed.

The *Sporting Life*, which initially refused to accept advertisements offering a lesser percentage deduction, changed tack and began to take them from newly-formed bookmakers. Had I been a younger man, I would have been delighted to form the Punters Protection Association, but I realise that if it prospered in a big way, to the detriment of the large firms, they would reduce their tax deduction temporarily, and the punters might drift back to them.

When my association collapsed, they would probably raise the tax again. For in the end the big bookmakers always win. They were unabashed at my protests over the extra tax deductions they were making from winnings.

Peter George of Ladbrokes announced in *The Times*: 'I can think of a number of bookmakers Bird could purchase for a nominal amount and he wouldn't be able to buy his wife a hat off the profits!'

The bookmakers justified the ten percent take by saying that on top of the Chancellor's eight percent, they had to contribute 0.9 percent of their takings to the Horserace Betting Levy Board, which uses the money to boost prize money and finance racecourse improvements. They also said their costs were rising. The *Sporting Life* which adorned the walls of every shop went up from twenty five pence to forty pence and staff were demanding higher wages, they said.

But they could not pull the wool over my eyes. I pointed out that there was still no justification for them in taking the extra half percent; for more than half the money staked in off-course bets was placed 'tax paid'! That meant that the bookies collected ten percent of what the punter staked – not what he collected.

That year I was pleased to learn that Beard, my trusted loyal butler at Aintree, was still working, even though he was in his seventies. He was still helping the Royals on the big occasions, such as the trooping of the colour or state visits, like American President Ronald Reagan's historic trip to England.

It was on 26 April, 1983 that I sat at home reading an article in the *Sporting Life* that sealed the Gorytus case for me. It was about Charles Frank M.R.C.V.S., one of Britain's leading veterinary surgeons, and an expert on horse doping. Frank, giving his views on the Gorytus affair, said: 'I have only ever seen one horse exhibit similar symptons to Gorytus, and that was Ribofilio, when he was short-priced favourite for the 2,000 Guineas in 1969.'

When I read the next sentence I was stunned. For he went on to reveal that Ribofilio had purged himself too, just before the classic race. I had never known that, but Frank rejected the view of myself and Richard Baerlein that Gorytus was got at. He said: 'If you give a horse a purgative, it will not purge just once. It will go on purging for several hours afterwards.' However, the eminent vet did not know the background to the Ribofilio case as I did. Now I was sure that Ribofilio too had been given croton oil. I wondered whether to go back to the Jockey Club again and report my suspicions. I decided against it, even though I had heard a report that, if it were true, prompted me to be even more suspicious.

On the month of Gorytus's pathetic run in the William Hill Dewhurst Stakes a vet's van was raided near his Berkshire stables. Several large bottles of croton oil were taken.

As I reflect on the racing dopers I have begun to put another horse into that sphere too. He was the £3 million Try My Best, ridden by Lester in the 1978 2,000 Guineas at Newmarket. He shocked the racing world and his trainer Vincent O'Brien when he was unplaced behind the 28–1 outsider Roland Gardens which cost only 3,200 guineas as a yearling. In the enclosure after the race, Try My Best's owner Patrick Gallagher could only say to O'Brien, 'Come on Vincent, it's brandy time.'

The trainer's explanation for the horse's dismal performance was: 'He was sickening when he ran, he must have been, otherwise he would never have gone as badly as that! He was listless and lost weight after the race.'

Gallagher said: 'The horse was not right on the day. Of that, there is no doubt. He purged himself on the way to the ring itself. He was also sweating up and was very much on his toes, behaving quite differently from any previous race. I believe he was the victim of a virus. His performance could not be explained away by the going alone.'

So was Try My Best got at too? The debate goes on. The horse never ran again, and was retired to stud. O'Brien explained: 'After the Guineas I had to give him a rest. When I started to do a bit with him again, he didn't stand up to anything.'

11

WHEN PEOPLE ASKED me what I would do when I retired I always used to reply: 'Go racing!' At the height of my career I went racing six days a week on the flat. I did not go so often in the winter because I always went abroad for two months holiday.

Today I go racing fifty days a year, which I suppose one could call semi-retirement. Because of the betting tax, I have drastically curtailed my betting activities and my turnover does not exceed £250,000 a year, a big drop from the years when I turned over two million pounds. My staking method is similar, but I have to be more selective. I now have one bet for every eight I had in those pre-tax days.

Today I understand that the Big Four members of BOLA want more control over starting prices now that the contract between EXTEL and the *Sporting Life/Sporting Chronicle* has expired.

For more than forty years the men from the *Life* and *Chronicle* have had their representatives on the course jotting down bets and prices and returning them to their customers, with a little give and take. Although the *Chronicle* no longer exists, their men are still retained for the job.

As I have explained in my book, the punter has been hit time and again by the bookmakers trimming the place odds from a quarter to a fifth and to a sixth if the favourite starts at odds on. He has seen the bookies take more of the cream for themselves when the tax went up, and to top it all along came computerised betting, introduced for straight forecasts.

Now the bookmakers want to inflict this new starting price imposition on the punter, but if they ever get a say in the starting price return, I have vowed to retire from betting altogether, and I believe fifty per cent of the punters would go with me.

I sold the last of my racehorses when trainer Rae Johnstone died and I thought that would be the end of my non-clinical approach to the form book. I say that because, no matter how hard one tries, it is human nature to make geese out of swans, and perhaps that is why I never made a lot of money with my own horses.

I have had my odd big wins on them, the biggest of course being Signification on that memorable Grand National Day in 1952. Precious Heather landed me quite a few big bets, but on the whole I lost money with my own horses, by the time I add up the cost of training fees and other extras like payments for jockeys.

Of all the National Hunt jockeys I have studied one is outstanding – John Francome. His quiet style of riding is most deceptive. He never hurries a horse in the early stages of the race, but always has him handy and does not give an inch to others. He is a rails man. His very nonchalance makes him a ready target for the stewards, and I lost count of the number of times he has been in front of them for apparently 'not trying'. Many jockeys would let such experiences affect them psychologically, but not John. He will never resort to pushing and shoving in the early stages of a race no matter what the stewards think. In fact, the more times he faces the stewards the more patient, quiet and skilful he becomes.

Had anyone said to me in my youth that I would go ten years without attending a football match I would have considered it an impossibility. I realize that soccer has speeded up and is now a different game. Matt Busby has said to me more than once that the teams of yesteryear would have no chance with the players of today and that not even the genius of men like Tom Finney and Stanley Matthews could balance the scales. I did, however, prefer the open play of those days and the only player of the last two decades who gave me untold delight was that wayward character George Best, who I considered the greatest footballer of all time.

I saw the last six cup finals at Wembley before the war and I have been about sixteen times since, but now I have become disenchanted with the big event in the soccer calendar. I enjoyed the community singing before the match, especially 'Abide With Me'. In those days everyone took their hats off, stood up and sang. Now there is so much noise and hooliganism, that even that moment is spoiled. Peoples' cars are no longer safe in the car parks, radio aerials are bent out of shape and paintwork scratched by the mindless vandals. The last time I went to see Manchester United at Old Trafford there was an argument between a middle-aged driver and a crowd of youths. One of the youngsters picked up a brick and smashed the windscreen of his family saloon.

Soccer players also love racing, I have discovered.

I remember in August 1982 sitting next to former England and Liverpool captain Emlyn Hughes during the William Hill luncheon at York races; he told me: 'Alex, people will never understand this, but I got a bigger thrill out of owning a little horse that won a race at Uttoxeter, than any of my great footballing moments.'

Apart from me, I cannot think of anyone who could enter into the same league of oyster eaters in the racing world, other than the *Observer*'s top racing journalist Richard Baerlein. A little while ago he invited me to an oyster party at his home in Chesham, Bucks. As I was at Haydock races during the day, I had a plane waiting to take me to his house, but during the afternoon the weather deteriorated. By the time the last race was run, the low cloud and mist obliterated all but the last furlong on the course. It was impossible to make the trip south. The next morning I telephoned Richard to see how the party had gone.

'Pretty well,' he said. 'We finished one barrel of oysters but the second is still unopened. I'm very disappointed you couldn't come. You and I could have finished it.' We would have as well. Even if there are forty dozen oysters in a barrel!

I wonder whether if I owned a racehorse nowadays I would be treated differently by many officials in the racing game. The Jockey Club has gone through a difficult time, and today has

finally realised that there is a need for change and a more repre-
entative membership. The stewards are now, in the main, a vast
improvement on the old brigade. I have vivid memories of the
days when it was necessary almost to go down on bended knees
before a steward of the Jockey Club to beg a counter signature
on a voucher, before a guest of a member could be admitted into
the Members Enclosure at Newmarket. A frosty-faced old gentleman would finally grudgingly oblige. No pleasantries would be
exchanged. Many of the sons of the last generation of stewards
are now friends of mine, particularly in the north. However,
memories linger and owning a horse would no longer give me any
pleasure.

Many well-schemed tactics have been tried to beat the bookies.
Even as I write some master plan is being formed. Not long ago a
leading owner and backer I shall call Mr X had a horse running at a
small National Hunt meeting. He was faced with my age-old
problem – how to get enough money on his horse. Finally, he
decided to enter two of his other horses in different races at
different meetings on the same day. Then he organised a team of
men to take in scores of betting shops and back his horses in three
doubles and a treble. That meant there was no big single bet on his
first horse. All the bets were linked and the bookmakers were
disarmed, but although Mr X had declared his other two horses he
never ran them. When the horse he backed in the first place won,
the bookmakers discovered they were holding a big stake, and hit
the roof.

Had there not been such a huge outcry from them Mr X would
merely have been fined twenty five pounds for not running his two
horses. Instead the case went to court and the man lost. The
stewards of the Jockey Club warned him off the Turf. Apart from a
few isolated instances, the bookmakers did not pay. Had the horse
lost, the bookmakers would have kept the money however.

I would not dispute the fact that the stewards had to take a
serious view of the case, but the warning off was severe. Had Mr X
carried out his plan twenty years ago nothing would have been said.

The bookies must learn that they cannot have their cake and eat it every time.

When my friend, builder Tony Kelly, asked me not long ago to hold a watching brief on his horses, not to manage them, but to advise him generally, I agreed. He has had phenomenal success in those few years and the horses were initially prefixed by the name Beldale, taken from his company Beldale Homes. I kept telling him that in this day and age, he had no chance of continuing to buy and sell horses at a profit as he had been doing. However, I am delighted to have been proved wrong. All of his horses are purchased in America and his trainer Michael Jarvis and Joss Collins of the British Bloodstock Agency, buy them for him. But they have got to agree on breeding, conformation, action and price. Those horses do not all win races but the percentage rate of their success is high, when one considers that some owners have horses for twenty years and never have a winner. I would not dare interfere in the face of such professionalism, but I do feel that I have helped in advising Tony on the various times put up by his horses.

Today, apart from meetings easily accessible to me such as Haydock Park, Chester, Liverpool, Doncaster and York, the only time I go racing is with Tony when he has a runner. Then we will fly to the course.

I live, as I have said, in a fifteenth century mansion house. In the summer I am up at 5.00am when I feed my pointer Patch, the trout, ducks and geese. I have always said that if worrying did any good, I would be the world's greatest worrier. They say that it is the worriers who cannot sleep, and yet I, who have never worried about anything, have never been a sleeper. Early in the morning while everyone else is slumbering I wander around looking rather like a tramp. One day I came across two youths fishing, and I rushed across to them while restraining my dog.

'Haven't you seen this notice?' I roared, pointing to the board that said: 'No fishing, guard dog patrol!' They hurriedly gathered their tackle together, nervously eyeing Patch. Panic-stricken they leapt over the wall, onto the pavement. Then, looking up at me through their manes of unkempt hair, they shouted:

'Anyone would think you owned the bleedin' place!' I was furious, and almost chased them. Then I looked at myself and realised my appearance was that of a tramp. I could not even be mistaken for one of the gardeners!

One of my problems is that I cannot get a window cleaner for the hundred or so windows in The Old Hall. Every six months Evelyn threatens to leave me unless they are cleaned. I keep trying to explain that a misty window is in keeping with our fifteenth century home. One day even I could stand them no longer. So I got the punt out and made my way across the moat with my bucket, window leather and ladder. Slowly I manoeuvred the boat alongside the mansion and tied it by rope to a drainpipe. Then I jammed the bottom of the ladder in the punt and the top reached the second storey windows nicely. Bucket in left hand, window leather in right, I started my cleaning. It was so easy I wondered why I had left it so long. Suddenly to my alarm, I felt the ladder coming away from the wall. The rope had frayed right through. My worst fears came true and I plunged into the murky water between the house and the boat. I swam ashore, vowing never to clean the windows again.

Nancy Thornton later sent me this rhyme.

> The horses don't run so fast any more,
> and growing potatoes can be such a bore,
> So Alex decided he might have a go
> At the job that George Formby did once long ago.
>
> He gathered his tackle but forgot what he ought'er
> That no one but Jesus could walk upon water.
> The rope came adrift and quick as a wink,
> He slid down the ladder and fell in the drink.
>
> Down in the village his splashdown was heard,
> And the ducks in the lake said
> 'Here comes a strange "BIRD"'

He rose to the top with some well chosen phrases,
Weeds festooned his head and some other strange places,
He stripped off his clothes and he ran round the lawn,
Looking nearly the same as the day he was born!
Although it was cold, he kept his composure,
But the Cops ran him in for Indecent Exposure.

Now it's dark and it's gloom inside The Old Hall,
If you look through the windows you can't see at all,
But when next they are cleaned, between you and me,
Whoever may do it, it won't be A.B.

Dear Nancy, her poems have always helped me see the funny side
of life. Her husband, my great friend Bill Thornton, died recently.
For thirty years he rang me every day. How I miss those calls, and
how I wish I had Nancy's gift of words so that I could somehow ease
her sorrow.

FOLLOW THE BIRD

ONE THING I did not want to do when I started this book was to advise readers on how to bet and win. Today betting tax has curtailed the profits of those who want to make racing pay. My publishers, however, asked me to devote a chapter to what the future holds for dreamers of fortune – although I almost called them 'compulsive gamblers'.

If the non-backer, who pays me the compliment of reading my autobiography, will bear with me for the next few pages, I will attempt to show how punters will be made to feel unwelcome in their local betting shops. Should this book stray to parts of the world where betting on English racing is legal, and no betting tax is chargeable, the chances of showing a profit are great. But remember these golden rules . . .

The punter must never back in handicaps. Handicaps are now computerised and these days there is less chance of a handicapper making a mistake. If he does so the bookmakers who formulate the odds will be well aware of this. The aim of handicappers is to adjust the weights so that the whole field will dead heat. That is obviously impossible but with the starting price bookmakers betting to a profit margin of between ten and fifty percent, betting on these races is strictly for the mug punter.

If your calculations are based on times, do not rely on times which are not electrically operated. There are very few watch holders reporting for the sporting press who are one hundred percent reliable. A high wind, a slight diversion or bad visibility could make a difference of a second or more and when one considers that a second is equivalent to five lengths, it does not take

244

a mathematician to work out what effect that would have on one's calculations. Even electric timing could have its pitfalls in that heavy rain during racing may affect the going considerably, and the difference between the first race and the last is incalculable. So if a backer is placing full reliance on times, it is important that he should read an account of the day's racing in a paper like the *Sporting Life*. On this subject never compare times for races run on different days, even if the going report is the same, as conditions such as wind and humidity can change so rapidly in Britain.

Finally, do not rely on times when the fields are very small because a false pace can be set as jockeys wait on each other.

If you have backed a horse which has become involved in a photo finish, never hedge or save your money if your horse is on the near side. If the horse on the far side *has* won, the odds will be prohibitive and virtually unbackable. If you are standing on the finishing line at a race meeting and you think the horse nearest to you has won, you will be right nine times out of ten.

Do not make a habit of backing horses on the first show. The opening prices are generally cramped as the bookmakers are virtually sparring for an opening, and the percentage of profit is very high. One has only to look at the prices on TV. Almost all of the runners increase in price, especially on a Saturday when there are several meetings where the market is weak.

There are certain races where the punter has a definite advantage. These are non-handicap races where the bookmaker is reluctant to bet on an each-way basis. The punter risks having his account closed or being turned away from the betting shop if he is seen to be too success-ful. Where the punter scores is to confine his betting each way in fields not too unwieldy; say eight, nine or ten runners, with a limited number of form horses. Then, opposing the favourite, he should back the second or third fancy each way in a single bet, doubles, trebles or accumulator. Imagine for example that the horses he nominates for the day average 5–1 for a win, the place position works out at evens, which saves the win stake. Two horses placed 3–1, three horses placed 7–1 and the four placed 15–1. If we accept the fact that on the law of averages one of the 5–1 horses wins one in six, the win portion of the bet will show a slight loss. But this is more than made up by the profit on the place bets if we calculate that three out of four will be placed. But he must omit the first and last months as it is generally early May before the form settles down and in mid-October and early November the heavy going unsettles form.

There is of course no guarantee that this method of backing will show a profit. The most important factor is to exercise patience, as one can go several days without the requisite form horses engaged. For instance the week of Royal Ascot is hopeless, and if one has to have a bet I would advise cutting one's stake to a tenth of normal and forgetting about my system.

Do not bet at meetings where the percentage of profit to bookmakers is unfair to punters. On Grade One courses like Newmarket and Haydock, it is generally fair, averaging fifteen to twenty percent in the bookmakers' favour. At holiday meetings and grade three courses, especially in winter when the attendance is sparse, we get a different picture. I noted at a northern track in early January 1984 that it was over one hundred per cent against the backer on the starting price returns. Those figures speak for themselves, and anyone who bets and accepts such prices is in my opinion a candidate for the lunatic asylum.

When the going changes from firm to heavy, the punter must button up his pocket. My bookmaker father used to look up at the sky in mid-summer and say: 'Will it never bloody rain again?' His profits increased by one hundred per cent in a wet summer.

Punters should always be on the look out for up and coming jockeys and spot them before the next man.

Having said that one should not back in handicaps, there is no way that I could encourage punters to make an exception to that rule. But in the years long ago, before the introduction of the betting tax, I did show a substantial profit backing horses ridden by apprentices who were showing great promise. At that time I was racing six days a week and had the advantage over the average punter who was only able to watch racing occasionally on TV. I well remember spotting a young boy in his early teens who impressed me tremendously. Claiming the 7lb apprentice allowance, then 5lb and ultimately 3lb, he had a terrific advantage over the seasoned jockeys. I won a lot of money on him. His name was Lester Piggott.

At Epsom about that time I was watching a race, disinterested financially, and I saw a horse going terribly well. However, it was the jockey's style and composure that made me lower my binoculars and look at the number board. The rider was Paul Cook, a 7lb claimer. I did not need to jot his name in my notebook (a must for racegoers). He was imprinted on my mind. It later gave me great satisfaction to see him go to the top of the tree.

At Haydock Park a few years ago I saw a similar cool exhibition. As the horse passed the post, with the jockey sitting still as a mouse, I looked to see who was riding. The jockey was Kevin Darley and the horse was trained by Reg Hollinshead. At that moment Reg, who was standing a few steps higher on the stand, eased his way past me.

'Who is that boy, Reg?' I asked.

'He's one of mine and that's his first winner,' he replied.

'That's better than money in the bank, Reg,' I said.

The trainer smiled as he went to the unsaddling enclosure. Darley was to become the champion apprentice that season.

When I saw jockey Martin Moloney at Doncaster a couple of years ago with his brother Tim who was champion jockey several times, I recalled the day he rode a horse at Leicester for Bobby Renton. That day I asked Bobby who this unknown jockey was. When he told me it was Martin Moloney, I said: 'Surely that is a mistake. It is obviously Tim Moloney who is riding.'

'No Alex, it's Tim's kid brother,' he replied. 'And Tim assures me that he is only twice as good as he is!'

It was an extravagant claim. No one could have been that good as Tim was then the reigning champion – but good he certainly was. Martin was the best steeplechase jockey I ever saw and that includes masters like Bryan Marshall and the present day artiste John Francome.

I have discussed in a previous chapter the day I convinced my local tax inspector how I followed Martin religiously and won in balance £60,000. Only one other jockey since those far off days have

I followed with such a staking method. His name was Peter Scudamore. When I attended the Bollinger Dinner some years ago I saw Peter's father Michael talking to Terry Biddlecombe. I went across and told him how impressed I had been with Peter's riding, so much so that for only the second time was I using the system I had devised to follow Martin Moloney, and was already many thousands of pounds in front.

'In that case I'll introduce you to Peter,' said Michael. 'He hasn't arrived yet however because he has been riding today.'

Biddlecombe, as witty as ever, exclaimed: 'You'll be sending him a case of champagne for Christmas then Alex!'

It was Peter's first full season and he had ridden a wonderful percentage of winners, later becoming joint champion jockey. That was thanks to the unselfish gesture of John Francome who forfeited rides in the last days of the season, because Peter was injured.

I hope that what I have related does not sound big-headed. It is not meant to be. I tell these stories to illustrate what can be done by spotting an up and coming jockey early in his career. After all, the only horse I ever rode pulled the coal cart in Newton Heath!

Finally, I must stress that in this day and age with some bookmakers deducting ten percent there is no way a punter can make a real profit. I had the advantage of betting on the racecourse both before the introduction of tax, and afterwards where the deduction was only four percent. But if my advice is followed I am sure that would-be backers will get a lot of pleasure without losing too much.

INDEX